PORTUGUESE SOCIETY IN THE TROPICS
The Municipal Councils of
Goa, Macao, Bahia, and Luanda, 1510–1800

by C. R. Boxer

As the great colonial empires of the European nations crumble, a whole pattern of life vanishes. Historians are faced with the important and difficult task of recording and studying the elaborate institutional structures, the councils and committees, the complex methods by which European countries organized their remote dominions. Of all European powers, the Portuguese were the forerunners in establishing an overseas empire, and appear to be the last to maintain one. Their navigators were the first to reach India, their colonists conquered and held vast areas of South America. In *Portuguese Society in the Tropics*, C. R. Boxer explores a relatively unknown aspect of the Portuguese Empire: the municipal governments of their Asian, Latin-American, and African colonies.

The author shows that these infrequently considered governmental bodies were of crucial importance in holding together the far-flung and ramshackle Portuguese Empire. Unable itself adequately to administer its domains, the over-extended and financially undernourished Portuguese Crown allowed local councils great latitude in the raising and administering of funds for a wide variety of purposes. The councils were often responsible for naval and military establishments and expeditions, and were actively concerned with the economic sinews of Portugal's maritime empire. The entrepôt trade of Goa, the silver and sandalwood trade of Macao, the sugar trade of Bahia, the slave trade of Luanda — all these fell in part within the compass of the councils.

Although this book is basically a study in institutional history, forty-five years of research in Portuguese colonial history have given Professor Boxer intimate knowledge of the society and social attitudes of those colonies. In the course of his examination of the municipal councils — their composition, their relationships with the Crown and with the local civil,

ecclesiastical, and military authorities — he offers a colorful and many-sided portrait of colonial society. His comparison of the Portuguese councils with the better-known Spanish town councils, and his analysis of the way national character affects colonial settlement, will be of interest to students of all colonial attempts as well as to students of comparative tropical history.

Professor Boxer is widely acknowledged as a leading authority on the history of the Portuguese Empire from the time of its establishment to the beginning of the nineteenth century. Since 1947 he has been Camoens Professor of Portuguese at the University of London, and he holds honorary degrees from the Universities of Utrecht, Lisbon, and Bahia. Among the most important of his numerous books are *The Christian Century in Japan* (1951), *The Golden Age of Brazil* (1962), and *Race Relations in the Portuguese Empire, 1415–1825* (1963). The present book formed the subject of the 1964 Knaplund Lectures at the University of Wisconsin.

PRIVILEGIOS

DOS CIDADÃOS DA
Cidade do Porto.

Concedidos, & confirmados pellos Reys deftes Rey-
nos,& agora nouamente por el Rey dom The-
lippe II. noßo fenhor.

Sendo Iuiz de fora o Lecenceado Rodrigo de Camera.

Vereadores.
Manoel Tauares Pereira.
Diogo Leite de Azeuedo.
. Afonfo Correa de Azeuedo.
Aluaro Ferreira Pereira.
Procurador da cidade Baptifta da Cofta de Saa.

Com licença da Santa Inquifição, & Ordinario.
Imprelfos com licença do dito Senhor, à cufta das
rendas da cidade. Anno de M. D C. X I.

NO PORTO. Em cafa de Fruftuofo Lourenço de Bafto.

Title page of the original edition of the Privileges of the
Citizens of Oporto, 1611. These privileges were later conferred
on the citizens of Bahia (1646) and Luanda (1662).

PORTUGUESE SOCIETY IN THE TROPICS

The Municipal Councils of

Goa, Macao, Bahia, and Luanda,

1510-1800

C. R. BOXER

THE UNIVERSITY OF WISCONSIN PRESS

MADISON AND MILWAUKEE, 1965

Published by
The University of Wisconsin Press
Madison and Milwaukee
P.O. Box 1379,
Madison, Wisconsin 53701

Printed in
the United States of America by
North Central Publishing Co.,
St. Paul, Minnesota

Library of Congress Catalog
Number 65–18878

Foreword

The Paul Knaplund lecture series was named to honor an outstanding and long-time member of the History Department of the University of Wisconsin. Paul Knaplund (1885–1964), whose field of scholarship was the British Empire, served during the years 1932–1938 and 1942–1949 as chairman of the History Department; he retired in 1955. It is for his distinguished services in both teaching and research, spanning a period of four decades, that the University of Wisconsin has wished to honor him. The lectures themselves in recent years have been sponsored by the Comparative Tropical History Committee of the History Department, with occasional assistance from the Graduate School.

The program in Comparative Tropical History, established in 1959 and supported by a grant from the Carnegie Corporation, undertakes to provide specialized training for historians of Latin America, Africa, North Africa and the Middle East,

South Asia, and Southeast Asia, in order to meet the growing need for research scholars and teachers in these fields. By combining historical study with interdisciplinary area studies, the program aims at increasing both the scope and the analytical depth of scholarship on the subject of tropical history.

The coherence of the program derives from recognition of the central importance of European influence in the modern history of the non-Western world. The Western impact upon the temperate zones often resulted from a blanket immigration of Europeans — as in Canada, Argentina, or the United States. Other parts of the temperate world — such as China or Japan — have experienced a degree of Westernization, but without losing political independence for long periods. In the four major culture areas of the tropical world, however, European powers established colonial administrations. Europeans exercised political control, but settlement was rarely so intensive that non-Europeans ceased to constitute majorities of the population. The historical experience in these four areas in the modern period is therefore comparable. They have become the "developing nations," in some cases the "new nations," of the 1960's, sharing a common set of problems and aspirations.

While the common factor of the European intrusion provides an element of comparability, the Wisconsin program in tropical history does not focus exclusively on European activities. Instead its emphasis lies with the changing patterns of society in each of the tropical areas. No historian can ever discount the profound impact of European cultural influences on these areas, but neither can the social roles of the non-Western peoples be abruptly dismissed, as has sometimes been done. The comparative approach seeks a balance, by giving more attention to the non-Western ethnic groups. We visualize the Ibero-American world, in particular, as the development of multiracial societies in which European and non-European cultural influences interacted to produce a result that was neither wholly European nor wholly Indian or African.

Traditionally the Ibero-American world has been viewed either as an extension of Europe or as a component in the history of the Americas. The former view originates in the undeniable fact that European elites, numerical minorities though they were, dominated these societies, at least on the surface. The Bolton thesis of common history for all the Americas — Anglo-Saxon as well as Latin — has yielded useful insights in that the two cultures did to some extent share common colonial experiences and that Latin America did fall under the sway of the United States from the early nineteenth century onwards. Both approaches were justified in terms of the *Zeitgeist* in which they were conceived. Recent events and trends, however, have challenged the premises which support both perspectives. Comparative Tropical History can offer new perspectives on the development of these multiracial societies, through meaningful and responsible comparisons in which Latin America is viewed as a part of the non-Western world. It is not the only approach to Latin America's history, but it is new, it is viable, and it merits exploration.

The Portuguese Empire lends itself to this comparative approach in that there was an intensive Lusitanian presence spanning centuries in several areas of the tropical world. In the lectures being published here, treating the municipal councils of Goa, Macao, Bahia, and Luanda, Professor C. R. Boxer has made another of his distinguished contributions to the history of the Portuguese in the tropics, and has enriched the tradition of the Paul Knaplund Lectures.

JOHN LEDDY PHELAN
For the Comparative Tropical History Committee

Preface

The four chapters of this book comprise the text of the four Paul Knaplund Lectures which I delivered at the University of Wisconsin in September and October 1964. I chose this topic because I do not know of any other book that has dealt with it, and because I think that the overseas municipal councils played a greater role in Portuguese colonial history than is generally realized. Publication of these lectures has given me the opportunity to add footnotes, an annotated bibliography, and translations of selected documents which help to illustrate my theme. If these translations read rather awkwardly in places, I can plead in mitigation that so do the originals. The minutes of the council meetings were evidently sometimes written by tired, or hurried, or frankly incompetent scribes, who affected long, straggling, ungrammatical sentences with highly capricious punctuation. Even so, I hope these documents will be found of interest as illustrating the composition of the municipalities, their routine functions, their action in times of crisis, and the kind of people with whom they had to deal.

A word about the system of transliteration — or the lack of it — is in order here. Portuguese and Brazilian official spelling and accentuation differ from each other in many respects. Both national forms have undergone changes within the last forty years, and there is no certainty that they will remain as they are for long. A few examples will suffice. For centuries, *Antonio* was written without any accent on both sides of the Atlantic, but it has latterly become *António* in Portugal and *Antônio* in Brazil. Similarly, *historia* became *história* in Portugal after World War I, but in Brazil only very recently (and not invariably). My friend Frazão de *Vasconcellos* (*sic* in 1924) now spells his surname *Vasconcelos*. *Macao* has gradually become *Macau* within the last fifty years; but Bahia still rings the changes on *Bahia–Baía–Bahia*. As a general rule, I have tried to give the titles of the works quoted in the footnotes and bibliography in the original (or first edition) form, which accounts for such apparent inconsistencies as *Historic Macao* (1902) and *Arquivos de Macau* (1929), or even *O Município de Loanda* (Luanda, 1919). In footnote citations publication facts are omitted for works listed in the bibliography.

It remains to thank my numerous friends and colleagues at Madison who made my stay in "America's Dairyland" so pleasant. To name them individually would read like a faculty roll-call, but I am particularly indebted to the following: Professors Merrill Jensen and Irvin Wyllie, successively chairmen of the History Department; Professors John Phelan and Philip Curtin of the Comparative Tropical History Committee; and Mr. William Vogel, for typing much of the manuscript.

C. R. BOXER

December 1964

Contents

Introduction, 3

I

The Municipal Council of Goa, 12

II

The Municipal Council of Macao, 42

III

The Municipal Council of Bahia, 72

IV

The Municipal Council of Luanda, 110

Conclusion, 141

Appendix, 153

Bibliography, 219

Index, 232

Illustrations

Frontispiece

Title page of the original edition of the Privileges
of the Citizens of Oporto, 1611

Pages 32–33

East map, showing Goa and Macao

Between pages 64 and 65

The city and island of Goa in the seventeenth century
The city of Macao in the seventeenth century
Panoramic view of the city of Salvador, Bahia, 1759
Partial view of the city of São Paulo de Luanda, 1755

Pages 96–97

West map, showing Bahia and Luanda

Documents in Appendix

1 Summons to a meeting at the Town Hall, Goa, 21 April
1535   153

2 Qualifications laid down for municipal officeholders at
Goa, 24 March 1542   154

3 The Senate of Goa and the working-class representa-
tives, 1595–1607   155

4 The *mesteres* of Goa and the Feast of Corpus Christi in
1618   158

5 Election of the municipal councilors of Goa for the year
1602   159

6 The Senate of Goa and the Armada da Collecta,
1623–68   160

7 The Senate of Goa and the decay of the city in 1680 . . .   165

8 Election of the municipal councilors of Macao for the
year 1718   167

9 Refusal to serve the office of *almotacél* at Macao in 1639   168

10 The Senate of Macao and the sandalwood trade with
Timor, 1689   169

11 Bribery of the Mandarin of Ch'ien-shan by the Senate
of Macao, 1690   170

12 The Senate of Macao and the payment of ground-rent to the Chinese government in 1691 171

13 The Senate of Macao and the municipal budget for 1691 172

14 Qualifications laid down for the municipal councilors of Macao, 1689–1709 174

15 Election of the municipal councilors of Bahia for the year 1682 176

16 New system for the election of the municipal councilors at Bahia, 1697 177

17 Down-grading of the workers' representatives by the aldermen of Bahia, 1650 179

18 The *mesteres* of Bahia and the Feast of Corpus Christi, 1673 181

19 The Senate of Bahia and the sale of rum in 1672 183

20 The Senate of Bahia and the crisis in the sugar trade, 1687 186

21 Election of the municipal councilors at Luanda for the year 1677 189

22 Two routine sessions of the Senate of Luanda, 1670 and 1716 191

23 The Senate of Luanda and the quota for the Anglo-Dutch indemnity, 1672 191

24 The Senate of Luanda and the slave trade with Brazil in 1711 193

25 Paucity of qualified citizens at Luanda in 1711 196

26 Typical deportees from Brazil and Portugal to Angola, 1714–48 197

27 Accounts of the procurator of the Senate of Luanda for the year 1699 209

PORTUGUESE
SOCIETY IN THE
TROPICS

Introduction

If we consult the carefully compiled index to the collective *História de Portugal* published under the editorship of Professor Damião Peres at Barcelos, 1928–37, we will not find any references to the functioning of the Portuguese *Senado da Camara*, or municipal council, in the overseas territories before the nineteenth century, although this work includes the history of the colonies as well as of the mother country. The Barcelos *História* is still the best general history of Portugal and her empire, and its neglect of the part played by the colonial municipal councils probably reflects the lack of an adequate Portuguese study of this subject. The standard English-language *History of Portugal* by H. V. Livermore (Cambridge, 1947), based as it is largely on the Barcelos *História*, likewise ignores this topic. Understandably enough, Brazilian historians have been more active in this field, but they have devoted most of their attention to the municipality of São

Paulo, which is the best documented in print, thanks to the archival publications and the secondary works of the late Affonso de E. Taunay. While it would be presumptuous to claim that I am doing anything substantial to fill this particular gap in Portuguese colonial history, I hope to show that the overseas municipal councils are worth studying in their own right. For this purpose I have selected four of the most typical, in that they all functioned in seaports — and the Portuguese colonial empire was essentially a thalassocracy until the development of the interior of Brazil during the first half of the eighteenth century. I will not consider them in the chronological order in which they were founded, but deal first with Goa and Macao, which were two vital centers of the Portuguese presence in Monsoon Asia, and then with Bahia and Luanda, which were the nodal points of Portugal's commercial empire in the South Atlantic. Moreover, Macao was in some respects a political dependency of Goa, whereas Luanda's economy depended to a large extent on Bahia.

It is obviously impossible to cover adequately the story of these four municipal councils in the compass of four lectures. I shall therefore limit myself to a discussion of some aspects of their organization and development. In this way we can, perhaps, obtain some light on such problems as the following, which were common to a greater or lesser degree to all of them: How far did their development diverge from that of their metropolitan models of Lisbon, Evora, and Oporto? How far were they subordinated to, or overawed by, the local viceroy, the High Court judge, or the governor? How far did they represent the general interests of all classes, or did they only reflect those of the "ruling few"? To what extent were they self-perpetuating oligarchies, and did they allow men of colour in their ranks? Apart from these problems, their records must inevitably reflect the daily life of the time and place concerned, as well as the more spectacular triumphs and disasters experienced by the citizens. Lastly, a study of the Portuguese colonial municipal councils may suggest some interesting contrasts and comparisons with the more intensively studied, and hence better known, *cabildos* in the colonial Spanish-American world.

Without discussing the problem of whether the feudal Portuguese municipality can be traced back to Roman times, the organization and functions of the Senado da Camara at the dawn of the sixteenth century can be sketched in broad outline as follows: Municipal authority was invested in two kinds of officeholders, comprising three or four *vereadores* (councilors or aldermen), two *juizes ordinarios* (justices of the peace, or magistrates), the *procurador* (municipal attorney), and four *mesteres,* or representatives of the working-class guilds (cf. old English "art, craft, and mystery"). These were collectively known as the *oficiais da Camara,* all of whom had voting rights in council meetings. The *escrivão* (clerk or secretary), though he had no voting rights originally, was often included in the *oficiais da Camara,* and at times this term was loosely extended to include subordinate municipal officials such as the *almotacéls* (market-inspectors) and the *tesoureiro* (treasurer). Other municipal functionaries who did not have voting rights included the *juiz dos orfãos,* who looked after the interests of widows and orphans; the *alferes* (herald ensign or standard bearer); the *porteiro* (doorkeeper or porter), who sometimes acted as archivist; the *contador* (accountant); and the *veador de obras* (foreman of works).

The *oficiais da Camara* were elected through a complicated system of annual balloting from voters' lists which were drawn up every three years in accordance with the procedure laid down in the *Regimento dos ofiçiaaes das çidades villas e lugares destes Regnos* of 1504.[1] About Christmas week at the

1. For the above and what follows, cf. *Regimento dos ofiçiaaes das çidades villas e lugares destes Regnos. Cõ preuilegio del Rey nosso senhor* (Lisbon, 1504), the facsimile edition edited with a preface by Marcello Caetano; Eduardo Freire de Oliveira, *Elementos para a História do Município de Lisboa,* particularly Vol. I, *passim.*

end of each triennial period, the outgoing municipal councilors and all the respectable — and respected — householders of the town assembled in the town hall or senate house. This body of electors was termed the *homens bons* (lit. "good" or "worthy" men) or, more loosely, the *povo* (people). The Crown judge (*ouvidor*) or the senior local magistrate presided at this meeting, and he obtained from each individual secretly and separately the names of those citizens considered to be fittest to choose the members of the new municipal council. He scrutinized the lists of the names thus obtained, and he then nominated as electors the six men who had secured the most votes. These six electors were then sworn to draw up lists of those persons whom they considered fittest to hold municipal office, excluding those individuals who had just finished serving. They also swore to keep secret the names of the persons for whom they voted. The six electors were then grouped into three pairs — each pair, in theory at least, not closely connected by blood, family, or occupational ties. Secluded from each other, each pair then drew up three electoral rolls of three persons whom they nominated to fill each of the impending municipal vacancies. The presiding official, who was likewise under oath not to reveal the names of any of the persons listed, then collated all the electoral rolls and wrote down the names in a comprehensive list known as the *pauta*. He also compiled three other lists of the most popular candidates for each of the vacant posts, these lists being rolled up inside small wax balls, from which they were known as *pelouros*. The *pauta* and the *pelouros* were then placed in a sack or bag containing as many pockets as there were municipal offices to be balloted for, and one more pocket for the *pauta* and the original electoral rolls. This sack was kept in a coffer with three different keys which were held by the three outgoing aldermen.

On New Year's Day, or sometimes on New Year's Eve, the

annual results were balloted for in a ceremony known as the *janeirinhas*. A small boy, called in at random from the streets, put his hand into each pocket of the sack in turn; and, after shuffling the *pelouros*, he took out one from each pocket. The names of the officeholders thus selected to serve in the ensuing year were then read out at a general meeting of the *homens bons*, and they were formally inducted into office if they were present, after taking an oath to do their duty without fear or favour. They were not allowed to excuse themselves from serving the municipal offices to which they had been elected, save only when they could adduce a good and sufficient excuse, such as a serious illness. Following on their election, the municipal councilors assembled in conclave to choose such of their number and the subordinate officials who had not been balloted for. These included the *almotacéls*, a title of Arabic origin for which I do not know the exact English equivalent, but which, following the dictionaries, I have translated as market-inspectors. Their chief duties were to inspect the foodstuffs brought into the town for sale; to see that they were sold at the market price where this was fixed; to ensure that the vendors used standard weights and measures; and to ensure that artisans and journeymen did not charge more for their labour than was authorized by the municipal and the guild regulations. They were also supposed to see that the streets were kept clean, and that the Camara's orders regarding public hygiene and sanitation were properly enforced. In course of time, the exercise of the office of *almotacél* gave the holder the status of a gentleman and a citizen (*o fôro de cavalleiro e cidadão*), rendering them eligible for subsequent service as *vereadores* and *juizes ordinarios*.

Working-class representation on the Lisbon municipal council was based on the guild system. The leading trades and handicrafts (armourers, goldsmiths, masons, coopers, cobblers, tailors, etc.) elected annually from their guild members twenty-four representatives, known as the *Casa dos Vinte e Quatro*. These men in their turn nominated four from among their number, called the *procuradores dos mesteres*, to represent their interests on the municipal council.[2] They had the right to attend all meetings and to vote in all matters which affected the workers' guilds or corporations and the economic life of the city. They advised the Camara as to what prices artisans and journeymen should charge for their respective services, and they also laid down the conditions for apprenticeship, guild membership, and so forth. In the year 1512 a royal decree was promulgated ordering that one of the four *procuradores dos mesteres* on the municipal council should be a *Christão-novo* (i.e., of converted Jewish origin) and the other three *Christãos-velhos*, or "Old Christians." This measure was certainly not enforced for very long; and the New Christians were soon discriminated against and barred from holding municipal office, as they were from all other official posts. The guilds were organized in *bandeiras*, so called from the square banners which they carried in religious processions and on festive occasions. These banners were usually made of crimson damask or brocade, bordered with gold or silver tinsel, and bore the device of the patron saint or of the craft which they represented. A *bandeira* might consist of the practitioners of one craft only, or it might comprise several crafts, one of which was recognized as the *cabeça* or head.

Meetings of most municipal councils were usually held twice weekly, on Wednesdays and Saturdays, though more often when required. The Camara of Lisbon naturally had far more business to cope with than any of the others, and its regular meetings soon rose to four and then successfully to six and seven days a week. Proceedings were confidential, and the

2. Cf. Franz-Paul Langhans, *As Corporações dos ofícios mecânicos: Subsídios para a sua história* (2 vols.; Lisbon, 1943–46); and his *A Casa dos Vinte e Quatro de Lisboa: Subsídios para a sua história* (Lisbon, 1948), for detailed and documented studies of the Lisbon guilds and working-class corporations.

minutes were recorded by the secretary. He had no vote and was not elected on a yearly basis but for a long period, or even for life. In this way he provided an element of continuity in the Camara. Time-expired councilors were not normally eligible for re-election until after three years had elapsed. In some Portuguese municipalities, the junior outgoing *vereador* automatically continued in office as next year's *procurador*, in order to explain to his incoming colleagues the details of the business transacted in the previous year, thus providing another element of continuity.

The presidency of the Camara generally devolved upon each of the *vereadores* alternately, the one who took the chair being called the *vereador do meio*, from his seat in the middle. Councilors who failed to attend meetings were fined, unless they could give a good excuse, such as illness. Decisions were taken by a majority vote after the matter had been freely debated at the council table. The decisions of the Camara in municipal matters could not be set aside or revoked by superior authority, save only if they involved unauthorized innovations which might adversely affect the Crown's finances. The Camara acted as a court of first instance in summary cases, subject to appeal to the nearest *ouvidor* (Crown judge), or High Court (*Relação*). The retiring *juizes ordinarios* were supposed to be investigated by their successors, but in practice this does not seem to have happened very often. Similarly, the treasurer's accounts do not seem to have been submitted regularly for inspection to anyone outside the municipality. The Camaras of Lisbon and Goa were, indeed, specifically exempted by their privileges from having their accounts audited by any outside body, the audit being entrusted to their own *vereadores*. The Camara supervised the distribution and leasing of municipal lands; assessed and collected municipal taxes; fixed the sale-price of a wide range of commodities and provisions; issued building licenses; maintained roads, bridges, fountains, jails, and other public works; regulated public holidays and processions; and was responsible for the policing of the town and for public health and sanitation.

The Camara's income was derived chiefly from the rents of municipal property, including houses which were leased as shops, and from the taxes it levied on a wide range of foodstuffs and provisions exposed for sale, though the basic supplies such as bread, salt, and wine were originally exempted. Another source of income was derived from the fines levied by the *almotacéls* and other officials on the transgressors of the municipal *posturas* (statutes, regulations), such as vendors who were unlicensed or who gave short weight. Municipal taxes, like those levied by the Crown, were usually farmed out on contract to the highest bidder for an agreed cash payment. The successful contractor then collected the dues in the name of the municipality and kept the surplus (if any) after paying the agreed sum. Public services, such as street lighting or paving, and concessions for supplying the city with certain kinds of goods and provisions were also often farmed out to the highest bidder. In times of emergency, the Camara could also impose a capital levy on the citizens, scaled in accordance with their real or assumed ability to pay.

The *oficiais da Camara* were privileged individuals who could not be arrested arbitrarily, nor subjected to judicial torture, nor imprisoned in chains, save only in cases such as high treason which involved the death penalty and from which fidalgos were likewise not exempted. They were also free from military service, save only when the city was directly attacked, and exempted from having government officials and soldiers billeted on them, and from having their horses, carts, etc., confiscated for use by the Crown. They had the privilege of corresponding directly with the reigning monarch, and they enjoyed various judicial immunities. They received a salary in money and in kind (chiefly corn and barley) during their tenure of office, and *propinas* (perquisites) when they attended the statutory religious processions, the chief of which was the Feast of Corpus Christi. When walking in these processions or when engaged on official duties, the *juizes ordinarios* carried a red-coloured wand or staff with the royal arms (*quinas*) at one end, as the badge of their office.[3]

3. For the privileges enjoyed by the *oficiais da Camara*, in addition to the voluminous *Elementos* of Freire de Oliveira, see the succinct *Privilegios dos Cidadãos da Cidade do Porto. Concedidos e confirmados pellos Reys destes Reynos, e agora novamente por el Rey dom Phelippe II nosso Senhor* (Oporto, 1611). These privileges of Oporto were all copied from those of Lisbon.

CHAPTER I

The
Municipal Council
of Goa

I have not been able to find the exact date when the municipal council of Goa was founded by Affonso de Albuquerque, but it must have been shortly after his definitive conquest of that city from the Muslim Sultan of Bijapur on St. Catherine's Day (25 November), 1510, and before his departure for Malacca in April of the following year, as stated by João de Barros. The Camara was then organized on the basis of one *vereador fidalgo* and two *vereadores nobres*, with two *juizes ordinarios*, a *procurador da cidade*, and four *procuradores dos mesteres*, all these ten individuals having voting rights.[1] They were

1. Viriato A. C. B. de Albuquerque, *O Senado de Goa: Memoria Histórico-Archeologica*, p. 3, states that the Senado da Camara of Goa consisted originally of six *vereadores*, two *juizes ordinarios*, one *procurador*, and twenty-six *mesteres*, and that its composition remained unchanged down to 1755. Both of these assertions are entirely erroneous and are contradicted by the sources mentioned in the next note, as well as by the documents that Viriato de Albuquerque prints in his own book. This work is very rare and I am greatly obliged to the Director and Trustees of the Newberry Library, Chicago, for kindly furnishing me with a complete photocopy of the one in that institution.

presumably selected (or elected) from among the men whom Albuquerque had encouraged to marry Indian women and to settle down in Goa for life. In 1516, the Camara sent two representatives to Lisbon, in order to petition the Crown for confirmation of the charter and privileges granted by Albuquerque, which were closely modelled on those of the Portuguese capital city. The married citizens of Goa also asked for complete freedom of trade, "both for themselves, their associates, their slaves, and their factors," in all provisions and goods, whether of European or of Asian origin. Not surprisingly, the Crown jibbed at this demand and, while granting free trade in general terms, expressly reserved for itself the royal monopoly in spices and other selected merchandise. The Crown also rejected as unreasonable the petitioners' request that the municipal officeholders should be exempted from contributing to the upkeep of bridges and fountains. With these exceptions, all the thirty clauses submitted by the representatives of the Goa Camara were confirmed by the Crown, including the reservation of almost all the municipal offices for married Portuguese male citizens of Goa and their descendants. The one difference between the Camaras of Lisbon and Goa was that the captain of the latter city, who was appointed by the Crown, had the right and duty to attend the council meetings whenever he thought fit, or whenever the councilors asked him to do so, and he was given the privilege of a double vote. But it was also stipulated that neither he nor the viceroy, governor, or any senior judicial official could interfere in the day-to-day administration by the Camara, and that the rights and privileges of the Portuguese citizens of Goa must be scrupulously respected.[2]

2. The principal sources utilized for my account of the Senado da Camara of Goa are Albuquerque, *Senado da Goa*; J. H. da Cunha Rivara (ed.), *Archivo Portuguez-Oriental* (hereafter cited as *APO*), particularly Fascicles I and II, containing the "Livro das Cartas que os Reis de Portugal escreveram à cidade de Goa, 1529–1611," the "Livro dos privilegios da Cidade de Goa," and the "Cartas da Camara de Goa a Sua Magestade, 1595–1609." I was also

The municipal councilors of Goa jealously guarded their right to the privileges and liberties of their Lisbon colleagues, and they repeatedly sought and obtained confirmation of this right from the Crown. In January 1520, for example, their representatives at Lisbon obtained a copy of the *Regimento* given to the Camara of that city, for the better guidance of their principals at Goa. Another complete copy was obtained in 1542, together with full instructions as to how the Lisbon municipal councilors carried out their daily routine duties. Confirmation that the privileges of the Camara of Goa were identical with those of the Camara of Lisbon was solemnly affirmed by the Crown in 1559, in 1566, and by Philip II in 1582 after his accession to the Portuguese throne. Similarly, D. João IV renewed the same confirmation soon after the restoration of Portuguese independence sixty years later. These privileges were again formally registered at Goa in 1674 and in 1680, to mention only two of the other occasions. One of the most jealously guarded privileges was that when the councilors went to see the viceroy on official business they had to be treated as if they were gentlemen of the royal household.[3]

The Camara of Goa did not, however, automatically follow all the changes which occurred in the constitution of that of Lisbon, and the *mesteres* of the two cities were organized on a different numerical basis. This was presumably the case

---

able, in February 1963, to examine the 11 MS volumes of the original "Livros dos Acordãos e Assentos" of the Senate of Goa, covering the years 1535–1723, preserved in the Historical Archive at Goa-Pangim. Cf. also José Ignacio de Abranches Garcia (ed.), *Archivo da Relação de Goa, contendo varios documentos dos seculos XVII, XVIII, e XIX*, which despite its title is confined to the 17th century; *O Oriente Portuguez*, particularly Vol. XII, pp. 149–52, Vol. XIII, pp. 47–50.

3. ". . . quando os Vereadores dessa Cidade fossem a elle em forma da Camara, os trate como aos fidalgos da minha casa, posto que elles o não seião." — *APO*, I (1857), p. 122. Cf. also "Livro dos privilegios da Cidade de Goa," in *APO*, II (1857), especially pp. 20–39, 48–85, and 268–87; Abranches Garcia, *Archivo da Relação de Goa*, pp. 574–76.

from 1510, though in February 1534, D. João III promulgated a decree that "in the city of Goa there should be twelve *mesteres* as there are in the other cities of my kingdoms, although there are twenty-four in the city of Lisbon."[4] The *mesteres* of Goa were, the decree added, likewise accorded the privileges of those of Lisbon. In 1572 the Senado da Camara of Lisbon was reorganized as follows. The president was no longer selected from the *vereadores* in rotation, but had to be a leading and well-qualified fidalgo, and the three other *vereadores* had to be qualified and experienced Crown lawyers (*desembargadores*). These four *vereadores*, together with two *procuradores* and four *procuradores dos mesteres* now formed the *oficiais da Camara*, or core of the council. In the reign of Philip II (Philip I of Portugal) the number of qualified lawyer-aldermen was successively increased from four (1585) to six (1591). Council meetings were henceforth chaired by the fidalgo alderman, flanked by three of his legal colleagues on either side. The number of weekly meetings was also increased to six, and later to seven, as previously noted.[5] The predominance of lawyers in the Lisbon municipal council from 1572 onwards was not copied by any of the colonial Camaras, which continued to be served mainly by leading citizens who were not members of the legal profession.

The first major changes in the composition of the Goa Camara occurred in 1654, when its reorganization had been under discussion between the authorities at Lisbon and Goa for at least four years. The Crown now ruled that henceforth the triennial *vereadores* should consist of six fidalgos and

4. Eduardo Freire de Oliveira, *Elementos para a História do Município de Lisboa*, Vol. XV, p. 564n. In point of fact, the representatives of the *mesteres* who elected the four *procuradores* to serve on the Senate continued to be called the *Casa de Vinte e Quatro*, and they represented 29 separate trades and crafts down to 1755, when the right of representation was further widened. Cf. p. 27 below.

5. Cf. Freire de Oliveira, *Elementos*, Vo. I, pp. 13–14, for the changes in the composition of the Lisbon municipal council, 1572–91.

three *nobres*. These were to serve on a yearly rota of two fidalgos and one *nobre*, in addition to the two *juizes ordinarios* and the *procurador*, who were also *nobres*. At a later date, which I have not been able to ascertain, the annual *vereadores* were again reduced to three, comprising one fidalgo and two *nobres*, with the fidalgo always taking precedence and the chair at meetings. This practice was challenged by the two *vereadores nobres* in 1744, who wished to revert to the original system of casting lots and rotating the chairmanship; but as a result of some correspondence between the viceroy and the Crown it seems that the precedence of the fidalgo was confirmed.[6]

Despite the elaborate arrangements made in the Manueline code to ensure that municipal elections were not rigged and that persons closely connected by ties of blood or of business did not serve on the same *vereação*, there were, in fact, frequent complaints that the law was being circumvented or disregarded. These complaints provided the Crown with a pretext to exert closer control over the composition of the municipalities in Asia in 1688. A royal decree of that year abolished the balloting element in the triennial elections and ordered that henceforth the lists of candidates for municipal offices which were drawn up by the six electors should be forwarded to the viceroy for scrutiny. The viceroy would then nominate those whom he considered fittest to hold office, in sealed annual lists which would be opened at the beginning of each year. This system reduced the element of popular choice in the election of *vereadores*, but it did not eliminate it. As several viceroys later complained to the Crown, these lists were sometimes so organized as to severely limit that high official's freedom of choice. Such viceregal

6. *Provisão Real* of 10 March 1654, in *APO*, II (1857), pp. 260–61; correspondence of the Viceroy Marquis of Alorna with the Crown, 23 March and 23 December 1747, in Historical Archive, Goa, "Livros das Monções," Vol. CXX-A (1744–47), fls. 17–18.

complaints were made in 1715, in 1743, and as late as 1810, to quote only three of several instances.[7]

Naturally enough, the complaints were not all on one side. The Camara of Goa was never backward in writing to the Crown whenever it thought, rightly or wrongly, that the viceroy or anyone else was trying to interfere with its rights, duties, and privileges. The Camara was particularly resentful of the tendency of some viceroys or governors to appoint their own servants or hangers-on to municipal posts which were in the gift of the Camara, or which were reserved for the citizens of Goa. On one occasion, they even ventured to criticize the powerful Society of Jesus, writing in 1603:

We affirm to Your Majesty that if this State is lost, it will be the fault of the Fathers of the Company, who, having permission from Your Majesty as we will note and prove, have nowadays as big a revenue in this State as amounts to half of the revenue of your Treasury. They are absolute lords of the greater part of this Island, and they buy up everything, so that inevitably within ten years there will not be a house or a palm-grove which they will not own. The citizens are being dispossessed of them all, which is the reason why this State is so poor, since men cannot buy landed property, and so they adventure and lose all their capital at sea.[8]

Nor did the Camara hesitate to give the viceroy and the Crown advice or information on matters of high policy, on the strategic conduct of wars, on local defense, and on the behaviour or misbehaviour of high officials from the viceroy himself downwards.

The Crown usually took these compaints very seriously, and frequently reminded the viceroys that they should respect the privileges of the city and cooperate with the Camara. No doubt this attitude was partly motivated by the expedient of checks and balances in which the Portuguese colonial

7. *APO*, I (1877), pp. 130–31; Abranches Garcia, *Archivo da Relação de Goa*, pp. 120, 388, 441. Cf. also Edmundo Zenha, *O Município no Brasil, 1532–1700* (São Paulo, 1948), p. 85n20, for the law of 17 March 1688.

8. *APO*, I, Part 2 (1876), p. 128.

empire — like the Spanish — was so fertile, and which ensured that the Crown was kept regularly informed of what was going on. Some of the more authoritarian viceroys naturally resented the freedom with which the city of Goa corresponded with the Crown; and attempts to intercept or censor this correspondence were not unknown. In 1632, the Viceroy Count of Linhares suggested that the municipal councils in Portuguese Asia should be abolished altogether. He alleged that places where there were none, such as Moçambique and Diu, were better governed than any of the other Portuguese settlements. Not surprisingly, the Crown rejected this suggestion, partly, perhaps, because it had been informed a few years previously that Diu was the worst governed of all the Portuguese possessions in Asia.[9] The Crown must, indeed, often have been puzzled by the conflicting advice and information that it received from the *conquistas*, as the overseas possessions were termed, and the Camara of Goa not infrequently contradicted itself. For example, during the viceroyalty of Matthias de Albuquerque (1591–97), the Camara repeatedly complained to the Crown of his allegedly obstructive and tyrannical behaviour, only to hold him up as a model a few years after his return to Portugal. The Camara took just the opposite line during the first viceroyalty of D. Francisco da Gama, Count of Vidigueira, often praising him when he was in office, and criticizing him bitterly after he had left.

It would, however, be wrong to think that the viceroy and the Camara of Goa were invariably at cross purposes. Not seldom they were, particularly between 1595 and 1608, as the published correspondence of that period shows. But there were also many occasions on which they cooperated well enough, and in times of crisis the viceroys never sought help from the Camara in vain. The classic instance is, of course,

---

9. Abranches Garcia, *Archivo da Relação de Goa*, pp. 406, 441. Diu at one time had a Senado da Camara, which functioned only from 1603 to 1613, when it was abolished.

the loan which D. João de Castro raised from the city of Goa on the security of a hair from his beard in 1547, but there were many other enterprises in which the financial help of the Camara was forthcoming. The city of Goa provided the sum of 10,000 cruzados to help fit out the fleet under D. Paulo de Lima which sacked Johore Lama in 1587; it also contributed heavily to the expeditions for the relief of Ormuz in 1619–22 — in vain in the upshot though these proved to be. Other examples were the galleons bought and equipped by the city as part of the armada of D. Martim Affonso de Castro for the relief of Malacca in 1606; the contribution made to the fitting-out of the armada of Nuno Alvarez Botelho in the Persian Gulf in 1624–25, and another for his relief of Malacca in 1629. It was also the Camara of Goa which raised and administered the funds for the coastguard flotilla known as the *armada da collecta* which convoyed ingoing and outgoing shipping at the entrance to the river Mandovi. The Camara was likewise responsible for finding the money for the upkeep of the city walls and fortifications, as well as for the pay and maintenance of the sailors of the *carreira da India*, when these men were waiting at Goa for the Indiamen to load their return cargoes for Lisbon.[10]

In addition to its statutory responsibility for the upkeep of bridges, roads, and other municipal public works, the Camara was often saddled with the responsibility of financing in whole or in part more ambitious building projects. These included the great powder mill and magazine at Panelim and the embankment highway of Ribandar, constructed during the viceroyalty of the Count of Linhares. Last not least,

10. In its annual letter of 1597 to the Crown, the Camara pointed out that "de ordinario se não podem fazer as armadas, e prouer as fortalezas sem emprestimos dos cidadões desta Cidade." — *APO*, I, Part 2, p. 58. For the *armada da Collecta* cf. *APO*, II, pp. 243–44, 255, 257; Panduronga Pissurlencar, *Assentos do Conselho do Estado da India, 1618–1750*, Vol. I, pp. 431–37; Albuquerque, *Senado de Goa*, pp. 440–41; and original papers of Dr. Pedro Alvares Pereira (dated 1623) in the author's collection.

the Camara had its say in the various monetary reforms and revaluations of the Indo-Portuguese coinage. In 1582, for example, a projected debasement of the coinage was abandoned on account of the protests of the Camara to the viceroy against this measure. In short, the cooperation of the Camara was essential to the government of Portuguese India, as was explicitly recognized on more than one occasion by the Crown. On the eve of the restoration of Portuguese independence in 1640, the Princess Regent of Portugal wrote to the viceroy that the Camara of Goa should be favoured in every way, "so that its officers may continue working with the same loyalty and good will as they have always done hitherto." [11]

The Camara was also vigilant in curbing — or trying to curb — the activities of speculators, monopolists, and engrossers, whether Portuguese or Indian, who sought to take advantage of Goa's dependence on imports of foodstuffs, and particularly of rice. With this objective, the Camara frequently legislated about the price of rice and other provisions; but it must be admitted that these efforts to regulate food prices were not always very successful, particularly, it would seem, during the first half of the eighteenth century. The Viceroy Marquis of Alorna, in the instructions which he left for his successor in 1750, observed that the Camara should not be allowed to fix the price of rice without first obtaining the viceroy's consent, although various royal decrees gave it the exclusive right to do so. He wrote:

Withal, experience has taught me that when the Senate did this, it was the same as announcing to the people that famine was in the offing, which led to the difficulties, complaints, and riots which plagued me three years ago. Whereas after I had decided that the Senate should no longer fix the price of this foodstuff, and that anyone could freely import it and sell it here at whatever price he

11. *Boletim da Filmoteca Ultramarina Portuguesa*, No. 20 (Lisbon, 1962), pp. 124–26, 225, 228.

wished, so much rice was imported and sold at such a moderate price that famine and complaints no longer occurred.[12]

The same viceroy also alleged that the Camara was often swindled by the contractors whom it engaged for the upkeep and repair of the fortifications. He suggested that a qualified military engineer ought to supervise this work in cooperation with the Camara. This had, indeed, been the practice when one was available, as in the days of Giovanni Battista Cairatto and Julião Simões, in the late sixteenth and early seventeenth centuries. The fines levied on merchants, shopkeepers, and itinerant street-vendors who infringed the municipal price-fixing and licensing regulations went to swell a fund known as the *renda do verde*. The proceeds of this fund were mainly used by the municipality for charitable purposes, such as the upkeep of a leprosarium and a home for foundlings.[13] It may be added that although the Camara of Goa derived a good income from its landed properties and from buildings leased as shops, godowns, etc., its expenses increasingly tended to outrun its income, chiefly because of the more or less forced loans which it was induced or compelled to make to the Crown in time of crisis. In 1611, the Crown ordered the viceroy to see that money was not borrowed from the city of Goa, save only in the most urgent crises; and that in such cases, repayment should be made a top priority from the Crown's most reliable sources of revenue. This order remained a dead letter. By 1760 the Crown owed the Camara over 400,000 cruzados, exclusive of accumulated interest, for the principal of loans which had never been repaid.[14]

12. *Instrucção do Exmo. Vice-Rei Marquez de Alorna ao seu successor o Exmo. Vice-Rei Marquez de Tavora*, Part 1, p. 77.

13. For the *renda do verde* in Goa, cf. Abranches Garcia, *Archivo da Relação de Goa*, pp. 207–8, 247. For the Senate's revenue from the *renda do verde* and other sources, and the way in which it was spent, cf. *APO*, I, Part 2, pp. 176–80, and II, pp. 193–204; Albuquerque, *Senado de Goa*, pp. 3, 6–7n, 440–42.

14. Albuquerque, *Senado de Goa*, p. 179; *APO*, I, Part 2, pp. 128–29.

Apart from periodical friction with the viceroy, the Camara had even more frequent disputes with the law officers of the Crown, and particularly with the judges of the High Court or *Relação*. In 1602, the Camara complained to the Crown that the more ministers of justice there were in Portuguese India, the worse was justice administered. *Desembargadores* would arrive from Portugal with a salary of 1,000 cruzados and a chest of books, but within two or three years they had accumulated fortunes of 30,000 or 40,000 cruzados, through indulging in bribery and corruption. Here again, however, the Camara sometimes gave self-contradictory information to the Crown. In 1602, for example, in the course of this long tirade about the lack of justice in Portuguese India, the Camara made serious allegations of corruption and other irregularities against several of the Crown lawyers, including the Licentiate Julião de Campos Barreto. Five years later, however, the Camara informed the Crown that this official had always served with exemplary honesty and fidelity in all the legal posts which he had filled.[15]

Disputes over jurisdiction between the judges of the High Court and the *juizes ordinarios* of the Camara were probably inevitable, and were certainly common. The *juizes ordinarios* were not trained lawyers but ordinary citizens vested with legal powers in municipal affairs during their annual term of office, and the Crown lawyers naturally tended to think themselves vastly superior. Apart from this, there was a long-drawn-out argument in the last quarter of the seventeenth century between the Camara and the Relação over precedence at religious and state functions. Both sides appealed to the Crown, which in 1691 decided in favour of the Relação,

15. *APO*, I, Part 2, pp. 94–95, 215. For some typical complaints of the Camara about the lack of justice in Portuguese India and the abuses perpetrated by the viceroy and other high officials see *ibid.*, pp. 91–128, 135–92, *passim*; and the letters of the Camara of Goa to the Crown in 1522–48, published in the *Boletim da Bibliographia Portugueza*, Vol. II (Coimbra, 1882), pp. 169–86, 201–7, 244–51, 257–74, 289–304.

on the grounds that the High Court represented the majesty of the sovereign, whereas the municipal council represented only "the commonwealth of its vassals who are the residents of that city." Five years later, the Camara was still trying to dispute this ruling, for which it incurred a sharp reprimand from the Crown. In 1674, the viceroy, at the request of the Camara, compelled a reluctant Relação to register the privileges of the city of Lisbon as conferred on that of Goa, in order to prevent the High Court from handing down judgments which conflicted with those privileges. These were only two of the many occasions on which the Camara and Relação indulged in mutual complaints; and as late as 1707, the Camara successfully resisted an attempt to impose a high legal official as its president.[16]

We have noticed that one feature of the Goa municipality which seems to have been unique was that the captains of the city had the right to attend and vote at council meetings. On assuming office, the captain took an oath to respect and defend the rights and privileges of the city, and, on the whole, successive captains seem to have done this. From time to time, criticisms were made of this practice, and in 1557 and again in 1602, the Camara suggested to the Crown that the captain of the city should no longer be a voting member of the council. The Viceroy Count of Linhares suggested that the post should be abolished as redundant; but the Crown rejected these proposals and the captain continued to attend and vote at meetings. On the other hand, when the Camara asked the Crown in 1714 for the right to appoint a municipal procurator for life, the Crown enquired of the viceroy whether such an appointment would not amount to "authorizing one more public thief." This query recalls the cynical observation of Padre António Vieira, S.J., when D. João IV asked him whether the state of Maranhão-Pará should be divided into

16. Abranches Garcia, *Archivo da Relação de Goa*, pp. 431–32, 487, 525, 575–77, 688, 695; *Oriente Portuguez*, Vol. XII, pp. 45, 151, Vol. XVI, p. 48

two separate governments, and the Jesuit retorted that it was better to have one thief than two.[17]

The *procurador da cidade* who was one of the *oficiais da Camara* at Goa, should not be confused with the *procurador* who represented the Camara's interests at Lisbon. We have seen that the city of Goa sent two personal representatives to the Portuguese capital in 1516, and thenceforth it either maintained a resident *procurador* at Lisbon or else sent special representatives with this title to plead its case at court when necessary. During the "Sixty Years Captivity" of 1580–1640, the Camara also sent *procuradores* to Madrid for this purpose, although the Crown wrote to the Camara in 1583 that it was not necessary to incur such an expense, as the King always paid careful attention to the Camara's letters from Goa. After the restoration of Portuguese independence, the Camara of Goa obtained a seat and vote in the Cortes, or assembly of the three estates, at Lisbon in 1674. These representatives of the Goa municipal council at Lisbon were sometimes men who had previously served on the Camara, and sometimes influential individuals, such as ex-viceroys or governors, who had previously served in the East.[18]

Since the *oficiais da Camara* were composed of the leading citizens of Goa, that body naturally represented their interests first and foremost ("pois a Camara e os moradores são hũa mesma cousa e se reprezenta este corpo milhor pellos officiaes della," as the Crown acknowledged in 1588), but it was often mindful of the poor and the lowly. The Camara closely cooperated with the Santa Casa da Misericordia, or Holy House of Mercy, which did such admirable work in

17. *APO*, II, pp. 46–47, and I, Part 2, pp. 108–9; *Oriente Portuguez*, Vol. VI, p. 427; *Studia: Revista Semestral*, Vol. VIII (1961), pp. 171–72. For Padre António Vieira's observation in his letter of 4 April 1654, see J. L. d'Azevedo (ed.), *Cartas do Padre António Vieira*, Vol. I (Coimbra, 1925), p. 416.

18. *APO*, I (1877), pp. 45–47, 94, and I, Part 2, p. 135; Albuquerque, *Senado de Goa*, pp. 42–45, 403–4.

relieving the poor and needy. Occasionally, of course, their interests clashed, as in 1547, when the *Mesa* (Board of Guardians) of the Misericordia secured exemption from serving on the municipality for those of their members who were elected to it. This ruling did not prevent leading citizens from serving in the Camara and on the Board of the Misericordia alternately, as Padre Francisco de Sousa, S.J., noted in 1698: "The Brothers of the Misericordia are the most eminent and respected citizens, and many of them were aldermen of the city."[19] The social status of a municipal councilor and of a Brother of the Misericordia were both enviably high, as exemplified in the proverbial saying that if a man wanted to live high, wide, and handsomely, he should become one or the other — or both.[20]

Just as the Crown borrowed from the Camara when it was in difficulties, so the Camara sometimes borrowed from the Misericordia. In 1621, for example, the Camara borrowed 100,000 xerafines from that charitable institution to help pay for the galleons sent to the relief of Ormuz. Most of this money had been repaid by 1636, but the balance was only liquidated fifty years later. In 1653, the Camara borrowed 15,000 xerafines from the Misericordia for the relief of Colombo, and the liquidation of this debt likewise took many years and involved an acrimonious correspondence. At a later date, the Camara came to the rescue of the Misericordia, when the former agreed to an amalgamation of its own hospital of Nossa Senhora da Piedade with the hospital of Todos os Santos operated by the Misericordia. The combined institution was thenceforth known as the Hospital of the Poor, and the Camara provided most of the money for its upkeep. The

19. Francisco de Sousa, S.J., *Oriente Conquistado*, Vol. II, p. 222.

20. "Que se quizesse viver bem e á grande fizesse diligencia para ser vereador do Senado ou Irmão de meza da Misericordia," in *Instrucção do . . . Marquez de Alorna*, p. 78n, and José F. Ferreira Martins, *História da Misericordia de Goa*, Vol. I, pp. 172–73. This latter work contains a great deal about the connections between the Senado da Camara and the Misericordia of Goa.

hospital of Piedade had been founded by the Viceroy Count of Linhares, but Todos os Santos was nearly a century older, and was open to people of all races. With the great and increasing poverty of Goa after the disastrous Maratha war of 1737–40, it proved impossible to maintain this combined hospital on the scale envisaged at the time of the amalgamation in 1681. The number of adults admitted was reduced to twenty in 1745, and ten years later to twelve; and from 1755 onwards only white foundlings were admitted, whereas previously coloured babies had been received as well. Another charitable institution operated by the Misericordia, and to which the Camara also contributed, was the Leper Hospital of São Lazaro, founded in 1529. These hospitals were all distinct from the famous Hospital Real de Espirito Santo, described in such glowing terms by Pyrard de Laval, and which was intended mainly for the Portuguese soldiers serving in India.[21]

The white and Eurasian working-class people of Goa were represented in the Camara by the four *procuradores dos mesteres*, and in the Misericordia by the *Irmãos de menor condição*, or "Brothers of lower degree." Visitors to Golden Goa often commented on the contempt of the Portuguese for manual labour, and the fact that all such work was left to foreigners, natives, or slaves. Similar observations made by

21. Ferreira Martins, *História da Misericordia de Goa*, Vol. II, pp. 287–396, *passim*. For the origins of the leper hospital of São Lazaro, see G. Schurhammer, S.J., *Franz Xaver: Sein leben und seine Zeit*, Vol. II, Part 1 (Freiburg im Breisgau, 1964), pp. 206–7. There is much unpublished material in the archives of Lisbon and Goa referring to these various hospitals and their connections with the Camara and the Misericordia. Cf., for instance, the "Lista dos defuntos que falecerão no Hospital Real em Goa no anno de 1727, pobres, e que a Misericordia se enterrou por amor de Deus," and attached documents, in Arquivo Histórico Ultramarino, Lisbon, "Documentos da India," Maço 27 (anno 1729); the "Lista dos pobres pretos [e brancos] do Recolhimento do Hospital de São Lazaro," 13 March 1710, with the lists of the inmates and deaths for 1698–1702, in the Historical Archive at Goa, "Livros dos Acordãos e Assentos do Senado," Vol. X (1694–1709), fls. 291 ff.

many visitors to Portugal also showed to what lengths the desire for *fidalguia* was carried, and testified to the widely held conviction that it was less shameful to beg than to work with one's hands.[22] No doubt this was broadly true, but we must avoid exaggerating this state of affairs. The existence of the *mesteres* down the centuries at Goa shows that there was a sizable number of white, or near-white, artisans and crafts-men there, just as there was at Lisbon, Bahia, and elsewhere. In 1755 an order of the Viceroy Count of Alva stated that owing to the decline in population, the four *procuradores dos mesteres* need no longer be chosen from among the twenty-nine traditional crafts and trades to which representation had hitherto been confined, but could be taken from any other as well.[23] It is possible that by this time full-blooded (but Chris-tian) Asians were eligible to serve as *procuradores dos mes-teres*, in default of sufficient whites and Eurasians, but I have not been able to find proof of this.

The main function of the *procuradores dos mesteres* in the Camara was, as we have seen, to advise their senior colleagues on all matters concerning the economic life of the city in general, and on what concerned the artisans, shopkeepers, and traders in particular. They did not always confine them-selves to debating and voting on such concerns, but sometimes gave their views on matters of high policy. In November 1552, they wrote directly to the Crown, without the knowledge of their colleagues in the Camara, bitterly criticizing the viceroy for his cowardly sloth in neglecting to relieve Ormuz from its siege by a small Turkish raiding flotilla. They also complained of the lack of justice in Portuguese India, and alleged that the *vereadores* did not write the whole truth in their letters to the King, since they had been suborned by the viceroy. On the

22. M. Gonçalves Cerejeira, *Clenardo e a sociedade portuguesa do seu Tempo* (Coimbra, 1949), pp. 159–69, 203–21, for the classic account of Portuguese *desamor ao trabalho* by the Flemish Humanist, Cleynaerts.

23. Text in Albuquerque, *Senado de Goa*, p. 109.

other hand, two years earlier the *vereadores* had written to the Crown, suggesting that the *procuradores dos mesteres* should not be asked to sign the confidential letters of the Camara to the King, as these dealt with matters which were too serious for persons of their lowly social position. As early as 1522 the *procuradores dos mesteres* of Goa had complained to the Crown that they were being treated "like the whale treats the sardine," and not with the consideration that their colleagues received at Lisbon. Contrariwise, the *vereadores* complained to the Crown in 1595 that the four *procuradores dos mesteres* were getting ideas above their station, and "as men of little intelligence" could not be trusted to keep secrets. On the whole, however, the working-class representatives usually got on well with their colleagues in the Camara, and they were treated with due consideration by the latter. In 1605 the Camara complained to the Crown that when this body paid an official visit to the viceroy, Martim Affonso de Castro, he did not wish the four *procuradores dos mesteres* to be seated, so he kept everyone standing while the interview lasted. The *vereadores* protested against this unprecedented slight shown to the four *mesteres,* and they reminded the Crown that these men were an integral part of the municipality.[24]

It will be recalled that the original citizens of Goa were mainly those Portuguese soldiers, sailors, and artisans whom Albuquerque had married with the widows or daughters of the slaughtered Indian defenders. There were comparatively few fidalgos and *cavalleiros* among them, but in course of time many of these two categories did settle down as *casados* at Goa, the great majority of them being married to the Eurasian female descendants of the pioneer citizens. By 1540, there were about 1,800 *moradores,* or heads of households, in

24. António da Silva Rego (ed.), *Documentação para a história das missões do padroado português do Oriente: Índia,* Vol. V, pp. 218–22; *APO,* I (1877), p. 34, and I, Part 2, pp. 153, 174, 213.

Goa, including recent arrivals from Portugal and those descended from the original settlers of 1510–20.[25] The death rate among Europeans was very high in the East, but the ranks of the *casados* were continually reinforced by new arrivals from Lisbon. These men had mostly come out as soldiers in the service of the Crown, and subsequently renounced a military career for the pleasures of matrimony and the profits of the interport trade. As the Camara of Goa reminded the Crown in 1595 — and, for that matter, on many earlier and later occasions — the citizens of Goa all earned their livelihood by engaging in trade, "not having any other means of living, because, as it is notorious to Your Majesty, they can only live and sustain themselves by trading." The parents of Eurasian girls were anxious to marry them to European-born Portuguese whenever possible, even if these men were of lowly birth. In 1632 an Augustinian chronicler stigmatized the municipal councilors as being none of them locally born, "but all of them outsiders, and most of them persons who had amassed wealth by trading and had married and settled in the city, which qualified them for participating in the municipal government. Many of them could neither read nor write; and for this reason those of them who had some education were able to lead the others by the nose." Fr. Agostinho de Santa Maria was admittedly a prejudiced writer, and his allegation that some members of the Camara were illiterate can only have been true of the *mesteres*, as the signatures of the *vereadores* are on some of the documents which he reproduced in his book.[26] But his observation reflected the tendency at this period and for long afterwards to give preference to

25. Schurhammer, *Franz Xaver*, Vol. II, Part 1, p. 209n. The Camara of Goa, writing to the Crown on 31 October 1524, stated there were then at least 450 Portuguese *moradores* in Goa (*Boletim da Bibliographia Portugueza*, Vol. II, pp. 244–49).

26. Agostinho de Santa Maria, O.E.S.A., *História da Fundação do Real Convento de Santa Monica da Cidade de Goa, Corte do Estado da India, e do Imperio Lusitano do Oriente*, p. 239.

European-born Portuguese both in municipal office and in the service of the Crown.

Even though Fr. Agostinho de Santa Maria was obviously exaggerating the defects of the municipal councilors in 1632, there is no doubt that the *oficiais da Camara* were not always as fully qualified by birth and education as they should have been under the existing laws. Nor is this surprising in an unhealthy tropical city such as Goa was from about 1575 onwards, and where white women were always in such short supply. Following the precedent set by the Lisbon Camara, "New Christians," or persons of Jewish descent, were banned from holding municipal office at Goa, even though some of them were elected from time to time. The Camara's correspondence of 1595–1608 is full of complaints against New-Christian monopolists and engrossers, and also against crypto-Jewish retail-traders and commission-agents, and their working with Muslim and Hindu (*Baneane*) merchants to the detriment of Old-Christian Portuguese traders. A royal decree of 18 February 1519 had already barred New Christians from serving as municipal councilors at Goa, save only in very exceptional cases and with the express authorization of the Crown. The ban was later made more rigid and renewed in 1562, and on various other occasions, thus indicating that it was by no means always observed in practice. In 1595 the Camara protested to the Crown that it was not so much opposed to the New-Christian financiers who handled the royal monopoly-contracts as to "the pastry-cooks, shopkeepers, and other low-class people" of Jewish descent, who were monopolizing the local retail trade by virtue of their inherent mercantile abilities.[27] Despite this anti-Semitic attitude of the Camara, the New Christians infiltrated here as elsewhere.

27. See *APO*, I (1877), p. 59, and I, Part 2, p. 14, and the index to this volume under the heading of "Homens da nação" for the reiterated complaints of the Goa Camara against the *Christãos-novos* in India.

They included the *vereador*, Luís de Fonseca de Sampaio, who was the mainspring of the council's opposition to the Convent of Santa Monica in 1629–35.

The unhealthiness of Goa first became noticeable in the last quarter of the sixteenth century, and it continued at an increasing rate during the next two centuries, culminating in the abandonment of the Old City and the transference of the capital to Pangim (1760). The two main reasons for this progressive deterioration were the porous nature of the soil, which allowed the drainage to seep into the wells whence the householders drew their drinking-water, and the increase of the incidence of malaria. The economic decline resulting from the disastrous wars with the Dutch (1600–1663) and with the Arabs of Oman (1650–1730) further dimmed the tarnished splendour of Golden Goa. The Camara was already bewailing the decline in the population by 1618, and Fr. Agostinho de Santa Maria, writing at the end of the century, described the situation in 1632 as follows:

As regards the depopulation of the city, this was shown to be due to the bad climate of that region, where the prevailing diseases wiped out entire streets within a few years, leaving nobody to inhabit the empty houses. Someone who was in a good position to ascertain the facts was able to prove that in a large parish of the city, out of all the householders who had lived there in the twenty-six years before 1632, only two of the leading families were left, all of the others having died out, due to the pestilential and unhealthy nature of the climate. And so much so, that it has often been seen after the arrival of the Indiamen from Portugal, that when the people on board might be expected to recover ashore the health which they have lost on so terrible a voyage, many of them die of the diseases which they contract within a few days of landing. To which it may be added, that in the thirty years prior to this trial inflicted on the Convent of Santa Monica [1632], it was found from the muster-rolls that 25,000 soldiers had died in the [Crown] Hospital at Goa alone, apart from those who died in their billets, or

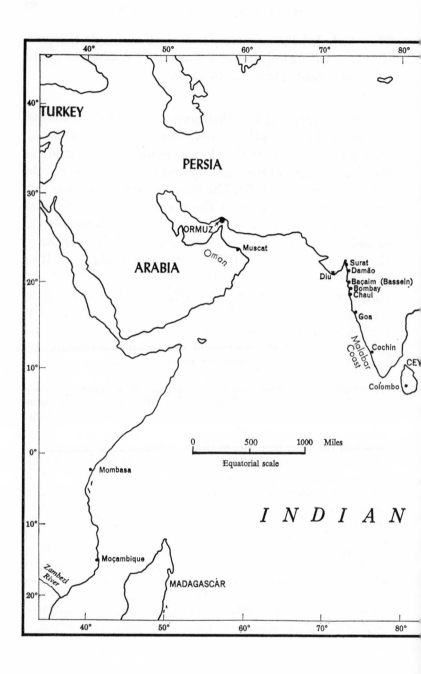

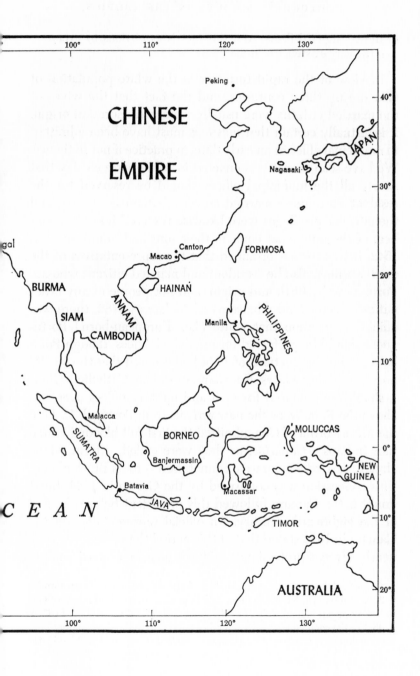

in the coastguard fleets. And this fact is as obvious to everyone as is the very existence of India.[28]

In view of the rapid turnover in the white population of Goa during three centuries, and the fact that the wives of the married citizens were usually women of Eurasian origin, it is virtually certain that *mestiços* must have been admitted to municipal office at an early date, in practice if not in theory. We have seen that it was enacted in Albuquerque's day that nearly all the municipal offices should be reserved for the resident Portuguese married citizens (*casados*) of Goa, and the citizens' privileges were likewise reserved for "the members of the municipal council, their sons and grandsons." In 1542, it was further ordained that the representatives of the *mesteres* must also be "resident and married citizens who are Portuguese by birth and origin, and not people of any other nation, race or kind whatsoever." As late as 1782, there was official notification that white (i.e., European-born) Portuguese should be preferred for municipal offices, though Pombal's famous instructions of 1774 had ordered that the locally born — whether whites, Eurasians, or Roman Catholic Indians — should be favoured for civil and military offices over and above the *Reinóis*, or the new arrivals from Portugal. In 1720 the Misericordia of Goa admitted the first full-blooded Christian Indians — *Canarins*, as they were called, a term which already carried a pejorative connotation — to its Brotherhood. This concession was confirmed by the Crown in 1743, but I doubt if the Camara followed this precedent before the end of the eighteenth century. An official representation of the Camara in 1812 stated that at this period the *vereadores* were nearly always professional military officers ("quasi sempre

28. Agostinho de Santa Maria, *História do Real Convento de Santa Monica*, p. 220. Writing in 1582, the Camara dated the increasing unhealthiness of Goa as having begun immediately after the great siege of 1571. — *APO*, I (1877), p. 95. For the complaint of 1618 and other references to the deteriorating sanitary conditions in Goa, see Albuquerque, *Senado de Goa*, pp. 423–25, 452–60.

militares graduados") and that the *naturaes,* or Goans with little or no admixture of European blood, were mostly priests and lawyers.[29]

It must be remembered that all the religious orders at Goa maintained a strict colour-bar against the admission of Indian vocations between about 1600 and 1750, when the Theatines broke a long-standing practice by admitting four Indian novices. The Convent of Santa Monica had admitted four *Brahmene* (high-caste Christian Indian) nuns before 1632, but it was bitterly criticized by the citizens of Goa for doing so. The indigenous secular clergy of Goa was kept in a strictly subordinate position by the European-born hierarchy and the Regulars down to the last quarter of the eighteenth century. In the absence of any proof to the contrary, I think it fair to say that seats in the Camara were reserved for whites and Eurasians only, with a decided preference for the former category. The Camara of Goa complained to the Crown in 1607, that when the government posts fell vacant they were given "to a few *Reinóis* who had not been more than one or two years in India, without their ever having seen active service, either ashore or afloat." This was an obvious exaggeration, but the royal orders promulgated in 1513 and 1559 that Indian Christians should be placed on a footing of absolute social and legal equality with the Portuguese *moradores* of Goa were very seldom, if ever, implemented in practice until over two centuries later.[30]

On the other hand, if the Camara of Goa consciously maintained the doctrine of white supremacy, it was not a self-perpetuating oligarchy in the sense that municipal offices

29. Albuquerque, *Senado de Goa,* pp. 113, 115, 120; *Oriente Portuguez,* Vol. VI, p. 426; Vol. X, p. 50; Gabriel de Saldanha, *História de Goa,* Vol. II, p. 144.

30. C. R. Boxer, *Race Relations in the Portuguese Empire, 1415–1825* (Oxford, 1963), pp. 57–85, and the sources there quoted, to which should be added *Instrucções com que El-Rei D. José I mandou passar ao Estado da India o Governador e Capitão General e o Arcebispo Primaz do Oriente no anno de 1774.*

descended from father to son, as they did, for example, in many towns of the eighteenth-century Dutch Republic. There were occasional complaints, some of them doubtless well founded, that the *vereadores* tended to become *compadres*, and so arranged matters that they and their friends rotated in office, despite the elaborate provisions of the *Ordenações* to prevent this being done. But such complaints alternated with others, perhaps more common in times of economic depression, that some people who were elected to municipal office were reluctant to serve, since they would be out of pocket by doing so, or because they were treated with insufficient consideration by the viceroy. This reluctance, however, seems to have been more evident in those elected to subordinate but exacting or time-consuming posts, such as those of *almotacél*, or *juiz dos orfãos*, than in that of *vereador* with the enviable social prestige which it conferred.[31]

"Golden" Goa was always proud of its other sobriquet of "The Rome of the Orient," and many visitors besides the Roman Catholic Pyrard de Laval, the Protestant Peter Mundy, and the Buddhist Siamese envoys to Europe in 1686, have left us their impressions of the magnificence of its churches, monasteries, and other ecclesiastical establishments. Prominent among these was the Convent of Santa Monica, the first institution of its kind in Portuguese Asia and one which was only paralleled later by the foundation of a Franciscan nunnery at Macao. Santa Monica owed its inception to the Augustinian archbishop, D. Fr. Aleixo de Menezes, who served as governor of Portuguese India in 1606–9. His proposal for the establishment of a nunnery was enthusiastically received by the Camara of Goa, which had vainly tried to persuade the Crown to allow the foundation of one many years previously.

31. For complaints that elected councilors were sometimes reluctant to serve and had to be compelled to do so, and for fraudulent elections, etc., cf. Abranches Garcia, *Archivo da Relação de Goa*, pp. 120, 194–95; APO, I (1877), pp. 106, 124, 130–31, and I, Part 2, pp. 98–99, 120–21.

In their session of 7 September 1605, the councilors recalled with pride the growth and opulence of "this city of Goa, which can nowadays be reckoned as one of the greatest belonging to the Portuguese Crown, both by virtue of its size and extent and by the number of illustrious fidalgos, knights, and very noble persons who are married and householders therein." They also recalled that four religious orders — Jesuits, Franciscans, Dominicans, and Augustinians — were established there; that many fidalgos could not afford to provide a dowry for more than one of their (often numerous) daughters; and hence there was a great need for a nunnery which could accommodate unmarried girls who would take the veil, in the same way as unwedded girls of noble birth usually entered convents in Portugal.[32] The foundation stone of Santa Monica was laid in 1606, and the building was concluded twenty-one years later; but the Camara soon repented of the support which it had given to this convent, and it failed to pay the annual subsidy which it had promised.

The number of the nuns at Santa Monica was limited by the original statutes to one hundred, and the number of indoor servants and slaves to one hundred and twenty. The dowry for each nun on admission was originally fixed at 2,000 xerafines, later reduced to 1,000 and then raised to 4,000. However, the Camara soon complained that there were more than one hundred nuns in the convent and that virtually all the wealthy heiresses and unmarried women of Portuguese Asia were anxious to be admitted, with the result that deserving citizens, fidalgos, and soldiers could not find suitable brides. The Camara further alleged that the convent was only interested in receiving wealthy spinsters and widows, and that it rejected poor but deserving applicants; that it possessed enormous wealth in land and property, particularly in the fertile "Province of the North" (the region between Chaul and Damão);

32. Historical Archives, Goa, "Livros dos Acordãos e Assentos," Vol. V, 1603–8, fls. 141–44, *assento* of 7 September 1605.

that it insisted on dowries much higher than the stipulated amount; and that it traded with the capital which it had accumulated, in direct competition with the merchant-citizens of Goa, whom it was forcing out of business.

The nuns and their Augustinian friar-spokesmen were not backward in refuting all these charges, and this acrimonious dispute reached its height during the viceroyalty of the Count of Linhares (1629–35), who openly supported the Camara and the other critics of Santa Monica. Both sides appealed to the Crown, which in 1636 took the convent under its direct patronage, conferring on it the title of "Royal." At the same time, the Crown stipulated that the restrictions in the number of admissions and of servants and the limitations placed on the dowries should be strictly observed. The Crown also ruled that the income from the convent's properties should not exceed 8,000 cruzados a year. The Augustinian chronicler of the convent, writing in 1696, complained that the Camara was still resentful of the wealth and influence of Santa Monica and that it contributed little or nothing to its support. This attitude did not prevent the *oficiais da Camara,* as individuals, from being very anxious to place their unmarried daughters inside; and many of them were, in fact, received as novices, sometimes without payment of a dowry.[33]

One interesting social sidelight which emerges from the controversy over Santa Monica is the vast number of slaves kept by the householders of Goa. The nuns, through their confessor and spokesman, Fr. Diogo de Santa Anna, O.E.S.A., complained that the stipulated maximum of one hundred and twenty was totally insufficient for them. An ordinary unmar-

33. The foundation and early years of Santa Monica, and the objections of the Camara of Goa and the Viceroy Count of Linhares to this institution are copiously documented in print. See Agostinho de Santa Maria, *História do Real Convento de Santa Monica; Diario do 3⁰ Conde de Linhares, Vice-Rei da India,* pp. 270–319; Saldanha, *História de Goa,* Vol. II, pp. 127–40; Germano da Silva Correia, *História da colonização portuguesa na India,* Vol. III, pp. 65–90.

ried European or Eurasian artisan would have fifteen or twenty female slaves; and the defenders of Santa Monica instanced a mulatto blacksmith who had twenty-six women and girls, exclusive of the male slaves in his household. A typical citizen of Goa, who served as a *juiz ordinario* in the Camara, had over eighty-five female slaves, and a typical Crown lawyer (*desembargador*) had over sixty. Rich ladies sometimes had over three hundred. These unnecessarily large slave households were maintained to give social status and prestige to their owners, and they were a feature of Portuguese colonial life from the Maranhão to Macao.[34] This example was followed later by the Dutch at Batavia, and to some extent by the English at Calcutta, though the latter employed servants rather than slaves.

Students of Iberian colonial history will hardly need reminding that the religious processions staged on certain church high-days and holidays formed one of the principal diversions for all classes of the population. The *oficiais da Camara* had a statutory obligation to participate personally in certain civic feasts, of which the most important was the Feast of Corpus Christi. This obligation originated in the Middle Ages, but it was during the reign of D. Manuel I that the Feast of Corpus Christi came to be celebrated with particular pomp and circumstance in all the cities of the Portuguese world, a distinction which it retained down to the nineteenth century. Ecclesiastics and laymen vied with each other in prodigal expenditure on this occasion, and the citizens of Lisbon hardly needed the reminder of their Camara on 7 May 1660, that this corporation "had always tried to increase the devotion and splendour of this Feast, celebrating it with all possible solemnity, decency, and reverence, so as to set an example not merely to this kingdom, but to the whole world." [35]

34. Agostinho de Santa Maria, *História do Real Convento de Santa Monica*, pp. 263, 358–59; Sousa, *Oriente Conquistado*, Vol. I, pp. 739–40.
35. Freire de Oliveira, *Elementos*, Vol. I, pp. 417–42.

The Senate of Goa was likewise very much to the fore in these religious processions when "the workers' guilds were accustomed to display their banners, castles, dragons, serpents, and giants, with the triumphal cars of the tanners and gardeners, etc.," as stated in a municipal decree of 1618. This same decree added that as the *mesteres* now found it too burdensome to stage these lavish displays in all the chief religious processions, they would henceforth be expected to provide them only on the two municipal feasts of Corpus Christi and St. Catherine. Their participation in the other festivals would be limited to walking in the procession with their banners and staves of office. As in Lisbon, each "art, craft, or mystery" was responsible for a certain section of the display. Thus the shipwrights and carpenters of the dockyard provided a ship or gallery, the tanners a castle or a tower, the cobblers a dragon, and the armourers an archer. Other guild members impersonated or depicted historical or mythological personages such as King David, various other kings, emperors, princes, devils, giants, wizards, and, on occasion, ladies of easy virtue.[36]

In surveying the development and the functions of the "very noble and always loyal" Senate of the city of Goa during the three centuries with which we are concerned, we are left with a strong impression that this corporation was one of the principal forces which held the ramshackle State of India (*Estado da India*) together. It certainly was not a mere rubber stamp in the hands of viceroys or governors, and it provided a strong element of continuity in a government whose head normally changed every three years. It jealously, and on the whole successfully, maintained the extensive privileges which it had been granted by the Crown; and successive monarchs undoubtedly valued it as a check upon both viceroys and archbishops. Even in the priest-ridden society of Portuguese Asia, where it usually needed no lusty blast on the ecclesiastical

36. Albuquerque, *Senado de Goa*, p. 426.

whistle to bring the laity humbly and crouchingly to heel, the Camara sometimes confronted the highest ecclesiastical authorities. In the course of a dispute over precedence with the Archbishop of Goa in 1747, the *oficiais da Camara* told him that as private individuals they recognized him as their spiritual pastor, but as a collective body they only recognized the King and the viceroy as their lawful superiors.[37] The Camara often came to the rescue of the perennially exhausted royal exchequer, and many coastguard fleets and armadas could never have sailed without the ships, men, and money which it supplied in whole or in part. If the *Reinol* element predominated among its members for much of the time, at any rate these were men who had married and had settled at Goa, thus helping to bind the Indo-Portuguese inhabitants closer to the mother country. Last not least, since the four *procuradores dos mesteres* always formed an integral part of the municipal council, this body did not reflect exclusively the interests of the "ruling few" but, more often than not, those of all classes.

37. *Ibid.*, pp. 187–88.

CHAPTER II

The
Municipal Council
of Macao

Much has been written on the origins of the Portuguese settlement of Macao, but nothing very definite has been established.
The oldest original documents in the archives of the Senado da
Camara date from 1712, although there are some nineteenth-
century transcripts of (incomplete) records going back to
1630.[1] The only piece of evidence by a participant in the
founding of the colony is a passing reference by Gregorio Gonçalves, *presbitero secular*, in an undated document in the
Archivo de las Indias at Seville, which, from the context, must
have been written about 1570. Padre Gonçalves implies that
the first settlers were unauthorized squatters, who spent some
months ashore on the "Water-lily peninsula" — to give it one
of its Chinese names — in the year 1555, between one trading

1. *Arquivos de Macau*; catalogue of the archives of Macao in *Boletim da
Filmoteca Ultramarina Portuguesa* No. 19 (Lisbon, 1961), pp. 331–1067,
especially pp. 339–46, for the "Lista dos códices existantes no arquivo do Leal
Senado."

season and the next. He goes on to state that within twelve years the Portuguese had built "a very large settlement on the point of the mainland, which is called Macao, with three churches and a hospital for the poor, and house of the Santa Misericordia, which nowadays forms a settlement of over five thousand Christian souls." Padre Gonçalves makes no mention of the Portuguese having helped the Cantonese authorities to suppress a pirate band, which is the traditional Portuguese version of the reason why the Europeans were allowed to establish themselves at Macao. It is, however, quite possible that they had done so, if mainly for their own benefit. In any event, the Cantonese authorities, in return for bribes, connived at the development of Macao from an obscure fishing-village into a flourishing port, which the Portuguese regarded as an integral part of the State of India.

Even so, it was some years before the viceroy at Goa realized the extent to which the place had developed, and still longer before the Chinese emperor knew that there were foreigners permanently settled in that remote corner of the Middle Flowery Kingdom. An ex-governor of the Philippines reported — not without a touch of malice — in 1582:

The Portuguese of Macao are still nowadays without any weapons or gunpowder, or form of justice, having a Chinese Mandarin who searches their houses to see if they have any arms and munitions. And because it is a regular town with about 500 houses and there is a Portuguese governor and a bishop therein, they pay every three years to the incoming viceroy of Canton about 100,000 ducats to avoid being expelled from the land, which he divides with the grandees of the household of the king [emperor] of China. However, it is constantly affirmed by everyone that the king has no idea that there are any such Portuguese in his land.[2]

2. For the reports of Padre Gregorio Gonçalves (*ca.* 1570), and Dr. Francisco de Sande (1582), see C. R. Boxer, *South China in the Sixteenth Century* (London, 1953), pp. xxxv–xxxvii, and the sources there quoted. A Jesuit visitor reported in 1578 that the population of Macao already comprised about 10,000 souls of various races and creeds.

The origin of the Senado da Camara of Macao dates from the time of the viceroyalty of D. Francisco Mascarenhas, Count of Santa Cruz (1581–84). Shortly after the settlement had agreed to take the oath of allegiance to Philip II of Spain, in June 1582, the citizens assembled in conclave and "decided to arrange the form of local government in the same way as was practiced in the cities of the kingdom and of the State of India; and in accordance with the *Ordenação* they elected [ordinary] judges and aldermen, a Procurator of the city, and a Secretary of the Camara. And they entitled it the City of the Name of God, which was the name by which it had been known up to then." Confirmation of this procedure was obtained by a viceregal decree signed at Goa on 10 April 1586, and at the same time the "City of the Name of God of Macao in China" was granted the same "privileges, liberties, honours, and pre-eminencies" as those possessed by the city of Evora in Portugal.[3] Not content with these privileges, the Camara subsequently tried to obtain those of Oporto, sending a representative to Lisbon as late as 1706, in order to petition the Crown for this purpose. These efforts failed, and successive royal decrees of 1596, 1689, and 1709 merely ratified the original viceregal concession of 1586. In 1736, however, the Camara secured the coveted privilege of the *Infanções de Santa Maria* — "grandsons of kings, and that as such they will not be put to the torture for any crimes," save only those such as high trea-

3. "Treslado dos apontamentos que se mandão pedir a Sua Magestade pelo D. [*sic*, for Padre] Gil de Matta para o bem desta Cidade, e bom governo delle no janeiro de 1592," MS quoted by José Feliciano Marques Pereira, *Ta-Ssi-Yang-Kuo: Archivos e annaes do Extremo Oriente Portuguez*, Vol. II, p. 526; Manuel Murias (ed.), *Instrução para o Bispo de Pequim e outros documentos para a história de Macau*, pp. 136–41; *Arquivos de Macau*, Vol. I, pp. 15–18; Diogo Caldeira do Rego, "Breve Relação do estado da Cidade do Nome de Deos Reino da China de seu principio até o anno de 1623," in Francisco Paulo Mendes da Luz, *O Conselho da India*, pp. 606–16. For Padre Gil de la Mata, S. J., the *procurador* of Macao in Europe, 1592, see Jesús López Gay, S.J., *El matrimonio de los Japoneses: Problema, y soluciones según un ms. inédito de Gil de la Mata S.J., 1547–1599* (Rome, 1964), pp. 79–130.

son, for which nobles and fidalgos could likewise be tortured. Similarly, they were normally exempted from being imprisoned when awaiting trial, but could only be placed under house arrest, as fidalgos were, "and in the same way they were granted all the privileges which were conceded to the City of Lisbon." These privileges were specifically granted to all past and present *vereadores, juizes ordinarios*, and *almotacéls* of the Camara, as also to their sons and grandsons.[4]

The main difference between the municipal council of Evora and those of Lisbon and Oporto was that the charter (*foral*) of Evora contained no provision for any representation of the *mesteres* of the *Casa dos Vinte e Quatro* on the Camara. The voting members of the Senate of Macao accordingly comprised three *vereadores*, two *juizes ordinarios*, and a *procurador da cidade*, who were elected by the method previously described. *Vereadores* had to be at least forty years of age and *juizes ordinarios* thirty. The secretary of the Macao Camara, who usually combined this function with that of *alferes* (ensign), was originally elected for a three-year term, later extended to six, and, after about 1630, often enough for life. In 1776 the Governor-General of Goa appointed António José Pereira as "Alferes Mor e Escrivão da Camara para toda a sua vida," in return for a cash payment of 2,600 xerafines, but this sale of office seems to have been exceptional. The *procurador da cidade* at Macao was a much more important figure than in any other of the metropolitan or colonial Camaras, relatively speaking. From early days he became the city's accredited representative in all dealings with the Chinese officials and was accorded the grade of a junior mandarin by the Chinese authorities. He also acted as treasurer of the Camara

4. Cf. the list of contents of the original "Livro dos treslados de todos os alvarás e privilégios concedidos ao Senado da Camara da Cidade de Macao," in *Boletim da Filmoteca*, No. 19 (1961), pp. 349–54. In 1717–21, the Crown granted the Camara of Evora the privilege that only the sons and grandsons of *vereadores*, or gentlemen of the royal household, would be eligible to serve as aldermen in future (*Gazeta de Lisboa*, 20 Feb. 1721).

down to the year 1738, when the two functions were separated, and hence he was the key man in the colony. To assist him in his dealings with the Chinese officials he had an official interpreter (*lingua*), who was presumably a local Chinese Christian, and two *jurubaças* or assistant interpreters.[5] The Camara also sent its personal representatives (*procuradores*) to Goa when necessary, besides maintaining a resident *procurador* there, and others at Lisbon, or at Madrid during the union of the two Crowns. As with all other municipal councils, refusal to serve an office was a punishable offense. On Christmas Eve, 1639, Manuel de Vasconcellos was deprived of all his citizenship rights and barred from holding any municipal office in future, owing to his refusal to serve in the post of *almotacél* to which he had been elected.

Thanks to its position as an entrepôt in the trade between China and Japan, Macao continued to prosper until the Tokugawa Shogunate put an end to its commerce with the island-empire in 1639–40, for motives which it is not necessary to discuss here.[6] A good review of the City of the Name of God in China in its heyday was given by the secretary of the Camara in November 1623, writing to the Crown a few months after the arrival of the first resident captain-general and governor, Dom Francisco Mascarenhas. The city was then in

size, in splendid buildings, and in number of householders [*moradores*] one of the most important in this Orient, containing more than 400 married Portuguese men, including some fidalgos, many gentlemen [*nobres*], and most of them persons who have served His Majesty for many years in the fleets and campaigns of this

5. Cf. J. M. Braga, "Interpreters and translators in Old Macao," in *Proceedings of the Congress of East Asian Historians at Hong Kong* (Hong Kong, 1964); António Feliciano Marques Pereira, *Ephemerides commemorativas da História de Macau*, pp. 101–2. The term *jurubaça* was originally applied to Chinese Christians born in Macao, but later was extended to include *mestiços* and Eurasians who spoke Chinese and Portuguese.

6. C. R. Boxer, *The Great Ship from Amacon: Annals of Macao and the Old Japan Trade, 1555–1640* (Lisbon, 1963), pp. 154–71, 330–33, for details and documentation.

State, besides many married men, sons of the soil, and outsiders who have settled here, as well as many people of various nations who come and go, living here for most of the year, on account of the great trade and commerce driven with many regions of the East. And the City has always maintained and fostered this trade in great peace and quiet with all concerned, spending yearly for this purpose a great deal of its money in bribes, embassies, and presents to the mandarins who govern China as well as the rulers of Japan and Cochin-China and with others, all of which must be done for the preservation of this city in the midst of so many and such powerful enemies.[7]

The Secretary further explained that the city likewise supported in whole or in great part a Jesuit college which was one of the finest in the East, and which contained at any given time between fifty and a hundred missionaries, as well as Augustinian, Dominican, and Franciscan monasteries and conventual churches, each housing from six to ten friars. There were a cathedral church and two parish churches, a couple of hermitages, a house of Misericordia with an orphanage and two hospitals attached, which catered for both Portuguese and Asians. "All this fabric of monasteries, churches, Misericordia, hospitals, charitable foundations and ministers of the church," continued this representation, "were built and maintained by this city with its ordinary and private almsgiving, and with some general taxes which were levied on the people with their consent for some years, without the royal exchequer contributing anything thereto, unlike it does in other parts." The only apparent exception was the bishop's stipend, which was supposed to be paid from Crown funds. But in point of fact, the money was seldom available, and the bishop and his household were likewise in practice a charge

7. Caldeira do Rego, "Breve Relação do estado da Cidade do Nome de Deos," in Mendes da Luz, *O Conselho da India*, pp. 606–16. At this period there were 437 *vizinhos e extravagantes* and 403 *jurubaças*, or Christian Chinese in Macao, apart from thousands of unconverted Chinese (papers of D. Francisco Mascarenhas, in the Evora Public Library, Codex CXVI–2–5, fl. 225).

upon the resources of the Senate. I may add that in later years the Crown abandoned all pretense of paying the episcopal stipend and made this officially a charge on the Camara, which vainly tried to shift the burden on to the viceregal government at Goa. As late as 1769, when the Bishop of Macao had been living at Lisbon for the previous four years, the Crown compelled the Camara of Macao to pay the whole of his stipend, although a successor to this absentee prelate was not appointed until 1772.[8] The Senate also organized the statutory religious processions, the chief of which, in Macao as elsewhere, was the Feast of Corpus Christi. By the mid-seventeenth century Macao had quite a plethora of patron saints: Our Lady of the Conception, St. John the Baptist, St. Francis Xavier, and St. Catherine of Sienna. It was resolved by the Senate in 1647 that all the municipal councilors would go to confession and holy communion on those feast days.

Friction between the captain-general or governor of Macao and the municipal council was frequent. In 1783 the Crown alleged that the Camara deliberately kept the governors and the garrison ill-paid and ill-found, in order to prevent them from exerting their full authority. This was probably an exaggeration, and the Camara often complained that the governors tried to interfere arbitrarily in municipal affairs, and that they were liable to run up large debts to the citizens which they made no effort to repay. In 1693 the Camara alleged that the governors had usually purchased their office for a fixed sum, which they had raised by borrowing money at Goa. Arriving in Macao heavily indebted, their one idea was to accumulate a large fortune during their three-year term of office, so that they could repay their creditors at Goa and leave

8. Biblioteca Nacional de Lisboa, Colecção Pombalina, No. 612, MSS "Documentos do Senado da Camara de Macao sobre a retirada do Bispo diocesano para Europa," 1765; Padre Manuel Teixeira, *Macau e a sua diocese no ano dos centenários da fundação e restauração*, Vol. II, pp. 156–276, *passim*, for the difficulties over payment of the *congrua* by the Senate to successive bishops of Macao.

something over for themselves.[9] There were, of course, instances when the governor and the Camara cooperated harmoniously; and there were times when the endemic friction between them culminated in armed clashes, as in the bombardment of the Town Hall by the governor, Diogo de Pinho Teixeira, in 1710. The history of Macao has been written largely in terms of the frequent conflicts between the Camara and the governors, as can be seen from the standard works of Montalto de Jesus, *Historic Macao* (1902 and 1926), Bento de França *Subsídios para a história de Macau* (1888), and Artur Levy Gomes, *Esboço da história de Macau, 1511–1849* (1957).

The Senado da Camara was proudly conscious of the fact that it was the real governing body in Macao, and that the governor or captain-general's duties were confined to the command of the forts and of the exiguous garrison. After the death of one governor and before the arrival of his successor in 1697–98, the Camara exercised the titular governorship of the colony — something which the Camara of Goa never achieved. It was the Camara, and not the captain-majors of the Japan voyage, nor the captain-general of Macao, who corresponded with foreign potentates such as the Tokugawa Shogunate of Japan; the kings of Siam, Tonking, and Annam; the rajah of Banjermassin in Borneo; and the Dutch governor-general at Batavia. It was the Camara which negotiated with the provincial mandarins of Kwangtung, and which petitioned the Chinese government through the intermediary of the Jesuit missionaries at the Court of Peking. Whenever Asian rulers had occasion to correspond with Macao, they likewise addressed their communications to the Senado da Camara, or "the Elders of Macao." In the years 1783–85, incited by the prompting of an ex-governor of Macao named Diogo Fernandes Salema de Saldanha, the Crown decided to make

9. Original MS representation of Pedro Cabral da Costa, *procurador* of Macao at Goa, dated 22 January 1693, in Historical Archive, Goa, "Livros das Monções," Vol. XCV, fls. 116–21.

the governor's powers more far-reaching and effective, while drastically curtailing those of the Senado da Camara. The municipal councilors reacted sharply to this new system, pointing out to the viceroy at Goa that the Camara had governed the colony for the previous 226 years "without any subordination to the governors thereof." Although the Camara's protests were rejected by the Crown, in practice the municipal council still continued to be the principal authority in negotiating with the Chinese officials, who would not recognize the governor's enhanced authority. It was only the enforcement of a royal decree of 9 January 1833, which reduced the proud Senado da Camara of the Name of God in China to the status and functions of a mere municipal council. Even then, the Procurator of the Senate still continued to be appointed from among the elected *vereadores*, and to handle all the negotiations with the Chinese officials, until the post was made a salaried Crown appointment in 1865.[10]

If for the period with which we are concerned, the Senado da Camara of Macao was certainly more important and more influential in the government of the colony than was the captain-general, they were both in a very difficult position vis-à-vis the Chinese authorities. Alexander Hamilton, the Calvinist Scots "interloper" who visited Macao at the turn of the seventeenth-eighteenth centuries, described the situation as he saw it with his slyly malicious wit:

The forts are governed by a Captain-General, and the city by a burgher, called the *Procurador*, but, in reality, both are governed by a Chinese mandarin, who resides about a league out of the city, at a place called Casa Branca. The Portuguese shipping that

10. Murias, *Instrução para o Bispo de Pequim e outros documentos*, pp. 1–114, 246, 356; *Arquivos de Macao*, Vol. I, pp. 337–38, 401–3, Vol. II, pp. 99–111; Artur Levy Gomes, *Esboço da história de Macau, 1511–1849* (Macao, 1957), pp. 280–93; Montalto de Jesus, *Historic Macao* (1902), p. 241; António Feliciano Marques Pereira, *Relatorio acerca das attribuições da Procuratura dos Negocios Sinicos da Cidade de Macau* (Macao, 1867); *Boletim da Filmoteca*, No. 19, p. 642.

come here, are admitted into their harbour, and are under the protection of the town; but the Chinese keep the custom-house and receive customs for all goods imported.

It may be added that although the Chinese always levied anchorage dues from Portuguese ships arriving at Macao, the erection of the *Ho-pu* or Chinese customhouse there dates only from 1688. It continued to function until its destruction by Governor Ferreira do Amaral in 1849, despite periodic urgings from Lisbon that it should not be tolerated. During its existence, the Chinese levied dues on all ingoing and outgoing Chinese shipping, and on all exports in Portuguese ships. Contrary to what Hamilton states, imports in Portuguese ships had to pay only the duties imposed by the Senate, unless they were intended for re-export to Canton, in which case they had to pay the Chinese customs as well.[11]

The Chinese government of Peking, once apprised of the existence of the Portuguese settlement at Macao, naturally continued to regard the place as an integral part of the Celestial Empire, although they allowed the Portuguese a large degree of internal self-government, just as they had done with the Arab and Persian trading communities at Canton and Zayton (Ch'uan-chou) in the Middle Ages. Chinese mandarins who visited the colony on official business were usually received with full military honours, long before this practice was belatedly sanctioned by the viceroy at Goa in 1689. The artillery of the forts fired salutes on imperial birthdays, and minute guns for the emperor's death, just as was done for corresponding events in the Portuguese royal family. In 1736, a minor mandarin, the *Tso-hang*, was appointed to assist the

11. Alexander Hamilton, *A New Account of the East-Indies, 1727*, ed. W. Foster (2 vols.; London, 1930), Vol. II, p. 116. "Casa Branca" was the name given by the Portuguese to the Chinese city of Ch'ien-shan (Tsin-shan, Ançião). For the Chinese customhouse (Ho-pu) and the duties paid by the shipping at Macao, cf. Murias, *Instrução para o Bispo de Pequim e outros documentos*, pp. 315–18, António Feliciano Marques Pereira, *As Alfandegas Chinesas de Macau*; and any of the standard histories of Macao.

mandarin of Tsin-shan in supervising the colony, and the consent of this official had to be obtained before any existing building could be repaired, the construction of new ones being forbidden. The Chinese gradually strengthened their control until the state of affairs was reached as described by the bishop in 1803: "This city of Macao belongs to the Portuguese in name only. The Portuguese do not own a piece of land here, nor can they buy it, nor build a wall, open a window, or repair the roofs of their own houses, without a license from the Mandarins, which has to be bought at a high price." However, these and other vexatious restrictions periodically imposed by the Chinese could usually be evaded by judicious bribery, and it was the Procurator of the Senate who handled the raising and the distribution of this "squeeze." [12]

It was not only the military governors, or the distant authorities at Goa and Lisbon, who were inclined to criticize the *oficiais da Camara* for their real or alleged subservience to the Chinese. In 1621 the Cantonese authorities demanded that the Jesuits should demolish some buildings which they were erecting on the Ilha Verde in the inner harbour of Macao. The senators were prepared to comply with this demand, which was backed by the threat of force, since they admitted that "this land in which we live is not ours but belongs to the emperor of China." They added that in any event they could not resist the Chinese by force of arms, nor could the colony survive a threatened ban on the trade with Canton. The rector of the Jesuit college, Padre Gabriel de Mattos, strongly denounced these arguments. He claimed that Macao was just as much Portuguese territory as was Cochin, "and, peradventure, Ormuz, and other cities in India which are situated in the lands of heathen kings but belong to the king of Portugal."

12. Marques Pereira, *Alfandegas Chinesas de Macau*, p. 33; Teixeira, *Macau e a sua diocese*, Vol. II, p. 310, for the Bishop of Macao's letter dated 20 December 1803.

He argued that payment of the annual *foro* (ground rent) to the authorities at Canton did not imply that the Ming emperor owned Macao as its true lord, but was merely the equivalent of what a landowner in Portugal paid to a count or duke. Vainly urging the Senate to take a strong line, he maintained that the Chinese were only bluffing, and would back down if they were stoutly resisted: "For they are such arrant cowards that they make an armed knight out of a mosquito." The senators rejected the bellicose Jesuit's arguments and settled this dispute as they settled all similar difficulties with the Chinese authorities by employing a mixture of simulated obedience, secret compromise, and bribery.[13]

The severest critics of the Senate's appeasement policy were usually the viceroys at Goa and the overseas councilors at Lisbon, who periodically urged the Camara to stand up to the Chinese and refuse to be browbeaten by them. But neither the viceroy nor the Crown ever sent — nor indeed could they have sent — the naval and military forces which made the "gunboat policy" of the European powers a practical proposition in the nineteenth century. The situation of Macao between 1557 and 1849 was essentially that described by António Bocarro writing in 1635:

The peace that we have with the king of China is as he likes it, for since this place is so far from India, and since he has such vastly greater numbers of men than the most that the Portuguese could possibly assemble there, never did we think of breaking with him whatever serious grievances we may have had; because the Chinese have only to stop our food-supplies to ruin our city, since there is no other place nor means of obtaining any.[14]

13. A set of the original documents on this affair of the Ilha Verde was captured by the Dutch and is now in the Rijksarschief at The Hague. Cf. C. R. Boxer, "Missionaries and Merchants of Macao, 1557–1687," in *Actas do II Colóquio Internacional de Estudos Luso-Brasileiros*, Vol. II (Lisbon, 1960), pp. 219–21.

14. António Bocarro's description of Macao, quoted in C. R. Boxer, *Macao Three Hundred Years Ago* (Macao, 1944), p. 37.

Unlike the Camaras of Goa, Bahia, and Luanda, the Senate of Macao possessed no landed property of its own from which it could draw rents. Such at least was the assertion made by the senators when they rejected a claim by André Lopes de Lavre, Secretary of the Overseas Council at Lisbon, that they should pay him certain annual *propinas* (emoluments, perquisites), as did the other colonial Camaras to the holder of this office. In rejecting this claim — and the royal order which accompanied it — the senators pointed out that their income was derived entirely from imposts levied on the local inhabitants which varied yearly and were calculated so as to cover the estimated annual expenditure.[15] As indicated above, the chief source of the Camara's income was the duties levied on all goods imported into Macao in Portuguese ships, there being no export duties save those levied by the Chinese customhouse from 1688 onwards, and an older tax known as the *caldeirão* (cauldron). This was originally a duty of about 3 percent levied on all goods exported to Japan, which was increased to 8 percent in 1634, and transferred to other goods after the loss of the Japan trade in 1640.

Out of these very fluctuating resources the Senate had to find the money to pay for the garrison, for the construction and upkeep of the fortifications, for artillery and munitions; for the support of the ecclesiastical authorities; for contributions to the Misericordia and its hospitals, and (after 1633) to the Convent of the Poor Clares. Above all, the Senate had to cope with the constantly recurring expenditure on bribes and "squeeze" to the local Chinese officials. The Senate also arranged for the policing of the city by mounting nightly patrols furnished by the *ordenança* or militia, which it paid and officered, steadfastly resisting the efforts of some governors to supervise this auxiliary force.[16] In this respect, as in some

15. Murias, *Instrução para o Bispo de Pequim e outros documentos*, pp. 317–18.

16. *Ibid.*, pp. 153–55; *Arquivos de Macau*, Vol. II, p. 264; Benjamin Vi-

others, Portuguese Macao offered a great contrast to Spanish Manila, which was only economically viable through the *situado*, or annual remittance of Mexican silver from Acapulco to balance the Spanish Crown's administrative expenses in the Philippines.[17] In Macao, on the other hand, virtually all military, civil, and ecclesiastical expenditure, with the partial exception of the Jesuits' college, had to be financed directly or indirectly by the Senate. Small wonder that the senators were often at their wits' end to raise the necessary money, and that they frequently had to call general meetings of all qualified householders in order to obtain the consent of their fellow citizens to increase the existing import duties, or to impose a form of capital levy, or to raid the funds of the Misericordia. On occasion, the Senate also borrowed heavily from Asian rulers and merchants, and in 1636 it owed some 70,000 taels to Kyushu capitalists and entrepreneurs. Owing to the closure of the Japan trade three years later, this debt was never discharged. In the year 1660, the King of Siam helped to finance the embassy of Manuel de Saldanha to Peking through a substantial loan to the Camara of Macao. This loan was eventually repaid in small annual installments over a period of sixty years.[18]

Like the Senate of Goa, the Camara of Macao often came to the financial help of the Crown in time of need. Thus, in spite of the loss of the lucrative Japan trade, the Senate managed to find the wherewithal to fit out three armed junks with supplies of men and provisions for beleaguered Malacca in 1640. But a century later, the Macao Senate was compelled

---

deira Pires, S.J., "A primeira polícia de Macau," 20-page reprint of an article in *Religião e Pátria* (Macao, 1962).

17. W. L. Schurz, *The Manila Galleon* (New York, 1939), pp. 181–82, for the *situado*.

18. *Arquivos de Macau*, Vol. I, pp. 152–75; C. R. Boxer and J. M. Braga (eds.), *Breve Relação da Jornada que fez à Corte de Pekim o Senhor Manuel de Saldanha, Embaixador del Rey de Portugal, e documentos contemporaneos* (Macao, 1942).

to turn down an urgent request for relief from Goa, then at the mercy of the invading Marathas, on the grounds that the citizens were so poor that they could contribute nothing more substantial than their tears. Some years earlier the Senate had raised the sum of 18,500 taels to finance the embassy of Dr. Alexandre Metello de Sousa to Peking in 1727, besides accommodating the ambassador and his numerous suite during their stay at Macao and paying all their expenses from the time of arrival.[19] This contribution had, however, compelled the Senate to mortgage its revenue, and crippled its finances for over thirty years.

As the governing body of a commercial entrepôt, the Camara was closely connected with Macao's overseas trade, and it had the major say in how it should be run, notwithstanding the orders which emanated from the viceroy at Goa. The senators were almost invariably merchants actively engaged in this trade, whatever airs they might give themselves of *fidalguia, nobreza,* and gentility in general. The essentially commercial nature of the Portuguese colonial empire, particularly the African and Asian sectors, was something that distinguished it rather sharply from the Spanish, though in this respect there was a striking similarity between Macao and Manila. In the evidence given at Macao by Portuguese and Macaonese eyewitnesses of the martyrdom of the Italian Jesuit, Marcello Mastrilli, at Nagasaki in 1637, they all, including the captain-major of the Japan voyage, described themselves as gaining their livelihood by trade, "as does everyone else here."[20] In 1664, the Jesuit rector at Macao wrote to his superiors: "The wealth of Macao consists of the sea, and all the city lives on this, there being nothing of value other than what is brought by the wind and the tides. If these

---

19. *Arquivos de Macau*, Vol. I, p. 309, Vol. II, pp. 25–56, 199–200.

20. See Boxer, in *Actas do II Colóquio . . . de Estudos Luso-Brasileiros,* Vol. II, pp. 221–22; also his *Fidalgos in the Far East, 1550–1770* (The Hague, 1948), pp. 157–73.

fail, then everything else fails, nor is it possible for this Province with its missions to maintain itself in any other way" than by engaging in this trade. He added that as long experience had taught the citizens the truth of this fact, they did not now grumble so much about the Jesuits' commercial activities as they had sometimes done in the palmy days of the Japan trade.[21]

After the loss of this profitable commerce in 1640, the Senate played a leading part in reorganizing and expanding Macao's trade with Southeast Asia, in search of new markets to compensate for that catastrophe. The Camara also regulated the trade with Spanish Manila and Dutch Batavia, when the respective authorities of these places allowed their inhabitants to trade with Macao. Admittedly, the senators were sometimes accused of abusing their privileged position by organizing the trade in such a way that the profits accrued to themselves and their cronies, rather than to their fellow citizens in general. It is difficult to ascertain how far such allegations were well founded; and when made by jealous governors they should probably be heavily discounted. But undoubtedly such abuses did occur, and a royal decree of 1728 forbade the senators from monopolizing the trade with Batavia and Manila as they were then trying to do.[22]

During the eighteenth century the trade with Timor and Solor for sandalwood, gold, beeswax, and slaves became the principal economic resource of Macao. From about 1695 this trade was operated by the Senado da Camara on the follow-

21. *Ibid.* Bishop Hilário de Santa Rosa wrote in 1748: ". . . Está a terra muita falta de gente Portugueza, e dos que ha moradores a maior parte são viageiros que sempre andão no mar." — Quoted in Teixeira, *Macau e a sua diocese*, Vol. II, p. 212. Another bishop, D. Frei Manuel de São Galdino, wrote to the Pope in 1803: "Assim tudo em Macao anda a risco do mar . . . em uma palavra afirmo a V. S. com toda a verdade, que em Macao quem não negoceia pede esmola."

22. *Arquivo das Colónias*, Vol. II, pp. 275–76; Montalto de Jesus, *Historic Macao*, p. 115.

ing basis, which lasted with minor modifications for nearly a century. One, two, or three small ships left Macao annually for Timor, sometimes calling at Batavia, and sometimes sailing direct. The Senate sent the names of all registered shipowners to Goa, where they were arranged by the government in sealed lists (*pautas*) on a rotating basis, so as to give all the shipowners their turn. These *pautas* were then sent back to Macao, where the list designated for the ensuing year was opened in a formal session of the Camara, and the owners of the ships named in them were told they could make the voyage. If, when the *pauta* was opened, the designated ship was absent and the owner had no other vessel available, then the next *pauta* was opened, and the ship specified therein made the voyage, being replaced by the other one the next year. Such at least was the theory, though it was alleged that the senators and the shipowners often came to mutually satisfactory arrangements irrespective of the order of the *pautas*.

One-third of the cargo space was reserved for the shipowner, the remaining two-thirds being distributed among the citizens of Macao, through the *bagues* (tickets or certificates of ownership) which might be held by one person only or by several conjointly, like the *boletas* of the Manila trade with Mexico.[23] The distribution of the *bagues* was organized by the Senate of Macao until the system was abolished in 1784. For the most of the eighteenth century, the Timor and Manila voyages were the only two regulated by *pautas*, the voyages to other places, such as Goa and Indochina, being open to all and sundry. As few of the merchants and shipowners of Macao had sufficient capital to make trading voyages entirely at their own risk and charges, they usually did so in partnership with relatives, friends, and associates. In this way, the whole of Macao participated in the sandalwood trade with Timor,

23. Schurz, *The Manila Galleon*, pp. 158–67, 172–77, 363, for the *boletas* of the Manila Galleon trade.

from the captain-general to the widows and orphans who ventured their mites in the *bagues*. People who wished to invest money in the voyage could also borrow from the funds of the Misericordia and the Cathedral Chapter, at rates of interest averaging about 20 or 25 percent, in the same way as the *obras pias* in Manila helped to finance a large part of the galleon trade with Acapulco.[24] Judging by the length of time for which it functioned, the *bague* system must have worked fairly well on the whole, though an ex-governor of Timor complained in 1708 that the principal profits of the Timor trade went to the municipal councilors. He alleged that they divided most of the *bagues* available among themselves, and subsequently bought up at low prices those they had distributed to the poor and widows.[25]

There was inevitably a close and continuous connection between the Camara and the Misericordia at Macao. The latter institution actually antedated the former, since the first bishop, D. Melchior Carneiro, founded the local branch of the Misericordia with a hospital for all races in 1569. The *compromisso*, or statutes, of the Misericordia as revised in 1627 recognized that it should theoretically consist of 300 Brothers (*Irmãos*), of whom 150 should be gentlemen (*nobres*) and the other 150 artisans (*mecanicos*). "But as there are no Portuguese in this city who exercise manual labour, all the Brothers are recognized as being of equal status." In this way the Misericordia of Macao differed from the parent institution and from those of Goa, Bahia, and elsewhere, whose Brothers were divided into the two categories of *nobres*

24. *Ibid.*, pp. 166–72, for the role of the *obras pias* in the Manila Galleon trade.

25. For the function of the *pautas* and *bagues* in the Macao-Timor trade cf. Murias, *Instrução para o Bispo de Pequim e outros documentos*, pp. 192–94, 209–11, 229–32; *Boletim da Filmoteca*, No. 19, pp. 390–91, 614, 774; Humberto Leitão, *Os Portugueses em Solor e Timor de 1515 a 1702* (Lisbon, 1948), pp. 173–81, *passim; Arquivos de Macau*, Vol. II, pp. 353–55.

and *mecanicos,* termed, respectively, *melhor* and *menor con-dição,* or higher and lower social status.[26]

Both the Misericordia and the various hospitals which functioned in Macao were supported largely by funds which were supplied or secured with the cooperation of the Senado da Camara. These charitable institutions included a Leper Hospital attached to the Misericordia, which contained 115 patients in 1726, though 60 or 70 seems to have been the usual number. The majority of the lepers were described as being "newly converted heathens" and were presumably Chinese. According to the regulations for the Hospital of the Poor, as revised in 1627, this institution admitted the poor and needy of all social categories and colours, including "the wretched sick slaves who had been abandoned and turned out on the street by their owners." These regulations also stipulated that the staff of Timorese and Negro slaves should be given ample rations of rice and fish "so as to ensure that they should be kept well-fed and contented." [27] This is an interesting as well as an intelligent and humane stipulation, since legislation to ensure the adequate feeding of slave personnel was seldom enacted by any of the slave-owning colonial powers.[28] Naturally, the numbers admitted to these hospitals were strictly limited at the best of times, and they were very small in the eighteenth century when severe poverty and unemployment

26. The revised *compromisso* of 1627 is printed in the *Arquivos de Macau,* Vol. IV, pp. 55–56, 113–18, 187–90, 223–28, 281–87, 371–79. It was modelled on that of Goa.

27. "Venciam de comer peixe e arroz, quanto basta para andarem fartos e satisfeitos," according to the *compromisso* of 1627. Cf. José Caetano Soares, *Macau e a Assistência: Panorama médico-social,* p. 150.

28. Cf. Richard Pares, *Merchants and Planters* (Cambridge, 1960), p. 39: "Many colonies made no laws at all about the feeding of the slaves before the humanitarians forced them into it at the end of the eighteenth century; and even where there were laws, the standards which they enforced were pitiably low." Pares was writing of conditions in the English and French sugar islands of the West Indies, but his observations are applicable to all European slave-owners in the tropics from the 16th to the 19th centuries.

were perennial at Macao for the reasons explained below. The Misericordia also arranged for a limited number of foundlings to be put out to paid foster mothers until they were seven years old. It likewise endowed a few poor but respectable orphan girls of marriageable age, and operated a short-lived *recolhimento* (home) for widows and orphans between 1727 and 1737.[29]

All these charitable activities and institutions were mainly financed by funds derived from the import duties which were voted annually by the Camara for this purpose, by the profits derived from lending money on *respondencia* (bottomry), and by testamentary bequests. José Lisboa de Almeida, a wealthy *juiz ordinario* who died in 1714, left the whole of his "great riches" to these "pious works," and the portrait of Martha Merop, the Macaonese widow of a rich foreign resident who was a generous benefactor of the Misericordia is still preserved there. It was a common practice for testators to bequeath slaves to work for the Misericordia (or for one of the hospitals) for a fixed number of years, after which they would automatically acquire their freedom. With the steady decline in the trade of Macao during the first half of the eighteenth century, save for a brief interval of prosperity in 1719–25, it became harder than ever for the Camara to help finance the Misericordia and the hospitals. Shipping losses in the typhoon-ridden South China Sea took a heavy toll, and many of the merchants and shippers who borrowed money from the Misericordia became insolvent debtors, or else simply made no effort to repay their loans.

The decrease in the population of Macao during these years of economic adversity was also accompanied by a decline in the quality of the persons who were eligible for office in the Camara and the Misericordia, as is attested by numerous com-

29. See Soares, *Macau e a Assistência*, for a documented study of the vicissitudes of the Santa Casa da Misericordia at Macao and its connections with the Senado da Camara.

plaints. In 1748, the Bishop of Macao informed the Crown that the *Provedor* (Guardian) of the Misericordia was a "huntsman of the late Infante Dom Francisco, who had been banished to India by Your Majesty. But as Macao is the asylum of these people who cannot stay either in Goa or on the coast of India, he came here, where he married and lives like a gentleman, as he is the brother-in-law of one of the leading citizens." [30]

Bishop Hilário de Santa Rosa further alleged that the senators of the Camara and the guardians of the Misericordia alternately rotated in office with each other and mutually covered up their financial and other misdemeanours. This was not the first nor the last time that such allegations were made, though it is difficult to ascertain to what degree they were well founded. In 1689, the Camara of Macao had obtained, at its own request, a decree from the Viceroy of India stating that men who had been sentenced for criminal offenses were not eligible to hold municipal office; but nearly a century later the viceroy alleged that the Macao Senate was mainly composed of "exiled convicts who have taken refuge there, and of similar undesirable individuals." [31] In 1789, we find a certain Manuel Pereira serving simultaneously as *provedor* of the Misericordia and as *vereador* and *juiz ordinario* on the Senate. He seems to have been an honest man, but there are intermittent complaints during the second half of the eighteenth century that *degredados*, bankrupts, illiterates, and similar unqualified persons were serving both in the Senate and on the Board (*Mesa*) of the Misericordia. The shortage of qualified persons at this period was presumably a by-product of the economic and demographic decline of

30. Cf. the extracts from Bishop Hilário de Santa Rosa's voluminous correspondence in Teixeira, *Macau e a sua diocese*, Vol. II, pp. 209–34, and Soares, *Macau e a Assistência*, pp. 236–43.

31. Murias, *Instrução para o Bispo de Pequim e outros documentos*, pp. 11, 53, 172–74. Similar complaints, probably with less justification, had been made as early as 1629. Cf. Gomes, *Esboço da história de Macau*, pp. 115–16.

Macao, which is reflected in the official dispatches of governors and bishops, as well as in the unfavourable impressions formed by visiting and resident foreigners such as William Hickey and Van Braam Houckgeest.[32]

One reason for this unsatisfactory state of affairs was the vast surplus of females in the population during the eighteenth century, noted by many other writers besides the Franciscan chronicler, Fr. Joseph de Jesus Maria, who stated that Macao was virtually "a city of women." Padre Francisco de Sousa, S.J., describing the condition of Macao at the end of the seventeenth century, wrote that there were then "150 Portuguese families, and a total of 19,500 Christian souls, of whom 16,000 are women." This excess of females was partly explained by the fact that the Chinese mothers of unwanted female babies deposited them in the Foundling Hospital. Since there was no room to keep all of them there, the foundlings were given out to poor foster mothers who received a small monthly payment for their maintenance for seven years. After that time, the Misericordia made no further provision for the foundlings, nor did it make any further enquiries about their welfare. The result was that the foster mothers sent the children out to beg in order to earn their keep; and the wretched girls almost invariably became prostitutes, "obliged by sheer necessity to surrender themselves to Chinese, to foreigners, and to everyone else."[33]

If the Misericordia and the Senado da Camara had both clearly fallen on evil days during the second half of the eighteenth century, another pious institution supported by the latter seems to have maintained a relatively high reputation, even in the eyes of the satirical poet, Bocage, who was rather uncomplimentary about Macao as he saw it in 1789.

32. See Boxer, *Fidalgos in the Far East*, pp. 255–68, for the relevant quotations from Hickey, Van Braam Houckgeest, and other visitors.

33. Quoted in Soares, *Macau e a Assistência*, p. 340. Cf. Francisco de Sousa, S.J., *Oriente Conquistado*, Vol. II, p. 374.

Um governo sem mando, um Bispo tal
De freiras virtuosas um covil
Três conventos de frades, cinco mil
Nhon's e chinas cristãos, que obram mui mal

Uma Sé que hoje existe tal e qual
Catorze prebendados sem ceitil
Muita pobreza, muita mulher vil
Cem portugueses, tudo em um curral

Seis fortes, cem soldados, um tambor.
Três freguesias cujo ornato é pau
Um Vigário Geral sem Promotor

Dois colégios, um deles muito mau
Um Senado que a tudo é superior
E quanto Portugal tem em Macao.[34]

The "virtuous nuns in a den," as Bocage described them, were the inmates of the Convent of the Poor Clares, founded by a group of Spanish Franciscan Sisters from Manila in 1633. The Senate had protected and supported the convent since that date, providing an annual income derived from a surtax of 1 percent levied on all *fazendas grossas* imported into Macao.[35] By a later agreement of 1692, the Senate promised "to pay this 1 percent punctually, while the nuns on their side are obliged to receive every five years one daughter of a citizen without a dowry." By the original agreement of 1633, the number of nuns was limited to forty, and preference was always given to the daughters of the *moradores* who had served, or were actually serving, on the Camara. This arrange-

34. Quoted in Soares, *Macau e a Assistência*, pp. 292–93. *Nhons* were Macaonese.

35. *Fazendas grossas* included a wide variety of commodities such as sandalwood, sharks' fins, cotton, putchuk, coarse cloth, etc. For the Poor Clares and their relations with the Senate of Macao, cf. the documents published in Murias, *Instrução para o Bispo de Pequim e outros documentos*, pp. 213–19, 224–28, 233–38, 347–48; *Arquivo das Colonias*, Vol. II, pp. 287–89, Vol. III, pp. 17–21; *Arquivos de Macao*, Vol. I. p. 25, Vol. III, pp. 175–78, 187–88.

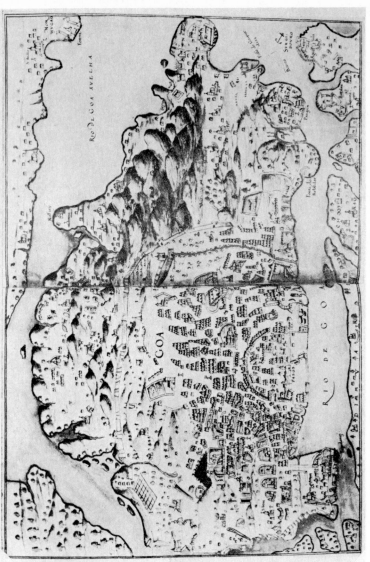

The city and island of Goa in the seventeenth century. From the MS "Livro do Estado da India Oriental," dated Goa, 1635.

Panoramic view of the city
of Salvador, Bahia, by José
Antonio Caldas, 1759.

Partial view of the city of
São Paulo de Luanda, by
Guilherme Joaquim Paes de
Menezes, in 1755.

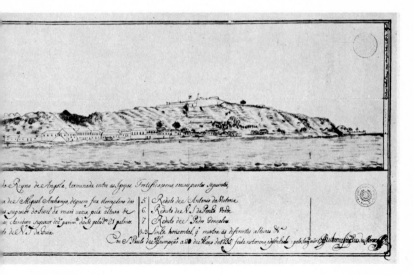

CIDADE DE MACAO.

The city of Macao in the seventeenth century. From the MS "Livro do Estado da India Oriental," dated Goa, 1635.

ment worked satisfactorily on the whole, though at times the Senate made complaints which recall the charges lodged by the Camara of Goa against the nuns of Santa Monica. In 1746, for example, the Senate complained that the nuns took all the local rich girls with dowries, thus spoiling the marriage market for expectant bachelors. The senators also alleged that while the nuns were lending substantial sums on *respondencia* to Armenian, Spanish, and French traders, they refused to lend any money to the Senate, on the plea of poverty. At this period the senators even demanded the closing of the Convent, but the storm of criticism soon blew over and amicable relations were resumed.

Although the Senado da Camara of Macao might be defined as a self-perpetuating oligarchy when considered as an institution, very few families in Macao remained in the social stratum from which the senators were chosen for more than two or three generations. There were probably no white women among the original settlers of 1555–57; and nearly a century later, after being hospitably entertained in a senator's home, the reliable Peter Mundy noted "by report but one woman in this town that was born in Portugal; their wives either Chinesas or of that race heretofore married to Portugals." [36] The first settlers did not mix with the Chinese population of Heungshan, and the women with whom they lived were Japanese, Malays, Indonesians, and Indians, many of them being slaves. Some African Negresses and numerous female Timorese slaves were later imported, and their blood contributed to the racial cauldron. Padre Alonso Sánchez, S.J., who spent some months at Macao in 1582–83, noted that: "The Chinese women are naturally reserved, honest, humble, submissive to their husbands, hard workers and house-proud.

36. Quoted in Boxer, *Macao Three Hundred Years Ago*, p. 64. A Jesuit apothecary at Macao in 1625 wrote: "as mulheres dos portugueses, as mais delas são chinas ou tem parte disso." — Quoted in Soares, *Macau e a Assistência*, p. 30.

. . . The Portuguese of Macao marry with them more willingly than with Portuguese women, because of the many virtues which adorn the former." These respectable Chinese women must have been the daughters of Christianized Chinese settled at Macao, for, as the chronicler António Bocarro emphasized in 1635, the mainland Chinese women "are so retired that the Portuguese never see them." [37]

The considerable admixture of Chinese blood which the Macaonese absorbed in the course of centuries derives largely from the cohabitation of Portuguese and Eurasian householders with their *muitsai* — the unwanted Chinese female children who were sold by their parents into domestic service for a fixed number of years (normally forty), or for the term of their natural lives. The practice of selling such girls to the inhabitants of Macao started very early, and it continued for over two centuries despite reiterated prohibitions by both the Portuguese and the Chinese authorities. A Portuguese naval officer at Macao in 1776 observed that while the upper-class women were virtuous, if lazy, "the common women who are either ransomed Chinese girls [*muitsai*] or else the daughters of female slaves, as they have not the stimulus of honour but are likewise dominated by idleness, are easily debauched, particularly by foreigners, on account of the money and clothes which the latter give them." [38]

Given the almost total absence of European-born Portuguese women for over three centuries, it was inevitable that all Macaonese families had a strong streak of Eurasian blood; but this did not mean that the majority of the men who served

37. *Tratado* and *Apuntamiento* presented to Felipe II by Padre Alonso Sánchez, S.J., in 1588, quoted in Pablo Pastells, S.J., *Catálogo de los documentos relativos a las Islas Filipinas* (9 vols.; Barcelona, 1925–38), Vol. III (1927), p. lix; António Bocarro quoted in Boxer, *Macao Three Hundred Years Ago*, p. 38.

38. Cdte. Nicolau Fernandes da Fonseca's account of Macao, January 1776, in Soares, *Macau e a Assistência*, pp. 231–32. For the *muitsai* problem at Macao, see Boxer, *Fidalgos in the Far East*, pp. 222–41.

as *oficiais da Camara* were locally born Eurasians. On the contrary, many of them and probably a majority, were *Reinóis*, or European-born Portuguese who had emigrated to Asia, just as they were strongly represented in the Senate of Goa. The viceregal confirmation of the city's privileges in 1689 reaffirmed that all of those eligible for municipal office must be "Christãos Velhos Portuguezes de Nação e geração"; otherwise the elections would be null and void.[39] If this stipulation had been enforced to the letter, it would have meant that virtually nobody born in Macao would have been eligible for municipal office. It is therefore significant that in 1709, when the city's privileges were confirmed, the Crown diluted this particular qualification by stating that as long as the councilors were *nobres*, no further investigation of their ancestry would be needed.[40] The qualification of *nobre* was excessively elastic in Portuguese Asia, being claimed by almost everyone with any pretensions to breeding and education, and it was certainly not confined to those of pure European birth. Moreover, in default of a large number of *Reinóis* in Macao, some Macaonese had to be admitted in the Senate on occasion. At the end of the seventeenth century there were only fourteen men in Macao who were, strictly speaking, fully qualified to hold municipal office.[41] In 1746 the Camara complained that there were only fifty Portuguese *moradores* all told in Macao, less than a dozen of whom had sufficient to live on. This meant that the senators constantly had to rotate in office, despite the illegality of this procedure, and that closely

39. Viceregal *alvará* of 30 April 1689, in Murias, *Instrução para o Bispo de Pequim e outros documentos*, pp. 174–75.

40. See *ibid.* for royal *alvará de confirmação* of 30 December 1709: ". . . com declaração porem que os ditos cargos da Çidade de Macao, não possa entrar os que não forem Nobres, sem que sejão neçessarias as outras qualidades, que no Alvará neste encorporado se declarão, as quaes se devem omitir. . . ."

41. Fr. José de Jesus Maria, O.F.M., *Azia Sinica e Japonica, 1745*, Vol. II, p. 128. The friar alleged that in his time (1742–45) illiterates were sometimes nominated as *juizes ordinarios* (*ibid.*, p. 237).

related people were serving in the same *vereação*, contrary to the stipulations of *Ordenõeçes do Reino*.[42]

Nevertheless, despite the difficulty of finding fully qualified men of European birth in the eighteenth century, *Reinóis* who married local women and became *moradores* had a better chance of serving on the Senate than had many of their Macaonese contemporaries. Of the numerous instances which could be quoted, it will suffice to mention Francisco Xavier Doutel, Manuel Vicente Roza, and Manuel Leite Pereira, three of the most important personalities in eighteenth-century Macao. The same applied to some inferior posts, and orders from Goa in 1751 enjoined that "poor but honest Portuguese" should be preferred to "the sons of the soil" as watchmen or tide-waiters for shipping in the harbour.[43] An anonymous account of Macao compiled about 1698 alleged that the *Procurador da Cidade* was nearly always a *Christão-novo*. This does not mean, I think, that he was a Chinese convert to Christianity but that he was of Jewish descent and, presumably, of European origin. Even if this particular assumption is correct, it does not mean that this was the result of a government order, or was more than a local social phenomenon.[44]

The determination to maintain white superiority is exemplified by the following instances, among others: An order pro-

42. *Arquivo das Colonias*, Vol. III, pp. 17–21. The decadence of Macao at this time and the shortage of qualified Portuguese is attested by Fr. José de Jesus Maria, *Azia Sinica e Japonica*, Vol. II, pp. 128, 229–40.

43. Murias, *Instrução para o Bispo de Pequim e outros documentos*, p. 267.

44. Biblioteca da Ajuda, Lisbon, Codex 51–viii-40, 24, "Memoria do que contem a Cidade de Macao." Mr. J. M. Braga kindly sent me a complete list of all the *procuradores do Senado*, 1594–1884. In an accompanying letter (17 June 1964), he writes: "It is possible that there were periods when the post of Procurador was held by men of Chinese descent or extraction, but from the accompanying list you will see that there were periods when the men holding the post were men from Portugal, especially in the earlier and later times. Personally, I feel that in Macao they would have tried to keep the post almost exclusively, if they could, for *pukka* Portuguese."

mulgated by the Camara to the sound of drum and trumpet through the streets, in October 1744, prohibited all the inhabitants of Macao "who are not Europeans by birth or descent" from wearing wigs and carrying sunshades. The pretext of this *bando* was that "the common people of this city" were wasting their substance on imitating their social betters in this way. The *naturaes*, or Europeanized natives, promptly protested to the Viceroy of Goa against this edict, pointing out that for generations they had been intermarrying with the Portuguese and that they were foremost in paying taxes and imposts. They also claimed that they were not a subject race, since neither they nor their ancestors had ever been conquered by the Portuguese; and they reminded the viceroy that the Roman Catholic natives of Goa were allowed the use of these adornments. The viceroy agreed with their representation and ordered the Camara to withdraw the offending edict as being illogical and unfair.[45] Thirty years later, in pursuance of the Marquis of Pombal's policy of breaking down the colour-bar in Portuguese Asia, the Macao Senate was ordered to include six of the leading *naturaes* among the *almotacéls*, as proof that the Crown recognized no distinction of race or colour as between its Roman Catholic vassals. The Senate evaded compliance with this decree, which remained a dead letter. Civic honours remained, in fact if not in theory, the exclusive privilege of the *moradores*, who were either full-blooded Portuguese or else had only a relatively slight mixture of Asian blood.[46]

There is no doubt but that the Senado da Camara of Macao was the most important and influential of all the Portuguese colonial municipalities during the three centuries with which

45. I have copies of the original *bando* of 16 October 1744, petition of the *naturaes de Macao*, and the viceregal *portaria* of 13 May 1745, in the Macao Archive. Cf also Soares, *Macau e a Assistência*, pp. 230–31.

46. Montalto de Jesus, *Historic Macao*, pp. 163–64.

we are concerned. Since the Chinese government, whether in the Ming or in the Manchu dynasty, recognized the Camara and not the captain-general as the responsible local authority, the Crown at Lisbon and the viceroy at Goa had to do the same, however reluctantly. The fact that Macao was to all intents and purposes a self-governing colony was as much a source of pride to its citizens as of annoyance to those viceroys and governors who tried to strengthen the Crown's excessively loose control over its distant vassals on the shore of the South China Sea. The Viceroy Count of Linhares writing to the Governor of Macao in 1634 denounced the citizens as being greater enemies to the Crown than were the Dutch.[47] Antonio Coelho Guerreiro, an ex-governor of Timor, declared in 1708: "The people of Macao are the most unworthy vassals that Your Majesty has in all your conquests, and whereas they deserve so little, they are withal those who enjoy the greatest freedom, since they are not subjected to any form of taxation." [48] Such allegations, which it would be easy to multiply, were manifestly unfair. There was more truth in the Senate's reminder to the Crown in 1635:

This city of the Name of God, situated in this Kingdom of Great China, has grown from humble beginnings to be one of the greatest that Your Majesty has in the State of India. And it has survived hitherto solely because of its trade and commerce, being maintained and developed at the cost of its citizens with lavish disbursements of their wealth, both in heavily bribing the Chinese, as in building walls and fortifications, something quite unprecedented in China, founding cannon, constructing a powder magazine, and providing the necessary munitions and war material for its defense.[49]

47. ". . . a soltura dos cidadões que eu considero serem ainda mayores inimigos que os de fora." — Quoted in Boxer, *The Great Ship from Amacon*, p. 135n.

48. Coelho Guerreiro's letter of 3 September 1708 from Bahia, quoted in Leitão, *Os Portugueses em Solor e Timor*, p. 181.

49. "Informação a Sua Magestade do Estado de Macao per mandar ver em seus concelhos," dated Macao, 21 April 1635. Original MS on Chinese paper

Viewed from this standpoint, the Senado da Camara certainly deserved the inscription reading "There is none more loyal" (*Não há outra mais leal*) which was placed over the main entrance to the Town Hall by order of the governor, João de Sousa Pereira, in 1654. The official title of *Leal Senado* was conferred on the municipal council by the Prince Regent of Portugal from his refuge at Rio de Janeiro in 1810, the Camara having previously used the prefix "Nobre," as did that of Goa. Whatever complaints the Macaonese may have had against the social discrimination exercised against them in some respects by the European-born Portuguese, they never wavered in their loyalty to Portugal. A distinguished Macaonese has recently reminded us that Macao is the only one of Portugal's overseas possessions which has not contributed a single individual to any of the so-called independence movements which exist, on however small a scale, in all of the others.[50]

---

in the Public Library of the Archive of Evora, printed by the present writer in the *Boletim Eclesiástico de Macau* (July 1937), pp. 30–43.

50. Carlos Estorninho, *Macau e os Macaenses, Divagações e achegas historicas* (Rotary Club de Lisboa, 1962), p. 15.

CHAPTER III

The
Municipal Council
of Bahia

The Municipal Council of Bahia was established in June 1549, when the City of the Saviour (Salvador) was founded on the shore of the Bay of All Saints, as the capital of colonial Brazil in general and of the captaincy of Bahia in particular, by the first governor-general, Tomé de Sousa. This was not the first municipal council in Portuguese America, for one had been established in the most southerly settlement of São Vicente in 1532; but the Camara of Bahia soon became of much greater importance owing to its location in the colony's nerve center.[1] The *mesa de vereação* was composed of three *vereadores*, two *juizes ordinarios*, and a *procurador da cidade*, elected annual-

1. Edmundo Zenha, *O Município no Brasil, 1532–1700*, pp. 24–25; Affonso Ruy, *História da Câmara Municipal da Cidade do Salvador*, pp. 1–8; Teodoro Sampaio, *História da Fundação da Cidade do Salvador* (Salvador, 1949). I have used, as did contemporaries, the terms Bahia and Salvador as being interchangeable for the city. Where the captaincy of Bahia is referred to, in contradistinction to the city, this is, I hope, evident from the context.

ly from the triennial lists, after the metropolitan model previously described (pp. 5–7 above). Working-class representatives in the persons of the four *procuradores dos mesteres* were only added to the Camara in 1641, although this representation had been authorized by the Crown eighty years earlier. These *procuradores dos mesteres* were dropped from the Camara in 1713, for reasons explained below.

The municipal councilors of Bahia are recorded as having participated in the procession of the Feast of Corpus Christi in June 1549, but it seems that it was not always easy to find properly qualified persons for municipal office in the pioneer days of the city. Out of a total of about one thousand original settlers, no fewer than four hundred were exiled convicts (*degredados*), and in 1550 the local *ouvidor* (royal judge) informed the Crown: "There are no men here who are fit to serve as ordinary judges or as aldermen, and the governors therefore place in these offices men who have been exiled for high crimes and misdemeanours, including some who have had their ears clipped." [2] This was probably a slight exaggeration; but in any event with the passage of time, the growth of the sugar industry, and the increased tempo of voluntary emigration to Brazil, better-qualified individuals soon became available. Although Brazil, like the Asian and African *conquistas* — or like Australia in the late eighteenth and early nineteenth centuries — continued to be a place of exile for convicts from the mother country during the whole of the colonial period, the *oficiais da Camara* were mainly drawn from the sugar-planters and growers of the Reconcavo, and from the richer residents of the city of Salvador who intermarried with them.

Contrary to what had happened at Goa and Macao, the Camara of Bahia was not originally modelled upon any specific metropolitan prototype, such as those of Lisbon or of

---

2. Quoted in Ruy, *História da Câmara do Salvador*, p. 32.

Evora, but merely on the general provisions regarding the municipalities as laid down in the Manueline codes – the *Regimento* of 1504 and the subsequent *Ordenações*. Soon after the accession of D. João IV, the Camara of Bahia asked for the privileges of the municipality of Oporto, a favour which was granted in 1646, in return for many financial burdens which the Camara had assumed during the war with the Dutch. The most onerous of these burdens were the payment, feeding, and housing of the local garrison, and the building and upkeep of the fortifications. The privileges of Oporto had already been granted to the cities of São Luis do Maranhão, Belem do Pará, and São Sebastião do Rio de Janeiro, and it is rather surprising that they were awarded so belatedly to the capital of Portuguese America. Some historians allege that the privileges of the city of Oporto were specially sought after, because they were more extensive than those of other Portuguese cities. So far as I can ascertain, this was not the case. Most of the privileges of Oporto were specifically copied from those of Lisbon, including the most valued provisions, such as the freedom from arbitrary arrest and from judicial torture, save in cases of high treason when fidalgos were likewise liable thereto.[3]

In 1696 the Crown altered the system under which the *oficiais da Camara* had hitherto been elected, doubtless with a view to strengthening the control of the government over the composition of the Camara, as it had done with that of Goa in 1688. The method of balloting with *pelouros* was abolished, and the judges of the High Court (*Relação*) at Bahia were entrusted with the task of scrutinizing the triennial electoral lists, from which the viceroy or governor then selected

3. ". . . logrando já o senado da Bahia por mercê do serenissimo senhor rei D. João IV, em provisão de 22 de março de 1646, os proprios privilegios que o da cidade do Porto, que são os mesmos que tem a Camara de Lisboa." – Sebastião da Rocha Pitta, *História da America Portugueza, 1500–1724*, Livro VIII, para 50, *Privilegios dos Cidadãos da Cidade do Porto*; Ruy, *História da Câmara do Salvador*, pp. 122–31.

annually, in the name of the Crown, those individuals who were to serve as *oficiais da Camara*. At the same time, the presidency of the Camara was no longer assumed by each of the *vereadores* in rotation, but was occupied by a senior Crown lawyer, the *juiz de fora*, or district magistrate. The posts of *juizes ordinarios* were likewise abolished, and the Senado da Camara of Bahia henceforth comprised the presiding *juiz de fora*, three *vereadores*, and the *procurador*. The secretary, or *escrivão da Camara*, also ranked as a Senate member in practice, though at Bahia as elsewhere he had no vote.[4] In 1704, the pay and emoluments of all the officers and employees of the Camara were placed on a regular footing, which made them in some respects the salaried servants of the Crown. Nevertheless, these administrative reforms did not mean that the senators became mere puppets of the Crown and of the viceroys, as is often asserted. On the contrary, throughout the eighteenth century they displayed nearly as much initiative and independence as had their more freely elected predecessors during the previous one hundred and fifty years. Strong-minded viceroys, such as the Count of Sabugosa (1720–35), continually complained about their clashes with the Camara; and Luis dos Santos Vilhena, writing at the very end of the eighteenth century, alleged that the presiding judge was often overruled by the *vereadores* who combined to outvote him.

4. Rocha Pitta, *História da America Portugueza*, Livro VIII, paras 50–51; *Documentos Históricos da Biblioteca Nacional do Rio de Janeiro*, Vol. LXXXVII (1950), pp. 10, 22, 50; *termo* of 20 April 1697 in *Atas do Senado da Câmara da Bahia, 1625–1700*, Vol. VI, pp. 336–37. Cf. also Eulália Maria Lahmeyer Lobo, *Processo Administrativo Ibero-Americano: Aspectos sócio-econômicos, período colonial*, p. 397. Oddly enough, José António Caldas in his eyewitness *Noticia Geral de toda esta capitania da Bahia desde o seu descobrimento até o presente ano de 1759*, states: "Ha tres vereadores e hum procurador da Camara, que anualmente são eleitos pelos pelouros, que se fazem na forma do estillo" (p. 85 of the facsimile edition, Salvador, 1951), as if the only change in 1696 had been the appointment of the *Juiz de fora* as president.

As mentioned previously, although Crown permission for the inclusion of representatives of the working-class guilds (*mesteres*) on the Camara had been obtained in 1581, this measure was only adopted eighty years later. These representatives comprised a *juiz do povo* (people's tribune or people's judge) and two other *procuradores dos mesteres* elected from among the twelve representatives of the following crafts and trades: tinkers, saddlers, tailors, barbers, stone-masons, cobblers, turners, goldsmiths, joiners, coopers, and blacksmiths. The three representatives of the *mesteres* coöpted to serve on the Camara had voting rights in all matters concerning their crafts and trades and the economic life of the city, and they originally participated in all the routine sessions of the *mesa de vereação*. Their social betters came to resent this, as they had done at Goa, and in December 1650 they decided that the bench on which these men sat (the *banco dos mesteres*) should be moved out of earshot of the high-table where the *vereadores* sat, so that the *mesteres* could not hear confidential discussions on matters which did not concern them, but they could speak up when relevant topics came on the agenda.[5] Despite this ruling, however, the *juiz do povo* often intervened, or tried to, in matters of high policy which the *vereadores* regarded as being above the limited intelligence of tradesmen and artisans. The power and influence of the *juiz do povo* and the *mesteres* reached their height in 1710–11, when the *juiz do povo* first led a riotous movement against a highly unpopular salt-contractor, and later incited a mob to force the governor and the Camara to prepare an expedition for the relief of Rio de Janeiro when attacked by the French. This truculent attitude so alarmed the *vereadores* that they petitioned the Crown for the abolition of these three working-class representatives on the Camara, since they were allegedly subversive of the maintenance of good order and discipline.

5. *Termo* of 30 December 1650, in *Atas da Câmara da Bahia*, Vol. III, pp. 111–12.

The Crown agreed with alacrity in 1713; and although the incoming *vereadores* of 1715 reversed their predecessors' attitude and petitioned for the reinstatement of the working-class representatives, the Crown maintained the ban on their representation.[6]

Affonso Ruy has published a list of the *oficiais da Camara* from 1549 to 1951, and although there are many gaps before 1625, the series is thereafter pretty well complete.[7] A perusal of these names shows that the Camara was predominantly officered by the sugar-planting aristocracy of the Reconcavo for the period 1625–1799, but that it was not a self-perpetuating oligarchy, in so far as the personnel was changed annually and thus fresh blood was brought in every year. This affords a striking contrast with many of the *cabildos* of colonial Spanish America, where the *regidores*, who were the equivalent of the Luzo-Brazilian *vereadores*, were often appointed for life, and seats on the council descended from father to son.[8] Since the *oficiais do Senado da Camara* at Bahia were recruited mainly from the ranks of the *senhores de engenho* and the more substantial tenant farmers, or *lavradores de cana*, it is very unlikely that mulattoes or men of colour were ever admitted, in view of the prejudice displayed by the upper classes at Bahia against *gente de cor* in the colonial period.[9]

6. *Ibid.*, Vol. II, pp. 14–18, 172–73; *Documentos Históricos*, Vol. XCVI, pp. 60–61; Ruy, *História da Câmara do Salvador*, pp. 173–88; Rocha Pitta, *História da America Portugueza*, Livro IX, paras 99–117.

7. Ruy, *História da Câmara do Salvador*, pp. 347–74.

8. For concise accounts of the *Cabildos* in colonial Spanish America see Bailey W. Diffie, *Latin-American Civilization: Colonial Period* (Harrisburg, 1947), pp. 305–7, 611–18; C. H. Haring, *The Spanish Empire in America* (New York, 1947), pp. 158–78; F. B. Pike, "The Municipality and the system of checks and balances in Spanish American colonial administration," in *The Americas*, Vol. XV (October, 1958), pp. 139–58. Cf. also Lahmeyer Lobo, *Processo Administrativo Ibero-Americano*, pp. 210–24, 344–69.

9. For the prejudice against mulattoes in colonial Brazil, cf. C. R. Boxer, *Race Relations in the Portuguese Colonial Empire, 1415–1825* (Oxford, 1963), pp. 114–19; *Anais do Primeiro Congresso de História da Bahia*, Vol. II, pp. 268 (no. 3256), 287 (nos. 3517–19), 301 (no. 3707); José Pinheiro da Silva,

I may mention here that in the course of time the office of *procurador do senado* evidently became socially down-graded, contrary to what happened at Macao. By the end of the seventeenth century at Bahia, *"pessoas da primeira no-breza"* were claiming that this post was beneath their dignity, and that even if they were elected to it they could not be compelled to serve. The point was referred to the Crown, which ruled that people who were not sons of the citizens of Salvador could be compelled to serve as *procurador*, and that service in this post would automatically qualify them to serve later as aldermen and judges.[10]

The Camara of Bahia seems to have been always in greater financial difficulties than those of Goa and Macao, although for about two hundred years Salvador was the capital of the wealthiest region in the Portuguese empire. This penury was, perhaps, partly due to the fact that the planters from whom the *vereadores* were recruited were a spendthrift lot who were nearly always deeply indebted to the merchants in the seaports. Probably the Overseas Councilors at Lisbon were not being entirely unfair when they observed in 1714 that the *vereadores* "were usually persons encumbered with debts of their own, and quite reckless in spending other people's money."[11] The first governor-general had made the Camara extensive grants of land in *sesmaria*, but the council either could not or would not collect adequate rents from those who leased or merely squatted on its lands. All the Camara's records were destroyed during the Dutch occupation of Salvador in 1624–25, and many people who resided or built houses on the municipal lands subsequently claimed the sites as their own, and the Camara was unable to prove them wrong in the

---

"A Capitania da Baía," in *Revista Portuguesa de História*, Vol. VIII, pp. 141–48.

10. *Documentos Históricos*, Vol. LXXXIX, pp. 50–53, 198.

11. ". . . eram ordinariamente pessoas empenhadas com dividas proprias, e sem reparo algum em gastar e dispender o alheio." — *Documentos Históricos*, Vol. XCVI, p. 128.

courts. Other householders were more honest, and they came to an agreed settlement with the Camara. But in such cases, this body was hardly in a position to charge high rents, and as late as 1730 it only received an insignificant sum from the rents of its lands.[12]

Other sources of the Camara's income included the verification of weights and measures for the sale of provisions; payments for the use of the municipal stockyards and abattoir; and taxes on various foodstuffs. The Camara also fixed the sale prices of many provisions, including meat, manioc, confectionery, fish, and fruit, as also on wines, brandy, rum, and other types of strong drink. The fines levied on shopkeepers and on street-vendors who ignored the official prices, or who neglected to take out a license from the Camara which authorized them to ply their trade, formed an important source of income for the *renda do verde*. In 1730, the Camara's income from all sources averaged about 15,000 cruzados a year.[13] This sum did not, as a rule, suffice to cover the routine expenses of the council, including the upkeep of public works, such as bridges, fountains, street-lighting, paving and sanitation, and the salaries of its employees.

From 1625 the Camara was partly — and from 1642 to 1714, wholly — responsible for the pay, rations, and clothing of the garrison, and it likewise had to find a large sum yearly as Bahia's contribution to the dowry of Queen Catherine of England and the war-indemnity paid to the United Provinces. This consolidated contribution, known as the *dote de Ingla-*

12. Waldemar Mattos (ed.), *Livro do Tombo de prefeitura municipal da Cidade do Salvador* (Salvador, 1953).

13. Letter of the Senado da Camara da Bahia, dated 28 June 1730, in A. J. de Mello Moraes, *Brasil Histórico*, 2d Series, Vol. II, p. 84, and the reply of the *Provedor-Mór*, dated 20 July 1730, in *ibid.*, p. 64. For details of the *rendas* of the Camara at the end of the 18th century, cf. Accioli-Amaral *Memorias Historicas e Politicas da Provincia da Bahia*, Vol. III, pp. 189–90; Luiz dos Santos Vilhena, *Recopilação de Noticias Soteropolitanas e Brasilicas contidas em XX cartas*, pp. 68–75.

terra e paz de Holanda, amounted to 90,000 cruzados per annum in 1688, and it was not finally paid off until the year 1723. To help find money for these two fiscal burdens, and others which were imposed by the Crown from time to time, the Camara was given the right to levy certain duties on the sale of wines, rum, and other strong liquors, and on the sugar exported. All these taxes, duties, and imposts were usually farmed out to monopoly-contractors, and there were constant wrangles between these tax-farmers and the Camara.[14]

Another difficulty in raising money was that although some of these taxes were supposed to be paid by all classes without exception, the religious orders and (to a lesser degree) the secular clergy usually evaded their obligations, or else flatly refused to admit their liability. Many laymen also evaded payment on the grounds that they were Familiars of the Holy Office of the Inquisition or otherwise privileged persons. Knights of the three military orders of Christ, Santiago, and Aviz tried to claim exemption until their pretensions were quashed once for all by royal edicts in 1657–58.[15] The result was that the burden of taxation was borne by the poor, who found that most of the necessities of life were taxed, and by the sugar-planters of the Reconcavo, whose sugars were subjected to rising duties at a period when the sale of Brazilian sugars in Europe encountered increasing competition from the French and English Antilles.

During the last quarter of the seventeenth century, the

14. Cf. Thales de Azevedo, *Povoamento da Cidade do Salvador,* pp. 328–449; Luiz Monteiro da Costa, *Na Bahia Colonial: Apontamentos para a história militar da Cidade do Salvador,* especially pp. 167–68, for detailed references to the 6 published volumes of the *Atas da Câmara da Bahia,* concerning the perennial problem of the "sustento da infantaria."

15. Cf. *Anais do 1º Congresso de História da Bahia,* Vol. II, pp. 136, 144, 147–48, 158, 177, 205, 208, 220, 244. Cf. also José de Wanderley Pinho, *História de um engenho do Recôncavo, 1552–1944,* pp. 189–90, and the numerous references to *Documentos Históricos* given there; *Cartas do Senado da Câmara da Bahia, 1638–1692* (3 vols.; Salvador, 1950–53), Vol. I, pp. 35–36, 55, 64, 116–17.

Camara's complaints to the Crown reached a crescendo of indignation, which sometimes struck a hysterical note. The effects of the heavy duties levied on the export of sugar and tobacco were aggravated by an outbreak of yellow fever, which ravaged Bahia in 1686–91, and by a severe financial crisis resulting from the drain of money to Portugal, since the Lisbon merchants now preferred to collect payment in specie rather than in sugar. The Camara repeatedly asked the Crown to lower the excessive duties on sugar and tobacco, and to reduce the garrison of Bahia from two regiments to one. It also suggested that many redundant senior officers could be dismissed, now that Portugal was at peace with all the Western world. But the Crown appeared to ignore these representations, which led the Camara to observe sourly that it might as well be abolished, since the misguided ministers at Lisbon seemed to be as determined to ruin the economic foundations of Brazil as their predecessors had done to Portuguese India, when they raised the price of pepper at Lisbon a century previously and thus induced the Dutch to go and seek it directly in the East. As João Peixoto Viegas, a leading sugar-planter and municipal councilor, pointed out in 1687, the root of the trouble was that heavy duties had been levied on sugar in the mid-seventeenth century, when its sale price in Europe was high; and these duties were maintained and even increased later, when the European price of sugar was falling, owing to the rising production of sugar in the English and French West Indies.[16]

The Senado da Camara, which represented above all the interests of the sugar-planters of the Reconcavo, may have deliberately exaggerated the economic depression at Bahia in the 1680's, but it did not exaggerate much. The same complaints were made by the governors and by the celebrated

16. *Cartas do Senado*, Vol. III, *passim*, especially pp. 104–8; Wanderley Pinho, *História de um engenho do Recôncavo*, pp. 196–203, for some typical extracts from João Peixoto Viegas' racy representations.

Jesuit, Padre António Vieira, S.J., who had a keen eye for the material as well as the spiritual side of life. Admittedly, the complaints were not all on one side; and if the Camara found it difficult to collect the money to which it was entitled, it did not always try very hard to do so. The viceroy informed the Crown in 1691 that the Camara was owed over 100,000 cruzados by persons connected with the contracts for the pay and provisioning of the garrison. Lawsuits for the recovery of these debts, he explained, "are tried by the *juizes ordinarios*, who are relatives and friends of the debtors, for whose sakes they spin out these suits interminably, and they will never be finished." [17] The protests of the Camara of Bahia against excessive taxation were closely paralleled at this point by those made by the Lisbon Municipal Council. This latter body drew up a forceful remonstrance to the Crown in July 1689, claiming that experience had shown that the yield from taxation had tended to decrease in proportion as the fiscal screw was tightened.[18] These representations had little effect on the Crown, which depended heavily on the revenue from its Customs and could not forego the immediate yield for the uncertain prospect of a larger income in a distant future. The Camara of Bahia was more successful with its request that a mint should be established in Brazil for the striking of pro-

17. *Documentos Históricos*, Vol. XXXIII, pp. 351, 359–60.
18. Eduardo Freire de Oliveira, *Elementos para a História do Município de Lisboa*, Vol. IX, pp. 126-40. On the other hand, the experienced diplomat, D. Luís da Cunha, who had lived for many years in England, Holland, and France, argued at a later date (1736) that the Portuguese people in general were the least heavily taxed in Europe (*Instrucções inéditas de D. Luís da Cunha a Marco António de Azevedo Coutinho* [Coimbra, 1930], pp. 168, 191). Pinheiro da Silva (in *Revista Portuguesa de História*, Vol. VIII, pp. 177–78) argues that the Camara of Bahia deliberately exaggerated the gravity of the economic crisis at Bahia in the 1680's and 1690's. It may have done so to some extent, but the seriousness of the situation is also apparent from the contemporary letters of Padre António Vieira, S.J., and the official correspondence of the Viceroy *Almotacél-Mór*, 1690–94.

vincial money for circulation in the colony. This was authorized in 1694, probably because the project was warmly
supported by the governor-general and by the influential
Padre António Vieira, S.J.

The Senado da Camara of Bahia was not merely the mouth-
piece of the sugar-planting aristocracy, but often represented
the interests of the population as a whole, as exemplified by its
opposition to the monopolistic chartered Company for the
Brazil Trade (*Companhia Geral do Comercio do Brasil*). This
company was founded in 1649, again largely owing to the ad-
vocacy of Padre António Vieira, S.J., who was at that time
D. João IV's *éminence grise*. In return for a monopoly of the
importation and sale of the colony's most essential provisions
— wine, flour, olive oil, dried codfish, and charcoal — and the
right to levy duties on the principal Brazilian exports — sugar,
tobacco, hides, and cotton — the Brazil Company bound itself
to maintain thirty-six warships for convoying merchant shipping between Portugal and Brazil, all vessels being compelled
to sail in its convoys. From the time of the arrival of the Brazil
Company's first fleet at Bahia in 1650, the Camara complained
that the Company did not import sufficient amounts of wine,
flour, olive oil, and *bacalhau*, and that it charged excessive
prices for what it did bring.

The Camara of Bahia later alleged that the Company never
maintained its annual sailings with any regularity and that it
had never once fulfilled its statutory obligation to maintain a
fleet of thirty-six warships for convoy duties. The protests of
the Camara of Bahia were echoed by the municipal councils
of Rio de Janeiro, Olinda, and other Brazilian seaports, and
the Company was equally unpopular with many people in
Portugal, if for different reasons. The growing volume of protests on both sides of the Atlantic forced the Crown drastically
to modify the terms of its charter in 1658, and in 1662–64 the
Company was incorporated in the Crown under the title of the

Junta do Comercio do Brasil. The protests, however, continued until the abolition of the Junta in 1720.[19]

The Brazil Company did not, it is true, satisfactorily fulfill its intended function of providing regular and secure annual convoys; although those which it did provide were undoubtedly an important and perhaps a decisive factor in the maritime struggle with the Dutch for the possession of Pernambuco in 1650–54. But the Bahia Camara's protests against the convoy system, and especially against its maintenance after peace had been concluded with the Dutch (1661), and even after the abolition of the Junta in 1720, were largely motivated by the fact that the sugar crop fluctuated widely from year to year, and that there was no way of accurately calculating it in advance. Consequently, sugars which could not be shipped straight away for Portugal when packed and crated at Salvador had to be kept in storage for months on end while awaiting the arrival of a convoy. This meant that they were apt to deteriorate badly, and so fetch lower prices in Lisbon. In 1739, for example, the homeward-bound fleet from Bahia exported not only the *safra* (harvested crop) of that year, but a large part of the *safras* of the preceding four years as well.[20]

There were also complaints that when the convoys did arrive in the Bay of All Saints, their turn-around in the harbour was either too long or too short, and that they arrived (or left) at times which did not coincide with the harvesting of the main crop. To some extent these complaints cancelled each other out. But the fact remains that whether the convoy system of annual fleets worked well or ill, and whether it was operated by the Company, by the Junta, or by the Crown, it was subject to continual criticism by the Camaras of Bahia,

19. For the complaints of the Camara of Bahia against the Brazil Company, cf. *Cartas do Senado*, Vol. I, *1638–1673* (1951), pp. 31–32, 36–46, 50–53, 57–59; and for the vicissitudes of the Company and *Junta do Comércio*, cf. Gustavo de Freitas, *A Companhia Geral do Comércio do Brasil, 1649–1720* (São Paulo, 1951).

20. *Documentos Históricos*, Vol. XCVI, pp. 10–11, 38.

Rio de Janeiro, and Pernambuco. Its final abolition by Pombal in 1765 was greeted with general approval on both sides of the Atlantic.

The freedom with which the municipal councilors of Bahia complained to the Crown on matters of high policy provoked the attorney general at Lisbon to observe in 1678 that those worthies should be severely reprimanded for acting as if they shared with the Prince Regent, D. Pedro, the responsibility of ruling the Portuguese empire.[21] Twenty years earlier the governor-general, Francisco Barreto, had told the Camara to reword a particularly outspoken passage in one of its many representations to the Crown concerning the evils of the Brazil Company; since, he said, this bluntness did not accord "with the humility and submission with which kings should always be addressed." [22] The Camara usually couched its criticisms in more respectful language, but it seldom failed to speak up boldly in defense of what it conceived to be the interests of the population of Bahia. In 1721, for example, it protested strongly and successfully against a project to establish a monopolistic company for the Brazil and West African trades; just as six years earlier it had vigorously protested against a proposal to close the Bahia Mint.

Since the municipal councilors were so outspoken to crowned heads, it is not surprising that they often did not mince their words about the local viceroys, governors, and judges of the High Court. In 1562, the Camara addressed a lengthy representation to D. João III, complaining bitterly of the misconduct of the senior Crown officials, including the governor-general and the senior Crown judge (*ouvidor*). Its

21. ". . . à Camara da Bahia se devia logo responder severamente de sorte que entendam aquêles vereadores que Vossa Alteza não tinha repartido com êles o cuidado de como há de governar a sua monarquia." — *Consulta* of the Overseas Council, 12 December 1678, in *Documentos Históricos*, Vol. LXXXVIII, p. 153.

22. Francisco Barreto to the Camara, 1 August 1657, in *Documentos Históricos*, Vol. LXXXVI, p. 134.

complaints may well have been exaggerated, but similar allegations were ventilated at frequent intervals throughout the whole of the colonial period. Perhaps the ill-feeling against the High Court judges was even greater than that against the governors. A leading citizen of Salvador, revisiting the place after an absence, wrote to the Crown in 1554:

I found the city well supplied with [manioc-]flour, and much more so with mutual enmity and ill-will between the principal authorities, which caused great trouble to the people and endangered the security of the land, owing to the want of many things which are needful, more especially of justice, for which everyone is clamouring.[23]

This complaint of the *falta de justiça* was a recurrent theme which runs like a thread through the history of colonial Bahia, as it does for that matter in the correspondence of the Camara of Goa with the Crown. In 1676 the Camara of Bahia was still asking for the abolition of the local Relação. Vilhena, writing at the end of the eighteenth century, commented on the long-standing rivalry between the municipal council and the High Court, and the tendency of the latter to give decisions against the Camara in all legal cases involving the municipality which were brought before it.[24]

There were, of course, some exceptions to this stream of complaints and remonstrances, which, in any event, cannot always be accepted at their face value. As the Count of Castanheira noted in 1553, *murmuração* (fault-finding) was the oldest and most typical sin of the Portuguese.[25] Life in the

23. Ruy, *História da Câmara do Salvador*, p. 72. Cf. also *ibid.*, pp. 74–76, 133–35; *Documentos Históricos*, Vol. LXXXIX, pp. 6–8.

24. *Anais do 1º Congresso de História da Bahia*, Vol. II, pp. 224–25; Vilhena, *Noticias Soteropolitanas*, pp. 77–78.

25. G. Schurhammer, S.J., *Franz Xaver: Sein leben und seine Zeit*, Vol. II, Part 1 (Freiburg im Breisgau, 1964), p. 207n. In 1736 D. Luís da Cunha deplored "o malicioso gosto, que tem os portugueses de se difamarem huns aos houtros." — *Instrucções inéditas*, pp. 93–94. It would be very easy to quote similar observations from João de Barros, Diogo do Couto, and Tomé Pinheiro

tropics certainly did nothing to discourage this national characteristic, but, even so, some of the governors and viceroys earned warm commendations from the Camara of Bahia. Among the most popular proconsuls were António Luís Gonçalves da Camara Coutinho, the *Almotacél-Mór*, and his successor, D. João de Lencastre. The latter's appointment in 1694 may have been due partly to the Camara's recommendation, since this body had asked for his promotion to Brazil, having heard such golden opinions of him as governor-general of Angola. In 1692, the Camara also wrote to the Crown extolling the merits of two of the leading Crown lawyers, one of whom was the Pernambuco-born attorney general (*procurador da Coroa*), Dr. João da Rocha Pitta, against whose appointment to a judicial post at Bahia the Camara had strongly objected sixteen years earlier. It is worth noting in more detail the Camara's inconsistency in this matter, since it shows how difficult it was for the Crown and its advisors at Lisbon to distinguish truth from falsehood in the conflicting advice and information which they received from Brazil.[26]

During the first half of the seventeenth century, the home government heard repeated complaints from Bahia that Crown judges who were Brazilian-born, though they received their legal training in Portugal, could not be relied on to administer justice impartially after their return to Brazil, since they were swayed and distracted by family ties or by family feuds. Influenced by these complaints, the Crown decreed in 1670 that henceforth judges who had been born in Brazil could only serve in a judicial capacity in Portugal itself. On hearing of this decision, the Camara reversed its former stand,

da Veiga, to name only three of the many classical writers who deplored this real or alleged national failing.

26. *Cartas do Senado*, Vol. III, pp. 109, 111; *Atas da Câmara da Bahia*, Vol. VI, p. 290; *Anais do 1º Congresso de História da Bahia*, Vol. II, pp. 317, 320, 328, 336–37; *Documentos Históricos*, Vol. XXXIII, pp. 357, 445, Vol. LXXXIX, p. 210.

and it protested strongly against this decree as unfairly and illogically discriminating against those born in Brazil, and, more especially, against those born in Bahia. Presumably influenced by this protest, the Crown did not at first strictly enforce this decree; but when it appointed two Brazilian lawyers to legal offices in the colony a few years later, the Camara of Bahia complained that though these lawyers were doubtless very capable and learned men, well qualified to serve the Crown elsewhere, they should not be appointed to Brazil, "where ties of family and friendship would pervert the impartiality which they should possess, since they would inevitably be influenced by the passions of hate and of love." [27] The Camara therefore urged that the decree of 1670 should be rigorously enforced and that Brazilian-born Crown lawyers should only be appointed to posts in the Portuguese empire outside Brazil. The Crown can hardly be blamed for ignoring the Camara's *volte-face*, and in the upshot with every justification, as we have just seen.

If there was often friction between the Camara and the leading representatives of the Crown, disputes between the Camara and the ecclesiastical authorities were less common. This is not surprising, for given the strength of religious fervour — not to mention religious bigotry — in the colonial period, Lusitanian laymen, however eminent or self-willed, were usually very loath to quarrel with their fathers in God. Such disputes as did occur were motivated by two principal reasons, which had nothing to do with dogma, nor did they affect the prevalent conviction of religious belief. Firstly, as I have already indicated, there was widespread resentment among the laity at the way in which the religious orders, some

27. ". . . suposto lhe concediam o merecimento, capacidade, e talento para servir a Vossa Alteza era em outras partes e não na sua pátria, aonde os parantescos e amizades pervertiam aquela inteireza que neles devia haver, por serem sujeitos ao ódio e ao amor." — *Documentos Históricos*, Vol. LXXXVIII, p. 132. Cf. also *Cartas do Senado*, Vol. I, pp. 100–101, Vol. III, pp.108–9; *Anais do 1º Congresso de História da Bahia*, Vol. II, pp. 7–8, 201, 222, 225.

of them obviously or apparently very wealthy, claimed exemption from paying many of the imposts, tolls, and taxes to which the citizens were subjected. To give one out of many such instances, the Crown in 1656 gave categorical orders that the regular and the secular clergy should not be exempted from paying their share of the taxes imposed for the payment of the garrison and for defense against the heretic Dutch, but the Camara of Salvador complained in the following year: "The Religious Orders, which in this captaincy possess much property and many sugar mills, estates, farms, houses, cattle and slaves, refuse to contribute anything at all to the expenses of the war, so that the rest of the people are heavily burdened, and the poor suffer continual oppression." In June 1661, Governor-General Francisco Barreto complained to the Crown that the religious orders, and particularly the Jesuits, refused to pay tithes on the plantations and estates which they possessed, although these lands were both extensive and profitable.[28]

The other main cause of friction between the Camara and the ecclesiastical authorities was mutual jealousy over problems of precedence and protocol in an age which was even more preoccupied with rank and status than is our own. On the occasion of the Feast of Corpus Christi in June 1543, the cantankerous old Bishop of Bahia, D. Pedro da Silva, insisted on the procession's moving off before the municipal councilors were ready to take their proper place with their banner. Not content with this, when the councilors caught up with the procession, the irate prelate "handed over the pyx he was carrying to the custody of the chanter, and sallying out from under the canopy to the astonishment of all beholders, he grabbed the ex-alderman who was carrying the Council's banner and pushed him forward by his arm, shouting at him in a loud voice that on pain of major excommunication he

28. *Cartas do Senado*, Vol. I, pp. 35–36, 64–65, 86; *Anais do 1⁰ Congresso de História da Bahia*, Vol. II, pp. 149, 158, 177, 244.

should take the banner to where those of the mechanical corporations were being carried, thus insulting and humiliating us." Admittedly, this incident was an exceptionally unedifying one, but there were many instances of bickering over such trifles as the seating arrangements in churches on festive occasions. In 1694, the Cathedral Chapter took great umbrage because the Camara had verbally invited the canons to participate in a procession, instead of sending them a formal written invitation.[29]

The municipal councilors at Bahia took very seriously their statutory obligation to participate in certain religious highdays and holidays with the maximum pomp and splendour, and with no expense spared. The three original civic Feasts, *Procissões del Rey* or *Festas del Rey* as they were called, were the Feast of Corpus Christi, and those of the Visitation of Our Lady (Santa Isabel), and the Guardian Angel. To these were successively added the Feast of St. Philip and St. James, to commemorate the recovery of Salvador from the Dutch (May 1625); the Acclamation, to celebrate the restoration of D. João IV (1 December 1640); St. Anthony of Arguim;[30] Our Lady of the Conception; and, finally, St. Francis Xavier, who was declared the patron saint of the city at the height of the yellow fever visitation, 10 May 1686. Of all these processions, the Feast of Corpus Christi was the one which maintained the greatest splendour during the colonial period.

Attendance at these principal feasts was compulsory for all the inhabitants of the city, and for those of the surrounding district to the distance of one league, on pain of a substantial fine for anyone who failed to appear without a good and suffi-

29. *Cartas do Senado*, Vol. I, pp. 18–20; *Documentos Históricos*, Vol. XC, pp. 253–55; *Anais do 1º Congresso de História da Bahia*, Vol. II, p. 172; Ruy, *História da Câmara do Salvador*, pp. 158–59.

30. For the origins of this feast and its miraculous image in 1595, cf. *Cartas do Senado*, Vol. I, p. 58; Ruy, *História da Câmara do Salvador*, p. 169; Frei Vicente do Salvador, *História do Brasil, 1500–1627* (São Paulo, 1954), pp. 335–36.

cient excuse, such as illness. In 1641, however, the shopkeepers of Salvador were excused by the Camara from walking in
these processions, save only in that of Corpus Christi. This
concession did not indicate any cooling in the religious fervour of most of the councilors. When the *procuradores* informed their colleagues towards the end of the same year that
there was no money in the treasury to pay for the celebration
of the forthcoming feast of St. Anthony, they voted unanimously to pawn or sell the silver salvers and inkstands belonging to the municipality, in order to provide the necessary
funds.[31]

In later years there evidently was some falling-off in their
enthusiasm, at any rate for a time. The Camara in its session of
22 March 1673, deplored that the processions had markedly
declined as regards the display of "time-honored insignia,
dragon, little horses, and old-time antiques, which helped to
foster the celebration and gaity which Christian piety renders
to God and his saints." [32] The Camara gave strict instructions
that the working-class corporations should contribute these
picturesque features of the procession on the former scale of
lavishness. Despite this ruling, it seems that in the eighteenth
century the master-craftsmen preferred to walk as "Irmãos de
menor condição" in the ranks of the Brethren of the Misericordia, leaving their own *bandeiras* to be accompanied "by
the wretched journeymen, who are too poor and miserable to
be able to dress up properly." [33] Nevertheless, these religious
processions continued to be the major diversion of the citizens
of all classes in colonial Brazil, being partly replaced as such
in modern times by the equally colourful and even less in-
hibited Carnival.

31. *Atas da Câmara da Bahia*, Vol. II, pp. 19–20, 59. For the celebration
of these feasts in general, cf. Ruy, *História da Câmara do Salvador*, pp.
155–71.

32. *Atas da Câmara da Bahia*, Vol. V, pp. 114–15, Vol. VI, pp. 374–76.

33. Carlos Ott, *Formação e evolução étnica da Cidade do Salvador*, Vol. I,
pp. 174–75, Vol. II, pp. 32–33.

In addition to the leading part it played in organizing and parading in the *Festas del Rey*, the Camara also had the obligation of arranging similar displays on the occasions of royal births, engagements, marriages, and coronations. These could likewise be very costly affairs, as instanced by the celebrations staged in honour of the marriage of Charles II of England with Catherine of Braganza in 1662. Despite the parlous state of the Camara's finances at this period, the governor-general, Francisco Barreto, ordered that these celebrations should last for ten days. They included bullfights, horse races, stage comedies, fireworks, salvoes of artillery, the illumination of the city at night, dances and fancy-dress processions in the streets, "in which all classes of people participate on such occasions." [34] The pleasure-loving Bahianos did not need much urging to join in such festivities; but they did not regard with the same enthusiasm the substantial monetary contributions which they were often called upon to remit to Lisbon on such occasions, under the euphemistic title of *donativos* or free gifts.

Like the municipal councils of Goa and Macao, the Camara of Bahia in the seventeenth century was anxious to have a nunnery in their city, where the daughters of respectable citizens, and, more especially, the daughters of the municipal councilors, could take the veil locally, thus saving their parents the expense of the voyage to Portugal. The Crown stalled for a long time on this request, since several of its leading advisers at Lisbon were anxious to promote marriages rather than life-long celibacy among the eligible maidens of Bahia, in order to foster the growth of the population. The Camara originally asked for barefoot Augustinian nuns as founding sisters, but was eventually given Franciscan nuns from Evora — "Poor Clares," like those of Macao. The number of resident nuns was first limited by statute to fifty, but this restriction was later relaxed. The Convent of Santa Clara de Nossa Senhora do Des-

34. *Documentos Históricos*, Vol. LXXXVI, pp. 151–52.

terro sometimes received not only those who took the veil but accommodated their poor relations and female slaves as well. It was at one time suggested that the nuns should be grouped into the two different social categories of *nobres* and *mecanicas*; but the Overseas Council rejected this proposal in 1719, observing that any such class-distinction would be bitterly resented in Brazil, "where the humblest individual gives himself the airs of a great fidalgo." [35]

The *oficiais da Camara* had originally promised the Crown that if their request for the authorization of a convent was granted, they would finance the institution entirely from their own resources, but this did not turn out to be so easy. In 1678 the governor-general ordered them to remove a tax on whale oil which they had just imposed to help finance the building of the convent, since only the Crown had the right to levy new taxes. His decision was upheld by the Crown, which rebuked the municipal councilors for trying to tax the common people of Bahia on behalf of an institution which was intended mainly for their own daughters. In 1683 the Lady Abbess who had come over from Evora with three companions to found the convent was complaining that funds were still inadequate and that the building was proceeding very slowly.[36] Soon after this, adequate dowries, alms, and legacies were forthcoming; and in the eighteenth century the Poor Clares of Salvador became celebrated for their lavish way of life, the splendour of their religious services, and the sumptuous entertainments

35. ". . . porque no Brasil será muito escandaloso, pois o mais humilde tem fumos de grande fidalgo, e neste reino não tem noticia que haja distinção senão em o convento de Vila do Conde, onde diferem as fidalgas das nobres e estas das mecanicas." The King minuted on 4 February 1722: "Não há que diferir a concessão que se pede." — *Documentos Históricos*, Vol. XCVII, pp. 189–94, 271–73.

36. *Documentos Históricos*, Vol. LXXXVI, pp. 223–24, Vol.LXXXVIII, pp. 163, 244–45, 255–61, 286, Vol. LXXXIX, pp. 82–83; *Anais do 1º Congresso de História da Bahia*, Vol. II, pp. 154, 221, 265, 269–70, 272; *Cartas do Senado*, Vol. II, pp. 28–37, 125–26, Vol. III, pp. 8–9, 26, 57–58. Cf. also Azevedo, *Povoamento da Cidade do Salvador*, pp. 219–22.

they gave on feast-days, which, if a French eyewitness is to be credited, were sometimes marked more by profane high spirits than by religious decorum.[37]

The Convent of Santa Clara do Desterro had been founded specifically for the benefit of Brazilian-born girls, and they were always the principal inmates and beneficiaries. Colonial birth was, however, a positive disadvantage in some of the religious orders in eighteenth-century Brazil. In 1780, the municipal councilors of Bahia complained to the Crown that during the previous sixty years the Brazilian-born members of the Franciscan Province had been systematically excluded from high office in the Order, "in favour of a faction of friars, natives of the city of Oporto." The councilors alleged that only three Brazilians had been elected as Provincials during this period, although plenty of pious and learned American-born individuals were available, whereas the majority of the Oporto-born Provincials were "inept, coarse, and foolish." [38] There may have been some unfairness in this complaint, as is suggested by the numerous denunciations of both Brazilian and Portuguese "frades atrevidos e soltos" which fill so much of the correspondence between the governors and the Crown; but it is significant that equally strong objections against the practice of promoting European-born rather than colonial-born clergy were made in the same period at Goa and in Pernambuco.[39] These complaints are all the more striking, when we recall Pombal's insistence on the abolition of the colour-bar as between all Roman Catholic vassals (Negro

37. Le Gentil de la Barbinais, *Nouveau Voyage autour du monde* (3 vols.; Paris, 1728). The author was at Bahia in 1717–18. For the nuns of Santa Clara do Desterro, cf. also Rocha Pitta, *História da America Portugueza*, Livro VI, paras 102–8.

38. Quoted in Ruy, *História da Câmara do Salvador*, pp. 157–58.

39. *Instrucções com que El-Rei D. José I mandou passar ao Estado da India o Governador e Capitão General e o Arcebispo Primaz do Oriente no anno de 1774*, Part 2, pp. 13–20; *Documentos Históricos*, Vol. XCI, p. 99; Francisco Augusto Pereira da Costa, *Anais Pernambucanas* (7 vols.; Recife, 1951–58), Vol. IV, pp. 282–84.

slaves excepted) of the Portuguese Crown, and the determined efforts which he made to abolish this form of racial discrimination from 1761 onwards.[40]

As in Goa and Macao, there was naturally a close connection between the Camara and the Misericordia at Bahia. The same individuals frequently served in both, and enjoyed the double distinction of Senator and Brother. Three typical instances will suffice. João Peixoto Viegas, one of the most prominent men in Bahia during the last quarter of the seventeenth century, whether as a sugar-planter, ranch-owner, or explorer of the interior, was active as *juiz ordinario* and *vereador* on the Camara, and as *provedor* of the Misericordia. Gonçalo Ravasco Cavalcanti e Albuquerque, nephew of Padre António Vieira, S.J., succeeded his father, Bernardo Vieira de Ravasco, as secretary of state in Bahia, and he was likewise active as a sugar-planter, rancher, senator, and as *provedor* of the Misericordia. José António Caldas, the celebrated Bahiano military engineer, was elected as *Irmão de maior condição* of the Misericordia in 1764, and as *procurador* of the Camara in the same year. In short, a perusal of the lists of the *oficiais da Camara* and of the *Irmãos da Misericordia* gives us the equivalent of a *Who's Who* of colonial Bahia. During the eighteenth century, both the Misericordia and the Camara were often accused of mismanaging their finances and rigging their elections to office. Vilhena, writing of conditions at the end of this period, asserted that the Misericordia of Bahia was one of the richest in the Portuguese world, "and for this reason the annual elections for its *provedores*, secretaries, treasurers, and other members of the Board of Guardians are carried out with even more legerdemain than those for candidates for seats on the municipal council."[41]

As was the case with the other colonial Camaras, the mu-

---

40. Boxer, *Race Relations in the Portuguese Colonial Empire*, pp. 57, 73–74, 83–84, 126, 98–100, and the sources there quoted.

41. Vilhena, *Noticias Soteropolitanas*, p. 125.

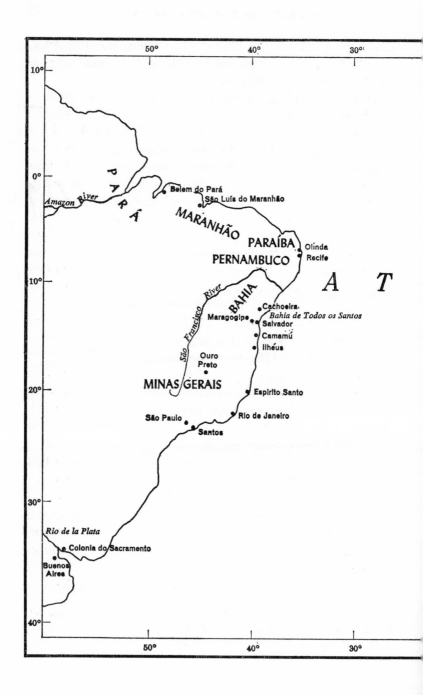

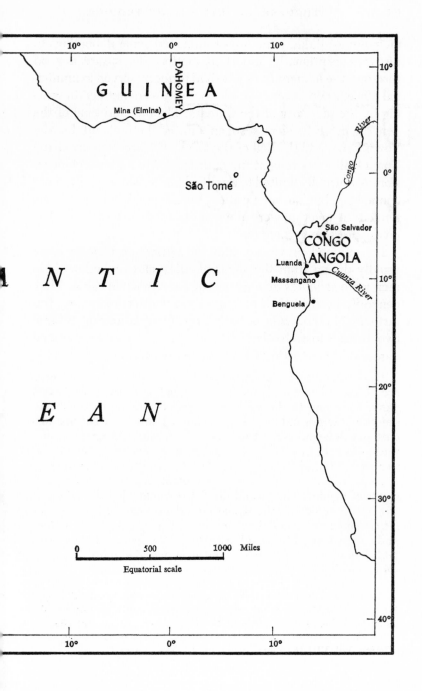

nicipality of Bahia sometimes summoned general meetings to discuss exceptionally important matters. To ensure a good turn-out, the *homens bons* who had formerly served in municipal office, or who were eligible to do so, were notified in writing by the secretary of the Camara. The day and time of the general meeting were also announced beforehand by the Town Crier, and the bell of the local jail (forming part of the Town Hall) was rung at the hour fixed. Voting on such occasions was usually limited to qualified householders and serving councilors; but on very critical occasions all those who attended the meeting were allowed to cast their votes as well as give expression to their views.[42]

I mentioned previously that the *oficiais da Camara* were usually drawn from the sugar-planting class, whether these men were *senhores de engenho* or *lavradores de canas*. They generally lived on their plantations in the Reconcavo, or even farther off in the *sertão*, or backlands. The relationship of these two districts to each other and to the city of Salvador, was well described by a visiting Crown judge in 1676:

The lands of the region of this captaincy of the Bay of All Saints are distinguished and divided by the inhabitants thereof into two parts, according to the different types of agriculture which are practiced therein and the different names given them. The first district, which begins immediately outside the city and extends along the seashore of this Bay for a space of thirty leagues in length, and to a breadth of ten or twelve landwards, is called the Reconcavo. It contains sugar mills, many sugar plantations, and some allotments of manioc. The second district is commonly called the *sertão*, and it comprises the whole hinterland extending westwards into the interior beyond the Reconcavo as far as the bounds of Peru and New Spain. This second district is being opened up by the establishment of cattle ranches, and it is provided with ample resources in the way of pastures and water for stock raising.[43]

42. Letter of the Camara to the acting governors of Bahia, dated 15 July 1761, in Mello Moraes, *Brasil Histórico*, 2d Series, Vol. II, p. 220. Cf. also Lahmeyer Lobo, *Processo Administrativo Ibero-Americano*, pp. 349, 355.

43. Dr. Sebastião Cardoso de Sampaio, quoted in *Revista Portuguesa de História*, Vol. VIII (Coimbra, 1959), pp. 57–58.

The highways and byways of colonial Brazil were notoriously bad, in so far as they existed at all, and communications between Bahia and various points in the Reconcavo were mostly by sea and river. The sugar and tobacco plantations were sited near navigable water wherever possible, since it was easier and cheaper to send the sugar to Salvador by boat than by slow and cumbersome ox-cart. In normal times, the Camara of Bahia met only twice a week, on Wednesdays and Saturdays, but it was not always possible to form a quorum. As a municipal representation of 1676 pointed out, "the people who serve on this Senate live on their plantations in the Reconcavo," and they did not always find it easy or convenient to attend even twice weekly. It was especially inconvenient for them at harvest time, when work in the mills went on round the clock. Nevertheless, a viceregal edict of January 1649 ordered that all those councilors who were absent on their plantations should come forthwith to carry out their municipal duties in the city, "regardless of the loss they might thereby sustain as private individuals in their sugar mills, since the service of His Majesty and the common weal is more important." [44]

Nor was it only the *vereadores* and *juizes* who were thus inconvenienced. In 1627, we find two of the elected *almotacéls* excusing themselves from serving on the plea that "they were often away on their plantations." On this occasion, the excuse was accepted and the *procurador* filled in for them; but more often only serious illness was accepted as a valid excuse. Thus in 1668, a *procurador* was excused from serving after having presented several medical certificates testifying that he was suffering from "a serious urinary disease and various other ills." More unusual was the case of a *vereador* who was excused from serving on the grounds that he was both re-

44. ". . . sem embargo da perda particular que tiverão em seus engenhos por importar mais ao serviço de Sua Magestade e beneficio publico." — *Portaria* of 13 January 1649, in *Atas da Câmara da Bahia*, Vol. III, pp. 7–8. Cf. *Cartas do Senado*, Vol. II, pp. 12, 15, 126–27.

lated to and the personal enemy of a serving *juiz ordinario.* "And they are not on speaking terms, nor do they take off their hats to each other, and if they meet in the municipality they might insult each other publicly to the prejudice of the common weal." [45]

In the second half of the eighteenth century the *senhores de engenho* tended to spend more time in their town houses at Salvador, so they were probably more assiduous in their municipal duties than were their predecessors of 1721, who drew upon themselves the following rebuke from the Viceroy Count of Sabugosa:

> Whereas I am informed that some householders of this city complain that the Senate is very lax in dispatching business, since sometimes the senators never meet for days on end, and at other times they begin so late that they only have time to deal with a few trivial matters, . . . I hereby order that the Senate must begin its meetings at 9 A.M. sharp, without fail. If the *Juiz de fora* is unavoidably prevented by legal business from attending at that hour, then the senators can carry on the meeting without him.

The Count of Sabugosa never lost an opportunity of keeping the municipal councilors up to the mark, but it may be doubted if his strictures were always very effective. At any rate, in admonishing the council over another irregularity two years later, he wrote as much in sorrow as in anger: "this will be the last time that I will write to the Senate on matters concerning the public weal, both because my recommendations avail so little, as to avoid lessening my authority owing to the way in which my reminders are virtually ignored." [46] I need hardly add that this was not by any means the last time that Sabugosa admonished or advised the Senate, and his succes-

45. *Atas da Câmara da Bahia,* Vol. IV, pp. 348–56. For arguments as to whether the post of *almotacél* automatically conferred the status of *nobreza* on the holder of this office, cf. *Documentos Históricos,* Vol. XCVIII, pp. 32–35.

46. Sabugosa to the Senate of Bahia, 30 May 1721 and 6 July 1723, in *Documentos Históricos,* Vol. LXXXVII, pp. 159, 185, 196.

sor had an even sharper tussle with this body. Irrespective of the rights and wrongs of these wrangles between viceroys and councilors, a perusal of their correspondence shows that the Camara still played an important part in the life of the city and that it was anything but a rubber stamp for superior authority.

One matter on which the Count of Sabugosa kept constantly prodding the Camara, and concerning which this body was as constantly promulgating rules and regulations, was the insanitary state of the city of Salvador. It must be confessed that this was a losing battle. The earliest extant proceedings of the Camara contain orders for householders to keep the street in front of their houses clean and to prevent the drains (where there were any) from becoming choked up, on payment of fines for non-compliance. Warnings were repeatedly issued by the municipality against householders or their slaves accumulating piles of night soil and offal in street corners or in public places, but the very frequency of such prohibitions shows how often they were disregarded. In 1672, the Camara complained that its order for all household filth and refuse to be dumped on the beach and nowhere else "was only obeyed by the poor and lowly, and completely ignored by the rich and by the soldiers." In 1694, the Camara alleged that one of the reasons for the insanitary state of the city was that the sanitary inspectors (*almotacés de limpeza*) were "persons of mean condition" ("*pessoas de menor condição*"), and so their instructions were disregarded by the householders, and even by the slaves. In 1759, the Camara tried to make all householders who had open drains cover them up in order to avoid the offensive smells, but this move was blocked by the acting governors, who informed the Crown that it was impracticable in all save a few cases.[47]

47. *Cartas do Senado*, Vol. I, pp. 19, 67, 92, 117; *Documentos Históricos*, Vol. LXXXVI, pp. 252–53; Ruy, *História da Câmara do Salvador*, pp. 149–53, where, however, on pp. 151–52, the dispatch signed by the acting governors

Other reasons for the insanitary conditions, which favoured the spread of disease during the smallpox epidemic of 1663 and the yellow fever visitation of 1686, were the habit of burying people in shallow graves under church floors, and the utter inadequacy (to use no stronger term) of the slaves' cemetery. In 1718, the Camara admitted that venereal disease (*morbo gallico*) was the most widespread of all the ills which afflicted the population. On this ground they asked for the retention of a French physician, who was a specialist in its treatment and cure, but who was threatened with expulsion in one of the round-ups periodically ordered by the Crown to expel all unauthorized foreigners.[48] As regards public hygiene at Bahia, a distinction must be drawn between the upper part of the city, where the more respectable inhabitants lived, and the crowded and filthy houses and tenements along the waterfront. All foreign visitors to Salvador noted this difference, which was succinctly expressed by Mrs. Kindersley in 1764:

> The town is large and populous, and the upper part of it is pleasant and airy, consisting of many good streets, broad and clean; the houses are large, but very ill-finished and of a mean appearance; all that part of the town next the sea, the streets are narrow and dirty, full of mean-looking shops, and crowded with negro slaves of both sexes.[49]

If the Camara was not successful in its efforts to keep the city of Salvador clean for any length of time, it was hardly more so in the unending struggle which it waged against the real or alleged "monopolists and engrossers" who supplied foodstuffs and provisions, including cattle on the hoof. Many of these complaints have a very modern ring, especially the

---

of Bahia, Dr. José Carvalho de Andrade and Colonel Gonçalo Xavier de Barros e Alvim (7 September 1761) is wrongly ascribed to the ex-viceroy Conde dos Arcos.

48. *Documentos Históricos*, Vol. XCVII, p. 124.

49. *Letters from the islands of Teneriffe, Brazil, the Cape of Good Hope and the East Indies*. By Mrs. Kindersley (London, 1777), p. 33. Cf. also Azevedo, *Povoamento da Cidade do Salvador*, pp. 214–18, "causas de morte."

allegations that up-country cattle-breeders periodically with-
held their beasts from the market with the object of creating
an artificial scarcity of meat and so getting higher prices.
Reading the fulminations in the local papers about the shortage of beef during my visits to Salvador in 1959 and 1963, I
was struck by their close resemblance to similar strictures
made during the viceroyalty of the Count of Sabugosa in
1720–35.[50]

Another problem which figured repeatedly in the records
of the Camara of Bahia for much of the seventeenth and
eighteenth centuries was the supply of manioc-flour for the
city and its garrison. The planters, tenant farmers, and share-
croppers of the Reconcavo devoted themselves above all to
the cultivation of sugar and tobacco. They did not always
grow enough manioc to supply their own households and
slaves, let alone the citizens and garrison of Salvador into the
bargain. They persisted in concentrating on these two profitable (actually or potentially) cash-crops, despite periodic
efforts by the Crown, viceroys, governors — and, on rarer occasions, by the Camara of Salvador — to make them plant
manioc on an adequate scale. The *moradores* of Ilhéus, a poor
and backward captaincy, made good this deficiency by exporting manioc to Bahia from the three townships of Camamú,
Cairú, and Boipebá. When the growers of these three townships tried to "horn in" on a more profitable market by growing tobacco for export as well, the viceroy ordered the
destruction of their tobacco fields in 1656.

It is not too much to say that successive viceroys and sen-
ates of Bahia "ganged up" on the unfortunate three townships
of Ilhéus, sending them peremptory and hectoring reminders
whenever the latter were, or appeared to be, remiss in shipping supplies of manioc and other foodstuffs to Salvador. In

50. Cf. *Documentos Históricos*, Vol. LXXXVII, pp. 44–45, 47, 62, 137,
180, 182, 185, 199–200; *Atas da Câmara da Bahia*, Vol. I, p. 250, Vol. II, pp.
349–50; Azevedo, *Povoamento da Cidade do Salvador*, pp. 350–78.

vain the three Camaras of Ilhéus pointed out to the Crown that the planters of the Reconcavo could grow much more manioc if they wanted to; and in vain they alleged that the Camara of Salvador sold the manioc to the soldiers of the garrison at a substantially higher rate than they paid the producers of Ilhéus. The planters of the Reconcavo retorted that they could not afford to divert enough of their Negro slaves from planting sugar to planting manioc without seriously lowering the production of the former, much more profitable export crop. The Camara of Bahia was mainly composed of *senhores de engenho,* or persons who were closely related with them, so their interests prevailed in the long run over those of the poorer and less influential *moradores* who practiced market-gardening and subsistence agriculture in Ilhéus.[51]

Although the Senado da Camara of Bahia primarily represented the interests of the sugar planters and growers of the Reconcavo, the councilors did not always present a united front. In September 1660 the *juiz do povo* and the working-class representatives on the Camara drew up a separate petition to the Crown, alleging that there were already enough sugar mills functioning in the Reconcavo, and that the establishment of new ones would result in the overproduction of sugar and consequently in the ruin of old and new plantations alike. The petitioners asked the Crown to promulgate a law prohibiting the establishment of any new mills by the seaside, and only allowing them in the interior provided they were placed well away from the existing plantations. When this petition was referred by the Crown to the authorities at Bahia for their consideration and advice, it provoked a violent reaction there in 1662.

51. *Cartas do Senado,* Vol. III, pp. 32–33; *Documentos Históricos,* Vol. LXXXVII, pp. 8, 9, 21, 30–31, 36, 42–44, 52–53, 58, 68–69, 73–84, 89, 91; Azevedo, *Povoamento da Cidade do Salvador,* pp. 299–310; *Revista Portuguesa de História,* Vol. VIII, pp. 202–16.

The *Procurador da Fazenda* and 108 of the "principal persons" of Bahia, including "fidalgos, knight-commanders of the Military Orders and other noble persons, colonels of infantry and other military officers, tenant farmers, sugar-mill owners, justices of the peace, and aldermen who are serving in the Senate this year," all combined to denounce this proposal. They alleged that it was inspired by the highly unpopular secretary of state, Bernardo Vieira de Ravasco, brother of the famous Padre António Vieira, S.J., who scandalously mismanaged his own sugar plantation and who was consequently deeply indebted and in no position to compete effectively with others. They claimed that the Camara as a whole had not been consulted, and that Vieira de Ravasco had induced an illiterate *juiz do povo* and his fellow *mesteres* to sign the petition without their having read it, as the culprits now freely acknowledged. The planters and growers argued that the more sugar was produced the better, because sugar was the economic mainstay of Brazil and the commodity which bore the burden of taxation for the benefit of the Crown. "Who says Brazil says sugar and more sugar, which cannot be produced in large quantities from a few mills, nor by restrictions on their location and numbers."[52]

Examining the list of names and occupations attached to this petition of 8 January 1662, it is interesting to note that many of the signatories who described themselves as being *lavradores de canas* were also knight-commanders of the military orders, senior military officers, and otherwise of equal or even higher social status than the *senhores de engenho* in whose mills their sugar was ground. One example will suffice: the "Lieutenant General of artillery, Luís Gomes de Bulhões,

52. ". . . quem disse Brasil disse açúcar e mais açúcar o qual se não pode fazer muito, em poucos engenhos, nem se pode limitar paragens nem numero." Cf. the documents dated Bahia, 8 January, 23 May, 20 September 1662, printed in full in *Anais do 1º Congresso de História da Bahia*, pp. 491–99, and those calendared in *ibid.*, pp. 147, 150, 154, 156, 161, 164.

knight of the Habit of São Bento de Aviz, and *lavrador de canas.*" Many of these *lavradores de canas* also served on the municipal council before and after 1662; and it is clear that the word *lavrador* in this connection did not carry the pejorative connotation which it usually did in Portugal, where we often find it prefixed by the adjective *vil.*

Despite the impressive array of signatures to this document of 1662, Bernardo Vieira de Ravasco had several supporters among the sugar-planters, and before long a modified form of his proposals was adopted. The enormous quantities of timber needed by the sugar plantations, both for stoking the mills at harvest time (which might last for several months) and for the construction of buildings, boats, ox-carts, and sugar chests, meant that the woods of the Reconcavo were being rapidly devastated and that the neighbouring *engenhos* were fiercely competing for timber. At the suggestion of the Camara itself, therefore, from 1677 onwards a series of laws was promulgated at Lisbon, specifying that no new *engenho* could be founded at a distance of less than half a league from the boundaries of any other. It was also enacted that tobacco plantations and cattle ranches must be situated at least ten leagues away from the seaside or riverside, so as to leave the intervening thirty miles available for the exclusive cultivation of sugar and manioc.[53] Protests and pleas for exemption periodically came from many places in the Reconcavo, such as Maragogipe, and Cachoeira; but the Camara (reversing its attitude of 1662) and the Crown usually stood firm and insisted on compliance with the regulations. As late as 1785, the Camara reiterated that "all the *lavradores*, whosoever they may be, who have land capable of bearing manioc, will be compelled to plant the number of *covas* they have been

53. Cf. Azevedo, *Povoamento da Cidade do Salvador*, pp. 299–303, 318–19, 454, 456; Wanderley Pinho, *História de um engenho do Recôncavo*, pp. 141–61; *Revista Portuguesa de História*, Vol. VIII, pp. 178–92; Frédéric Mauro, *Le Brésil au XVIIe siècle*, pp. 281–307.

allotted, so that if they produce more than is necessary for consumption by their households, they can bring the surplus for sale to the people of this city, as has been practiced up to now." Despite the assertion in the last sentence, we know from Vilhena's account of Bahia a few years later that, in point of fact, many *senhores de engenho* evaded compliance with this regulation and some even refused to plant any manioc at all.[54]

For most of the seventeenth and eighteenth centuries, the Camara was also closely connected with fixing the price of sugar, which naturally varied annually in accordance with supply and demand and with the success or failure of the *safra* (harvest). The Camara was fixing sugar prices and freight rates in 1626, and probably much earlier, apparently in consultation with a number of *louvados* (arbitrators, umpires, or referees) who were appointed annually. In 1642 these experts comprised two representatives of the sugar-planters, two of the merchants, two *mesteres*, and one magistrate, with the *ouvidor* as president. In 1677 the Crown ordered the Camara not to concern itself with fixing sugar prices; but this policy was soon reversed and the system of price-fixing by the Camara, after consultation with a commission representing the interests of producers, exporters, and consumers, was restored. In case of disagreement, the problem was referred to arbitrators drawn from the local High Court, whose decision was final. The prices agreed on were ratified by the Camara and publicly announced as binding for that year. In 1751, this system was supplanted by the establishment of a board of inspection (*mesa da inspecção*), staffed mainly by Crown bureaucrats, though the Camara was allowed to nominate one *senhor de engenho* or *lavrador de canas* to represent the interests of the sugar-growers.[55]

54. Cf. Azevedo, *Povoamento da Cidade do Salvador*, pp. 319–21; *Atas da Câmara da Bahia*, Vol. II, pp. 388–405.
55. *Atas da Câmara da Bahia*, Vol. I, pp. 31–32, 39, Vol. II, pp. 72–74;

To recapitulate, in addition to deciding, or helping to decide, the sale price of meat, manioc-flour, sugar, salt, tobacco, rum, medical supplies, and a wide range of other commodities, the Camara was actively concerned with revaluations of the currency, with the imposition and collection of local taxation, and with many other fiscal and administrative measures. For much of the colonial period, the Camara submitted lists of three names when a vacancy occurred in a militia officer's post, from which the viceroy chose one. Like its counterparts at Lisbon, Goa, and Macao, the Camara of Bahia often came to the rescue of the perennially exhausted royal treasury in time of need, as instanced by the money it raised for the maintenance and repair of the armadas commanded by the Conde da Torre (1638–40), and the Count of Villa Pouca (1647–50).[56] In 1699–1700, the Camara contributed a newly built warship, *Nossa Senhora de Bittencourt*, and three hundred men for the recovery of Mombasa; it was no fault of the municipal councilors that this stronghold fell to the Arabs of Oman before the expedition sailed.[57] These sacrifices continued throughout the eighteenth century, when the Camara frequently raised money, men, and provisions for the garrison of Sacramento in the Rio de la Plata, as well as sending soldiers, horses, and ammunition to Angola.

The Crown was not unmindful of the sacrifices made by the Camara of Bahia during the Dutch War. When in 1653, on the eve of the expulsion from Pernambuco of the heretic Dutch invaders, the *moradores* of Brazil asked for representation in the Cortes at Lisbon, D. João IV replied that the municipality of Bahia, as capital of the State of Brazil, could nominate in future two representatives to attend when the

---

Documentos Históricos, Vol. LXXXVII, pp. 6, 15–17, 24–25, 120; Wanderley Pinho, *História de um engenho do Recôncavo*, pp. 185–86, 309; Lahmeyer Lobo, *Processo Administrativo Ibero-Americano*, p. 510.

56. Azevedo, *Povoamento da Cidade do Salvador*, pp. 313–16.

57. C. R. Boxer and Carlos de Azevedo, *Fort Jesus and the Portuguese in Mombasa, 1593–1729* (London, 1960), pp. 66–74.

Cortes were held. It will be recalled that the Camara of Goa later enjoyed the same privilege, though neither city was able to make very much use of it, as the last meeting of the Cortes during the period with which we are concerned took place in 1698.[58] Nevertheless, Goa and Bahia were thereby placed on a level with the cities of metropolitan Portugal over a century before the principle of "no taxation without representation" became one of the reasons for the break between Great Britain and the Thirteen Colonies.

58. *Cartas do Senado*, Vol. I, pp. 118–21; *Anais do 1⁰ Congresso de História da Bahia*, Vol. II, p. 127; Pedro Calmon, *História do Brasil*, Vol. II, pp. 647–49.

CHAPTER IV

The Municipal Council of Luanda

In a handbook which the municipality of Luanda published in 1918, the officiating town councilors made the following observation:

It would be very interesting to compile the history of this municipality, in order to study its role in the colonizing movement of the province in bygone days, its civilizing influence in the historical evolution of Angola, and to draw therefrom lessons which might enable us to form correct ideas concerning the advantages or disadvantages of the system of municipal government in newly settled countries. But, unfortunately, it is not possible to study this history in the municipal archives of the early centuries, because, although the minutes of the council meetings (*vereações*) and many other registers and documents exist from the year 1649 onwards, the condition of the archives until far into the eighteenth century is not such as to facilitate their consultation, and some are entirely illegible. They are leaves riddled with holes, unreadable, enclosed in sheepskin bindings. Many of them, especially the oldest, have nowadays only the value of attesting that the Camaras promulgated their decrees, held their judicial and administrative meetings, met, discussed, and decided matters for the good of the common weal, but in ways which only their contemporaries understood.[1]

Two visits which I paid to the municipal archives of Luanda, in 1955 and 1961, respectively, enable me to state that this gloomy picture is somewhat exaggerated.[2] Admittedly, all the documents prior to 1649 are lost, with insignificant exceptions. The Dutch invaders of 1641 intercepted the convoy which was carrying the municipal archives and some refugees up the river Bengo from the city, and they threw all the documents into the river after killing most of the inoffensive fugitives. The Camara of Luanda was reconstituted shortly after the recapture of Luanda by Salvador Correia de Sá e Benavides, in August 1648, but it does not seem to have left written traces of its existence till the next year. It is also true that many of the documents of the period 1649–1750 are in poor condition and that many others are so eaten by the white ants (*salalé*), or so corroded by acid from the ink used, that they are completely unreadable and fall to pieces when they are touched. But many others have not suffered so much and these can be restored in whole or in part, as is now, in fact, being done. Some of the documents dating from the second half of the seventeenth century, and a still larger proportion of those in the eighteenth century, are perfectly legible. With the aid of these documents, and of others from Luanda and Lisbon which have been published in the series, *Arquivos de Angola*,[3] it is possible to form quite a good idea

1. *O Município de Loanda*, Chap. IV.
2. Thanks to the facilities given me by the authorities concerned, which enabled me to work in this archive and the others at Luanda. I am particularly indebted in this respect to the late Dr. Carlos Coimbra, to the President of the Municipal Council at Luanda in 1961, to Senhor Dr. José Redinha, and to Senhor Carlos Mendes Couto, who kindly copied several of the original documents for me. Needless to say, none of the above gentlemen are responsible for the deductions which I have drawn from this manuscript material.
3. *Arquivos de Angola*, 1st Series (5 vols.; Luanda, 1933–39), 2d Series (16 vols.; Luanda, 1943–59, in progress).

of how the Camara of Luanda functioned and to compare its power and influence with those of Goa, Macao, and Bahia.

I have not been able to ascertain the exact date when the Camara of Luanda was originally constituted; but there seems no reason to doubt the traditional account that Paulo Dias de Novais installed the municipality shortly after he had moved from his first settlement on the island of Luanda to the mainland on the opposite shore, where he founded the existing city of São Paulo de Luanda in 1576. However that may be, the Camara in its original form was modelled, like that of Bahia, on the general pattern envisaged in the *Ordenações do Reino*, and not on the prototype of Lisbon or any particular Portuguese city. The *oficiais da Camara* comprised three *vereadores*, two *juizes ordinarios*, and a *procurador*, with the usual subordinate officials such as the secretary and the *almotacéls*. So far as I can ascertain, there was no working-class representation, in the form of a *juiz do povo* and *procuradores dos mesteres*, on the Camara of Luanda, which in this respect resembled that of Macao. There are a few references to the existence of a *juiz do povo*, and I have found one such relating to the year 1670, but from the context it does not appear that he was a member of the Camara. In due course, the municipal council of Luanda petitioned for the grant of the privileges of the city of Oporto, as so many other colonial Camaras had done. These privileges were eventually conferred by a royal decree of 28 September 1662, in recognition of the sufferings endured by the citizens of Luanda at Massangano and elsewhere in the interior during the Dutch occupation of Luanda and Benguela in 1641–48.[4]

It is worth noting that anti-Jewish prejudice was as marked at Luanda as elsewhere in the Portuguese empire, although — or perhaps because — the Marrano element was strongly represented in the colony's pioneer days, and Paulo Dias de

4. *Alvará* of 28 September 1662, transcribed in *O Município de Loanda*, Chap. IV.

Novais himself had a "taint" of New-Christian blood. As late as 1656, the *oficiais da Camara* reminded the Crown that New Christians had been forbidden by law to serve in the municipal council or in the magistracy "since the time of King Philip of Castile." They alleged that some crypto-Jews had nevertheless wormed their way into such positions since the recapture of the colony, and they asked that the anti-Jewish regulations should be "observed inviolably." [5]

An *ouvidor-geral* was appointed for Angola in 1651, and he was given some supervisory authority over the Camara. At a slightly later date, this official assumed the presidency of the Camara, though the number of *vereadores* still remained the same. In 1722, a *juiz de fora* was appointed for Angola, and henceforth the presidency was vested in this functionary. As with the other colonial Camaras, the municipal council of Luanda often found that its income was insufficient to cover its expenditure, and it likewise experienced difficulty in collecting rents from such properties as it possessed.[6] Much of its income was also derived from license fees, taxes on market produce, and fines on shopkeepers, stall-holders, and street-vendors who transgressed the licensing and the price regulations. Sale prices of locally manufactured products were promulgated periodically, after due consultation with the elected representatives (the *juizes*) of the trades or crafts concerned (tailors, cobblers, coopers, jewellers, etc.), though these *mesteres* were not, as previously noted, given seats in the municipal council. The Camara also levied duties on consignments of wine, brandy, rum, and other alcoholic imports from Portugal and Brazil, and it had a share in the export duties levied on slaves — the "Black Ivory" which was the economic mainstay of Angola for some 250 years.

5. Camara to Crown, 19 February 1656, in *Arquivos de Angola*, 2d Series, Vol. VII (1950), p. 39.

6. "Registo de Termos de Posse, Arremetações, escrituras etc., 1650 a 1846," codex in the municipal archives at Luanda.

As happened at Goa, Macao, and Bahia, the Camara of Luanda was often called upon to help the Crown in times of crisis, and to arrange for the collection and disbursement (or remittance to Lisbon) of special taxes imposed during these emergencies. The first of these occurred in 1633, when the Camara reluctantly agreed to raise the equivalent of 40,000 cruzados to finance the construction of fortifications against an expected Dutch attack. These fortifications proved useless when the invasion materialized eighteen years later, as the defenders fled in panic; but the Camara agreed to place another surcharge on the export tax on slaves in 1651, in order to help pay for the expenses of the expedition which Salvador Correia had organized at Rio de Janeiro in 1647–48, for the recapture of Luanda and Benguela from the Dutch. The Camara of Luanda, like all the others, was called upon to contribute to the double indemnity of the *Dote de Inglaterra e paz de Holanda* in 1662. By pleading poverty and alleging various other excuses, the Camara managed to evade making any payments on this account until 1670–71, when an additional surcharge on the export of slaves was imposed for this purpose. As with Brazil, the collection of the total contribution (originally assessed at 360,000 cruzados) proved to be a slow and difficult business, and installments were still being remitted in 1728.[7]

The Camara of Luanda sometimes had a share in the government of the colony. It was regularly convened and consulted by the governors in emergencies, particularly on such occasions as making war or peace with the king of Congo — Portuguese relations with this nominally Christian kingdom

7. *Assentos* of 7 June 1670 and 24 December 1672, in municipal archives, Luanda. Cf. also Ralph Delgado, *História de Angola, 1482–1836*, Vol. III, pp. 264–71, 346–49, 361–63, Vol. IV, p. 390, for the payment of the *dote de Inglaterra e paz de Holanda*. For the levy of 1633, see the documents printed by Padre Ruela Pombo, *Anais de Angola, 1630–1635* (Lisbon, 1945), pp. 32–54.

having steadily deteriorated ever since the founding of Luanda. The Camara was also actively concerned in the deposition of the governor, D. Francisco de Almeida, in 1593, and
in the election of his brother, D. Jeronimo, as a substitute. The
Camara — or, rather, three successive *vereações* — actually
governed the colony for nearly three years in 1667–69, after
the governor, Tristão da Cunha, had been forced to flee from
Luanda by a mutiny of the garrison in January 1667. The
vereadores of that year were later accused of being the insti-
gators of this mutiny and they were sent to Lisbon, where
they were imprisoned for a time. After the death of the governor, Bernardo de Tavora, in 1702, the Camara again
governed the colony for a period of three years until the belated arrival of his successor. The Camara took over the reins
of government for the last time in 1732, after the death of
Paulo Caetano de Albuquerque, although only for a few days
on this occasion.

The Camara of Luanda, like the others, had a good deal
of friction with the governors at various times. Apart from
being implicated in the deposition of two governors, as mentioned above, the Camara was involved in open conflict with
a third, the half-mad João de Sousa Correia, who left Luanda
abruptly in 1623, having antagonized all sections of the community. In 1702, the Camara petitioned the Crown to extend
the councilors' period of service from one year to three, so
as to coincide with the triennial term of the governors. The
Camara explained that as the governors were more involved
in trade and commerce than anybody else, they were prone
to misuse their authority in order to further their own private
ends. The councilors who might venture to oppose a governor's malpractices or misdeeds were liable to refrain from
doing so, lest the governor should take vengeance on them
when their year in office had expired. The Camara concluded
its petition by observing sententiously that the common weal
should always take preference over personal interests, "these

latter being the total ruin of monarchies, whereas the former is the sole foundation of the preservation of all peoples." [8]

The Crown rejected or ignored this petition, which the Camara renewed in 1711, making the additional point that the citizens of Luanda who were qualified to serve as municipal councilors were very few and mostly related to each other. If, therefore, the *oficiais da Camara* were changed yearly in accordance with the procedure laid down in the *Ordenações*, either related persons would have to serve in the same year, or else "unworthy individuals" would have to be admitted. These included persons "who were married three days before the elections, and to girls who were not daughters of respectable citizens." This, in turn, led to the few qualified officeholders being reluctant to serve — a reluctance reinforced by the fact that they only held office for one year. The Camara repeated this request for the third time in 1714, but it must have carried even less weight at Lisbon, since in the previous year the Camara had warmly commended the governor, D. João Manuel de Noronha, and asked that his tour of duty should be extended for another three years. [9]

The Crown took evasive action on these petitions, which were only part of the stream of complaints that the Overseas Council at Lisbon had been receiving for many years on the tendency of colonial governors, whether in Asia, Africa, or Brazil, to act as commercial monopolists and engrossers. It is interesting to note that D. João Manuel de Noronha, the governor so warmly commended by the Camara of Luanda, owned about 30 percent of all the slaves exported from that port. [10] Stimulated, in all probability, more by the complaints from Brazil than by those from Angola, the Crown eventually

8. Camara to Crown, 22 April 1702, in Codex 483 (old numbering) of the municipal archives, Luanda.

9. Camara to Crown, 26 September 1711, and 7 May 1714, Codex 483, fls. 93–105.

10. Cf. Delgado, *História de Angola*, Vol. IV, pp. 303, 322.

promulgated a decree (29 August 1720) strictly forbidding all colonial governors, and all civilian and military officers above the rank of captain or its equivalent, to engage in any form of trade and commerce, directly or indirectly, "upon any pretext whatsoever." The governors and other officials were awarded higher pay and salaries to compensate for the loss of their commercial profits; but it need hardly be said that this decree was honoured more in the breach than in the observance by most of those at whom it was aimed, just as was similar legislation enacted by the Dutch, English, and French East-India Companies against the "private trade" driven by their employees.

Among the governors who proved to be popular with the *moradores* of Luanda were Salvador Correia de Sá e Benavides (1648–52), D. Francisco de Tavora (1669–76), and D. João de Lencastre (1688–91). The Camara kept up a correspondence with them after their return to Lisbon, asking them to intercede with the Crown through their friends in (or their own membership of) the Overseas Council, in support of the requests submitted by the Camara. D. Francisco de Tavora, later Count of Alvor and Viceroy of India, seems to have been the governor who made the best impression not only on the *moradores* of Luanda, but among all classes and races. Though only twenty-three years old when he was appointed as governor, his conduct earned him the sobriquet of *"o menino prudente,"* and a highly complimentary valediction in Kimbundu from the crowds of Bantu who came to see him off at the end of his seven-year term. When his successor promulgated the routine edict announcing that a judicial investigation would be made concerning his predecessor's governorship, at which anyone could come and lodge complaints, the Camara wrote indignantly to the Prince Regent of Portugal that there was no reason for anyone to submit any complaints, since all of Tavora's actions had been "most justifiable and in strict accord with his duty to God and to Your Highness."[11]

When the municipal councilors sent a *procurador* to Lisbon to protest against Angola's being made to contribute to the double indemnity of the *Dote de Inglaterra e paz de Holanda* in 1662, they somewhat tactlessly coupled this request with a petition for more extensive privileges and favours. These included the prohibition of offensive wars against the Negro tribes of the interior, with the corollary that the governors should only be allowed to wage defensive wars after prior consultation with the Camara; that exiled convicts (*degredados*) on arrival at Luanda should not be employed in official posts, but should be sent forthwith to serve their sentences in the interior, so as to prevent their embarking clandestinely for Brazil; that the governors should on no account interfere with the jurisdiction of the Camara, and that they should fill vacant posts and offices from among the *moradores* of Luanda and not from among their own servants and hangers-on; that the governors should not be allowed to send *pombeiros*, or slave-traders, into the interior; that all governors should be compelled to register their letters-patent and instructions with the Camara on taking the oath of office; and that the contracts for the collection of the Crown taxes should be auctioned at Luanda rather than at Lisbon.[12]

As previously noted, the Crown did grant the privileges of the municipality of Oporto to the Camara of Luanda in 1662, but otherwise its reception of these requests was not wholly favourable. The Camara was compelled to contribute to the *Dote de Inglaterra e paz de Holanda*, although, as we have seen, it continued to avoid making any payments on this ac-

---

11. Camara to Crown, 11 November 1676, in Codex 482 (old numbering), fl. 9. For Tavora's popularity, cf. also António de Oliveira Cadornega, *História Geral das Guerras Angolanas*, Vol. II, pp. 368–69.

12. Documents of 19 July, 8 August, 22 October 1664, in Delgado, *História de Angola*, Vol. III, p. 266n.

count until 1670–71. Offensive wars in the interior were prohibited by a series of royal decrees beginning in 1669, and, what is more, the citizens of Luanda were exempted from active military service save only if the place itself was attacked. The restrictions on the movements and placing of convicts were indeed ordered by the Crown, but these orders remained for the most part a dead letter. By the eighteenth century the bulk of the white population was made up of *degredados* or their descendants, and they necessarily filled many of the civil and military posts. The governors of Brazil constantly complained that convicts deported to Angola were finding their way back to Brazil, with or without the connivance of the authorities at Luanda. On their side, the governors of Angola and the Camara of Luanda periodically protested against the colony's being made a dumping ground for the "vicious criminals" (*degredados facinorozos*) of both Portugal and Brazil. During the eighteenth century the influx of these undesirables was reinforced by levies of gypsies whom the Crown strove to expel entirely from Portugal. The Camara of Luanda complained in 1720 that "all the gypsies who have been sent to Rio de Janeiro, Bahia, and Pernambuco, invariably end up in the kingdom of Angola." The Camara was responsible for registering the arrival of all convicts and gypsies, and for seeing that they served their sentences. The records kept of these deportees specify the offenses for which they were exiled, affording some interesting sidelights on eighteenth-century Luso-Brazilian society.[13]

As regards the other matters which figured in the Camara's representation of 1662, the governors continued to appoint

13. British Museum, Additional MS 15,183, fls. 165–66; municipal archives at Luanda, Codex 499 (old numbering), "Registo de Degredados condenados por varios crimes cometidos, que se desembarcaram nesta colónia, vindos de Portugal e Brazil, 1753 a 1793." Despite the title, the documents go back as far as 1663, but only become legible with those of 1714. See the extracts translated in Appendix 26, below.

their *criados* to official posts, as was the accepted practice everywhere in the Iberian colonial world. They also continued to take an active and often a leading part in the slave trade, whether directly or indirectly. They did indeed register their letters-patent and instructions with the Camara on assuming office, but this was merely the revival of a formality which had been standard practice in the sixteenth century. The corespondence between the Camara and the Crown in 1704–14, shows that the governors did try to bring pressure to bear on the Camara when they felt so disposed, though cooperation rather than conflict was the general rule. The suggestion that the Crown monopoly contracts should be farmed out in Luanda rather than at Lisbon came to nothing, as even the wealthiest *moradores* of Luanda could not compete with the Lisbon financiers.

The two main factors which stultified the healthy development of Angola were the concentration of virtually all efforts on the slave trade, and the use of Angola as a penal settlement for the *degredados* of Portugal and Brazil. Bento Banha Cardoso, one of the leading *conquistadores* of Angola, after noting some of the potential agricultural and mineral resources of the colony in 1622, added regretfully: "very little attention is paid to these things there, because most people being employed in the slave trade, they neglect everything else." This observation was profoundly true and it remained the keynote of Angolan history for the next two centuries, with the exception of a few interludes such as the enlightened administration of Innocencio de Sousa Coutinho in 1764–72.[14] From time to time, suggestions were made by higher authorities, whether at Lisbon or at Luanda, that sugar or cotton should be culti-

14. Bento Banha Cardoso's observation of 1622, in Luciano Cordeiro, *Viagens explorações e conquistas dos Portugueses, 1620–1629. Producções, comercio e governo do Congo e Angola* (Lisbon, 1881), p. 18. For Sousa Coutinho's governorship of Angola, cf. *Arquivos de Angola*, 2d Series, Vol. X (1953); Ralph Delgado, "O governo de Sousa Coutinho em Angola," series of articles published in *Studia: Revista Semestral*, Vols. VI, VII, X.

vated on a large scale in Angola, as they were in Brazil; but, in the upshot, little or nothing came of these ambitious plans.

The Camara of Luanda, when consulted by the Crown on this point in 1655, replied that large-scale sugar cultivation was impractical for the following reasons: The juice of the cane which grew in Angola was not nearly so good as that of Brazil; there was not sufficient firewood to keep the sugar mills grinding at harvest time, at any rate in the region round Luanda which was bare of trees; the citizens of Luanda had not got sufficient capital resources to develop the industry. If they grew cotton, they had no ships in which to export it to Lisbon, and they would have to send it via Brazil. This would involve paying double freight for each consignment, and make the transaction unprofitable. Some of the governors were inclined to blame the "*pouca curiosidade*" of the *moradores* for their unwillingness to undertake such enterprises.[15] But the basic reason was undoubtedly their resolve to concentrate on the slave trade, for which they had a ready market in Brazil — and a still more profitable one in Spanish America when slaves from Angola could be imported there. Portuguese agricultural enterprise was therefore mainly confined to the transplantation of various Brazilian food-plants (the most important of which was manioc) to Angola, and of African plants to Brazil. The *moradores* also established *arimos*, or farms, in certain favoured localities, such as the mouth of the river Bengo and around Massangano, where food-crops were grown for local consumption and the surplus dispatched for sale in Luanda.

A problem which figured largely in the triangular correspondence between Lisbon, Luanda, and Bahia in the second half of the seventeenth century was the export of Brazilian rum and sugar-cane brandy (*cachaça* and *geribita*) to An-

15. Cf. the documents cited in Cadornega, *História Geral das Guerras Angolanas*, Vol. II, pp. 510–12; Delgado, *História de Angola*, Vol. III, pp. 168–70.

gola.[16] The governor and Camara at Luanda complained to the Crown in 1678 that the importation of *geribita* from Brazil had noticeably increased in the last twelve or thirteen years. It was of such a fiery quality, "that the drinking thereof has caused great harm and sudden death among both slaves and white men, disabling the soldiers." The Camara of Luanda asked the Crown to prohibit the importation of Brazilian rum into Angola and this was done in the following year. The imposition of a ban on the distillation and sale of *cachaça* in Bahia itself had been advocated by the Camara of Salvador as early as 1628, and it had been enacted seven years later. But this ban had been lifted again in 1640, since experience had shown that the *"gente poderosa"* continued to distill and sell rum, undeterred by threats of fines and prison sentences. In 1646, a general meeting held at the instance of the *juiz do povo* and *mesteres* voted to reimpose the ban on *cachaça* owing to the ruinous effects of "Demon rum" on the health of soldiers, workers, and slaves. I do not know how long this prohibition lasted, but evidently it was not for long, since the ban was reimposed by the governor Count of Atouguia in 1656, this time on the grounds that the sale of Portuguese wines and brandy imported by the Brazil Company was adversely affected by the local production of *cachaça* and *geribita*. This ban proved to be as ineffective in practice as the previous ones had been. It was lifted at the request of the Camara in 1672, so that the stills and the *cachaça* itself could be legally taxed, though the exportation of rum to Angola was prohibited by the Crown seven years later, as we have seen.[17]

16. *Cachaça, geribita* (*gerebita, jerebita*, etc.), *aguardente de terra*, and *vinho de mel*, all seem to have been different terms for rum, or, perhaps, for different kinds of rum; *cachaça* being the most common term in Brazil and *geribita* in Angola.

17. *Atas da Câmara da Bahia*, Vol. I, pp. 111, 281, 431, Vol. II, p. 312, Vol. V, pp. 60–63; Thales de Azevedo, *Povoamento da Cidade do Salvador*, pp. 308, 331–34, 379n; correspondence between Luanda and Lisbon cited in Cadornega, *História Geral das Guerras Angolanas*, Vol. II, pp. 510–12,

The futility of this last ban, and the loss of revenue which it involved for the Camaras of Bahia and Luanda, induced both these municipalities to petition the Crown in the years 1687–89 for its revocation, but for some years without success. The Camara of Luanda pointed out that Brazilian rum was "the principal commodity for which numerous slaves were bartered on the borders of the [kingdom of] Congo, in the Dembos region, and in the remoter parts of the hinterland." When *geribita* was imported legally from Brazil, many people earned their livelihood by participating in this trade, which they could not do since the ban of 1679. The rum was now smuggled ashore in coves and bays at some distance from Luanda and sold to monopolists and engrossers, who resold it to retailers, who, perforce, had to charge high prices for it in their turn. The Camara was unable to collect duty on this contraband rum, which was nevertheless drunk in considerable quantities in Luanda, "without the drinkers coming to any harm, in spite of allegations to the contrary." The Camara of Luanda thus completely reversed its position on this problem between 1678 and 1688.[18]

Nor was the Camara of Bahia any more consistent. Forgetting or ignoring the representations of their predecessors in 1628 and 1646 about the harmful effects of *cachaça* on the workers, soldiers, and slaves at Bahia, the Camara of Salvador informed the Crown in 1687 that the restrictions placed on the production and export of Brazilian rum had been imposed at the request of the merchants of wine and brandy in Portugal, who thus hoped to corner the markets in Brazil and Angola for their own products. The Overseas Councilors at Lisbon, on their side, advised the Crown to reject these repre-

544–45. Cf. also Delgado, *História de Angola*, Vol. IV, pp. 125–26, 175, 185–88, 198.

18. Camara of Luanda's *proposta* of 5 January, and D. João de Lencastre's reply of 9 February 1689, in municipal archives, Luanda; *Arquivos de Angola*, 1st Series, Vol. III, p. 17; *bandos* of Camara of Luanda, dated 31 December 1688 and 12 January 1689, in municipal archives, Luanda.

sentations from Bahia and Luanda, and to maintain the existing ban on the export of Brazilian rum to Angola. They reminded the Crown that the problem had been carefully considered in all its aspects before the imposition of this ban in 1679, and that the petitioners had not adduced any new arguments. "On the contrary," they added, "the ban should be more rigorously enforced, because our information shows that the trade in Brazilian brandy with Angola is still going on; and it is being winked at, either through the power of the governors, or through the machinations of private individuals." The King agreed, and maintained the ban; but protests and appeals continued to reach Lisbon from both sides of the South Atlantic, the Camaras of Luanda and Bahia being warmly supported by their respective governors. The rum-trade suited all parties in Brazil and Angola, from the governors, distillers, and tax-farmers at the top end of the social scale to the slaves at the bottom. Either convinced by these economic facts of life, or else by the reiterated representations from Luanda and Bahia, the Crown finally yielded and authorized the exportation of Brazilian rum and sugar-cane brandy to Angola by a decree of November 1695.[19]

Writing to the Count of Alvor at Lisbon in February 1698, and thanking him for his help in bringing about this long-desired result, the Camara of Luanda observed:

Insofar as concerns the *gerebitas*, it is certain that there is no commodity more suitable for the Negro slave trade, nor can the ships from Brazil bring anything else in the way of cargo. If the *gerebitas* fail, then everything else is bound to collapse, and for these reasons we are most grateful to Your Excellency for the zeal you have shown in obtaining permission for them.[20]

19. *Documentos Históricos*, Vol. LXXXIX, pp. 80–81; *Revista Portuguesa de História*, Vol. VIII, pp. 192–95; Delgado, *História de Angola*, Vol. IV, p. 198.

20. Camara of Luanda to the Count of Alvor, 5 February 1698, in municipal archives, Luanda, Codex 483 (old numbering), fl. 74.

I have gone into this problem in some detail, because the importance of Brazilian rum in the West-African slave trade, and more especially in the trade with Angola, is not always sufficiently stressed, and it is sometimes wrongly assumed that firearms and gunpowder were more important. They may have been at certain times and in certain regions, but for most of the seventeenth and eighteenth centuries they took second place to Brazilian rum and brandy in Angola and Benguela. The Camaras of Luanda and Bahia both relied heavily on the duties they levied on wines and spirits. Their eighteenth-century records show that the captain or master of every ship entering those ports had to declare the manifest of his cargo to the Camara and pay the stipulated duties on those liquors before any goods on board could be discharged.[21]

Another problem over which the Camara of Luanda waged a long struggle with the Crown and its advisers at Lisbon was the need to substitute a copper coinage for the local form of barter money. This latter consisted of *libongos*, or square pieces of palm-bark cloth (*raffia*), also known as "straw money" (*moeda de palha*). Ten *libongos* made a *macuta*, which was originally valued at 500 reis, and from 1649 onwards they were all stamped with the letter *R* by the *procurador* of the Camara as a guarantee of authenticity. This system was adversely criticized by the Overseas Council in 1688, echoing the representations of the Camara of Luanda, which were summarized as follows:

The *macutas* which circulated as money in Luanda were so vile and base a commodity that outside of that city neither the Portuguese nor the barbarians used or valued them, and the heathen only made use of them in order to sell them in Luanda. A *macuta*

21. Original manifests of cargo registered with the Camara at Luanda are extant from about 1735 onwards in the archives of the municipal council there. For the corresponding MSS, "Livro do registro de entradas de navios no porto da Bahia," covering the years 1688–1752, cf. Azevedo, *Povoamento da Cidade do Salvador*, p. 414n.

[alias, *libongo*] consisted of a small square measuring about a hand's-breadth, made like a mat from a kind of straw or hay so fragile that it was worn out in a short time through passing from hand to hand as money, and the citizens in this way lost over 15,000 cruzados every three or four years.[22]

Shortly after the recapture of Luanda from the Dutch in August 1648, the governor, Salvador Correia de Sá e Benavides, convened a general meeting of the citizens, clergy, and officers of the garrison, which voted for the introduction of a copper coinage; but when this request was forwarded to Lisbon it was rejected by the Crown. Subsequent governors and Camaras renewed this request with increasing urgency and frequency, but the Crown hesitated for a long time before giving its assent. In a lengthy dispatch dated 30 December 1683, the municipal councilors wrote that they could not understand the reasons for this procrastination, as the Crown was morally bound to grant their well-grounded requests.

For as the municipal councils are, as it were, the tutors of royal personages, or, rather of the realms and peoples whom they govern, they are as such obliged not only to deliberate on matters concerning the common weal and mutual preservation, but also of the general welfare of all classes, which is the reason why we are in duty bound to send Your Highness, as we do, these continual petitions, so that casting your eyes on our representations you may grant us justice, since the reason for our request is such a justifiable one.[23]

In point of fact, the Crown had already agreed with the Overseas Council to authorize the issue of a copper coinage for Angola in 1680, but it subsequently failed to implement this decision. The appeals of the Camara had become almost hysterical by the time that the decision was belatedly imple-

22. Quoted in Cadornega, *História Geral das Guerras Angolanas*, Vol. II, p. 536.

23. Camara to Crown, 24 May 1679; ditto to ditto, 30 December 1683; ditto to ditto 7 August 1683; all in Luanda municipal archives, Codex 482 (old numbering), fls. 20–61, *passim*.

mented with the arrival of the first consignment of copper money at Luanda in 1694. As is the way with mankind the world over, no sooner had this long-standing request been granted than the municipal councilors began to express their disillusionment with the results. They alleged that too much money had been sent for the relatively modest needs of Angola, and that consequently its value was depreciating. They requested the Crown to check this depreciation by allowing Angola copper coins to circulate in Brazil, a request which was granted by the Crown in 1704. Even this was not the end of the colony's currency problems, as the *moeda de palha,* together with other forms of barter-money, such as blocks of salt and cowrie-shells, were used to pay some of the troops and officials at the garrison posts (*presidios*) in the interior until the middle of the nineteenth century.[24]

The correspondence of the Camara with the Crown, and with its own procurators and friends at Lisbon, is full of complaints about the increasingly heavy taxation to which the citizens of Luanda were subjected, and allegations of their extreme poverty and inability to pay the amounts demanded of them. In 1665, the Camara stated that there were then 326 white *moradores,* or heads of households, in Angola, of whom 132 lived at Luanda. Fourteen years later, the municipal councilors complained to the Prince Regent: "this people, whose name has come to Your Highness' ears as a kingdom, in fact comprise about eighty *moradores,* of whom less than forty are qualified to hold office in this senate." They added that these few individuals were burdened with taxes and imposts to the amount of 90,000 cruzados a year, and it was (they wrote) little short of miraculous that they could find

24. Cf. the documents cited in Cadornega, *História Geral das Guerras Angolanas,* Vol. II, pp. 484, 534–40, Vol. III, pp. 195–96; Delgado, *História de Angola,* Vol. IV, pp. 34–35, 83, 111–15, 130–31, 176–89; Frédéric Mauro, *Le Portugal et l'Atlantique au XVIIe siècle, 1570–1670,* pp. 396–97, 426; Gastão Sousa Dias, *Os Portugueses em Angola* (Lisbon, 1959), pp. 185–87.

this sum — or most of it.[25] The Camara's correspondence con-
tinues in this vein for some years, and it is interesting to note
that among the signatories of these pessimistic letters was
António de Oliveira Cadornega, the soldier-chronicler who
lived for over forty years in Angola (1639–85), and who
served in the Camaras of Massangano and Luanda.

Yet Cadornega in his classic *História Geral das Guerras
Angolanas*, which he compiled at Luanda in 1680–83, gives
us a very different picture of the city at this time.[26] He depicts
Luanda as a thriving, bustling seaport with considerable
financial resources. He enthuses over the "principal citizens
and ancient *moradores* of some hundred households, who
have produced prosperous families dwelling in costly and
sumptuous buildings, which greatly ennoble this city —
most of them being white men from our kingdom of Portugal,
and sons and grandsons of the original conquerors." Elsewhere in the same work, Cadornega extols the lavish charity
of the Brotherhood of the Misericordia, comprising "some
seventy Brothers, the most noble persons in the city." He adds
that there were "other *moradores* who helped to increase the
population with many young people, especially women and
girls, who live longer in this kingdom since they are not exposed to the calamities of the sun and the rigours of the backlands," as their menfolk were.

Cadornega admits that the chief demographic contribution
to Luanda came not so much from the respectable married
citizens as from the soldiers, sailors, and other "private individuals" mating "with black ladies for lack of white ladies."[27]
These unions, most of which were obviously fleeting and

25. Camara to Crown, 24 May 1679, in municipal archives Luanda, Codex
482 (old numbering), fl. 20, and other letters of later dates in the same codex.
26. *História Geral das Guerras Angolanas*, Vol. III, pp. 5–44, for Cadornega's description of the city and island of Luanda in 1681–83.
27. ". . . há muita producção que cauza a Infantaria e outra gente particular, em falta das damas brancas nas negras damas, de que há muitos
mulatos e pardos . . . ." — *Ibid.*, p. 30.

irregular, gave rise to a large mulatto and coloured population, the men being good material for soldiers, well able to
endure the short commons and other hardships of tropical
warfare in the backlands. Cadornega also tells us, what we
know from other sources, that white women were usually in
short supply in Angola [28] and that, with the exception of a few
married couples who had come with the original *conquistadores*, most of the later arrivals "had accommodated themselves with Mulatas, daughters of worthy men and conquerors
who had begotten them on either their female slaves or on
free Negro women." He concluded this panegyric of contemporary Luanda by stating that there were many resident and
transient merchants in the city, including some wealthy capitalists. They were all engaged in the slave trade, exporting to
Brazil about 8,000–10,000 slaves in an averagely good year.
There were seldom less than twenty slave-ships in the harbour
at any given time, some of them being large and well-gunned
vessels. There was also a flourishing coastal trade with Benguela to the south, as well as with Loango, São Tomé, and
even Guinea (São Jorge da Mina) in the north, as well as a
busy traffic on the rivers Kwanza, Bengo, and Dande. The
city was abundantly supplied with provisions of all kinds,
offered for sale in the *quintandas*, or daily markets, where
goods imported from Europe were also available.[29]

It is not easy to reconcile Cadornega's account of prosper-

28. In 1664, however, the Camara asked the Crown not to send any more
white girls or women to be married in Luanda, as there were plenty of marriageable females in the colony owing to their husbands and fathers having been
killed during the Dutch war, 1641–48 (Cadornega, *História Geral das Guerras
Angolanas*, Vol. II, p. 529). The Crown used to send out small parties of
women, either orphan girls or reclaimed prostitutes, as it did to India and
Brazil, but their numbers were too small to make much appreciable difference.
Cf. "alvará de lembrança a uma viuva que conduzira a Angola nove mulheres"
(14 August 1614) in *Arquivos de Angola*, 1st Series, Vol. IV, p. 111.

29. For a documented survey of the triangular Lisbon-Luanda-Bahia trade
at this period see Virginia Rau, *O "Livro de Rezão" de António Coelho Guerreiro*, especially pp. 42–69.

ous Luanda in his *História* of 1683, with the Camara's letter
to the Crown which he signed in December of the same year,
alleging the abject poverty of the place.[30] Presumably the
truth lies somewhere in between, but the basic fact is that
the prosperity of Luanda was closely connected with that of
the slave trade, which was itself liable to violent fluctuations.
The demand for Negro slaves from America was insatiable,
largely owing to their high death rate and low reproduction rate on the plantations and in the mines; but fashions
changed in slaves as in other *generos* (lit., "commodities").
Sometimes slaves from Guinea were preferred and sometimes
those from Angola. Moreover, shipboard conditions on the
Atlantic crossing varied widely, and the mortality was often
very heavy. Last but not least, slaves were often sold in whole
or in part on long-term credit; and buyers might (and often
did) default on their payments.[31]

After the discovery and exploitation of the gold-washings
and mines in Minas Gerais at the end of the seventeenth
century, better prices were paid for slaves of all kinds at Rio
de Janeiro than at Bahia and Pernambuco. This induced the
Luanda traders to ship more slaves for sale at Rio, and provoked an acrimonious correspondence with the Camara of
Bahia, which complained to the Crown on this score. The
Camara of Luanda retorted, no doubt correctly, that many
of the slaves exported to work in the sugar and tobacco plantations of the Reconcavo were, in fact, being re-exported from
Bahia to Rio de Janeiro by sea, or overland to Minas Gerais,
in both of which places slaves fetched higher prices. After
considering the mutual accusations of the Camaras of Bahia

30. Camara to Crown, 30 December 1683. The signatories were António
de Oliveira Cadornega, F. de Araujo de Azevedo, Paulo Valente, Manuel
Lobo Barreto, (?) de Abreu, Tomé Mattos Leitão (archives of municipal
council, Luanda).

31. Cf. Affonso de E. Taunay, *Subsídios para a história do tráfico Africano
no Brasil*; Mauro, *Le Portugal et l'Atlantique au XVIIe siècle*, for documented
accounts of the West African slave trade with Brazil.

and Luanda, the Crown in 1703 imposed a quota system for the importation of slaves as between Rio de Janeiro, Bahia, Recife, and Paraíba. This quota system was maintained until 1715, though one may doubt how far it was rigorously applied in practice.[32]

The slave trade between Angola and Brazil was also affected by the increasingly heavy duties and surcharges levied on it, which were more easily collected at Luanda and Benguela than in places like Loango, or at Mina and Jaquem on the Gold Coast, which were not under Portuguese control. It also fluctuated in accordance with the relative ease or difficulty with which slaves were obtained in the interior, which depended on such factors as internecine tribal wars, famines and food-crop failures, and the physical condition in which the slave gangs reached Luanda — not to mention exceptional hazards such as the smallpox epidemic of 1685 which took thousands of lives in Angola. All these factors, and others which I have no time to mention, meant that the slave trade was not always profitable to those who made their living by it at Luanda, despite the constant demand for slaves from all the European colonies in tropical and sub-tropical America and the West Indies.

It cannot be too often stressed that the whole economy of Angola was geared to the slave trade for over 250 years. As the Camara of Luanda reminded the Crown in December 1683, and on many other occasions, the prosperity of Brazil depended on the supply of slaves from Angola, and the prosperity of Portugal depended on the resources derived from its trade with Brazil. In other words, Angola was the keystone of the Portuguese Atlantic empire. The governor, the garrison, the bishop, and all the civil and ecclesiastical officials were

32. Camara's letters to the Crown, 1702–1715, in the original letter-book in the municipal archives, Luanda, especially the Camara's letter of 6 November 1711. Cf. also *Arquivos de Angola*, 1st Series, Vol. III, pp. 21–22; Delgado, *História de Angola*, Vol. IV, pp. 301–5.

paid directly or indirectly from the proceeds of the trade in "Black Ivory" — the export of white ivory, though considerable at times, being always a secondary consideration. The Camara and the Misericordia at Luanda both took their cut from this traffic, like everyone else. The municipal councilors were awarded a third part of the available shipping space for themselves and their fellow *moradores* in 1716; and the Misericordia had been granted a *preferencia* (annual surcharge) on five hundred Negroes in 1695. The slaves were purchased in the interior by itinerant traders known as *pumbeiros* or *pombeiros*, who were mostly mulattoes but could be free Negroes or even slaves themselves. The export trade was farmed out in the usual way to monopoly-contractors who issued licenses for export on payment.[33]

Another body which received a *preferencia* in the slave trade was the local branch of the *Junta das missões* which had been established at Luanda in 1682, with the object of fostering missionary work in the interior. This Junta does not seem to have been very active, and only missionaries who consistently worked in the *sertão* were the Italian Capuchin friars, who had been first admitted by Salvador Correia and the Camara in 1649. Though regarded by the home government with some suspicion at first, the Capuchins' self-sacrificing labours earned warm praise from virtually all of the civil, military, and ecclesiastical authorities in Angola. Writing to the Cardinals of the Propaganda Fide in December 1678, the *oficiais da Camara* observed that it was their bounden duty not only to thank their Eminences for sending these devout and holy men, who brought such immense spiritual benefits "to the inhabitants of these extensive provinces," but to beg insistently for more of these missionary friars. The Camara renewed this tribute on many occasions down to 1785 at least, by which time the mission was virtually extinct, for lack of

33. *Arquivos de Angola*, 1st Series, Vol. III, pp. 19–22, for the *preferencias* to the Misericordia (1695) and Municipal Council (1716).

personnel to replace those who died. Most of the governors of Angola likewise acknowledged that the Italian Capuchins were the only missionaries who dared to brave the dangers and diseases of the *sertão*, "which frighten away all the other Religious," as Governor Henrique Jacques de Magalhães wrote in 1695.[34]

If concentration on the slave trade was the chief obstacle to the sound development of Angola, another major drawback was the extreme unhealthiness of the colony, owing to the prevalence of malaria and other tropical diseases whose cause and cure were then unknown. Angola had earned the reputation of being a white man's grave before the end of the sixteenth century, and its ill-fame as a region where life was short lasted until well into the nineteenth century. This was one of the reasons why Angola became and remained the penal settlement of Portugal's Atlantic empire, since by the middle of the seventeenth century it was very difficult to induce anybody to go there voluntarily. This state of affairs, which involved the authorities in a losing battle with disease for over two centuries, was reflected in the largely unavailing efforts to keep the garrison up to strength.

After the recovery of Luanda in 1648, it became customary to send out drafts of recruits for the garrison with the incoming governor every three years. The drafts were mainly raised from the overpopulated islands of Madeira and the Azores,

34. Camara to the Cardinals of the Propaganda, 30 December 1678, in the original letter-book (Codex 482, old numbering), municipal archives, Luanda. Cf. also the documents published in *Arquivos de Angola*, 2d Series, Vol. VII, Nos. 27–29 (January–June 1950), dedicated to the "acção missionário dos capuchinhos no Congo e Angola"; Cadornega, *História Geral das Guerras Angolanas*, Vol. II, pp. 485–93; Delgado, *História de Angola*, Vols. III and IV, *passim*; Francisco Leite de Faria, O.F.M., Cap., articles on the "Capuchinhos" in West Africa in *Portugal em Africa*, Vols. X–XII (Lisbon, 1952–55), and his review of P. Mateo Aguiamo, O.F.M., Cap., *Misiones Capuchinas en Africa*, Vol. II, *Misiones al reino de Zinga, Benin, Arda, Guinea y Sierra Leone* (Madrid, 1957), in *Studia: Revista Semestral*, Vol. III (1959), pp. 289–308.

particularly the former. Writing to the Crown in 1702, the Camara of Luanda complained that these raw recruits were mostly teen-agers of poor physique, who died soon after their arrival. The Camara suggested that these islanders had better be sent first to Brazil, whence they could be transferred to Angola after becoming acclimatized to the tropics, these seasoned soldiers being termed *Baquianos*. In another letter of the same date, the Camara suggested that if recruits were raised in Portugal they should be drawn from the provinces south of the Tagus, which had a climate resembling that of Africa. A contemporary governor of Angola made the alternative suggestion that they should be recruited from what he termed the rougher provinces ("*não mimosas*") of Portugal, e.g. Tras-os-Montes, Alemtejo, and the Algarve. The Camara repeated these proposals, or variations of them, in later years, but a high percentage of the recruits continued to be raised in Madeira and their death rate continued to be disquietingly high. Very few soldiers, whether in Portugal or in Brazil, volunteered to serve in Angola, and most of the drafts which arrived in Luanda were composed of *degredados*. Brazilian-born or -trained soldiers certainly stood the change of climate better, but they were criticized on other grounds. It was alleged that they were ringleaders in the mutiny of the garrison in November 1694; and in 1729 the Governor of Luanda complained that the soldiers he received from Pernambuco and Ceará were the worst of the lot. "They are mutinous and unruly," he wrote, "and they are those who persuade the others to desert to Loango." [35]

The perennial shortage of white soldiers in Angola induced the Crown to decree in 1684 that no distinction should be made between whites, mulattoes, and free Negroes serving

35. Camara to Crown, 22 April 1702, in municipal archives, Luanda, Codex 483, fls. 84–85; Governor to Crown, 20 December 1729, in Arquivo Histórico de Angola, Luanda, "Governo, Ofícios para o Reino," No. 1, Gav. 1, Cod. 1. Cf. also Delgado, *História de Angola*, Vol. IV, pp. 150, 159, 200, 222–23, 234, 249–50, 384.

in the garrison, and that merit should be the sole criterion for promotion. I do not know how far this order was implemented, but it would seem that Luís Lopes de Sequeira, the victor of the decisive battle of Ambuila (29 October 1665), and the leading soldier in Angola during the seventeenth century, was a mulatto, or that his mother was at any rate a coloured woman.[36] On the other hand, the Camara of Luanda wrote to the Crown in 1713 that one of the companies of the local militia regiment (*terço de ordenança*) should be recruited exclusively from citizens who were eligible to serve in the Camara and from their sons, and not, as hitherto, from white and coloured persons indiscriminately.[37] I have not been able to trace the answer to this request; but during the dictatorship of Pombal the Crown ordered (in 1766–67) that three militia regiments should be organized on a basis of white, coloured, and black (*brancos, pardos, e pretos*), respectively. Their officers were given the same pay, privileges, and status as those of the regular troops, without distinction of colour.[38]

It is possible that the perennial shortage of qualified white *moradores* in Luanda resulted in the admission of *pardos* and mulattoes to serve as *oficiais da Camara*, but I am not sure of this. There are several references in the municipal archives of Luanda to a manuscript book in which were listed all the leading citizens who were eligible to serve in the municipality: "Livro em que se declarão as pessoas principaes que andavão na Governação desta Cidade," with their names, social status, and occupations; but unfortunately this could not be traced when I searched for it in March 1961. If Luís Lopes de Sequeira was a mulatto, as is often asserted but not (so far as I know) definitely proved, it is interesting to note that he was

36. For the career of Luís Lopes de Sequeira see Gastão Sousa Dias, *A batalha de Ambuila* (Lisbon, 1942); and for the decree of 24 March 1684, Delgado, *História de Angola*, Vol. IV, p. 58.

37. Camara to Crown, 2 August 1713, in municipal archives, Luanda, Codex 483 (old numbering), fl. 100.

38. *Arquivos de Angola*, 1st Series, Vol. III, pp. 25–30.

elected *almotacél* for the month of November 1669, as can be seen from the respective *termo* of 30 October.[39] The attitude of white Portuguese to their coloured cousins was certainly ambivalent. This ambivalence is reflected in the chronicle of Cadornega, who has transcribed some amusing if rather scurrilous verses on the progressive Africanization of his countrymen in Angola; though he adds that he thinks the anonymous poet went a little too far in this respect:

> Terra de gente tostada
> ou da côr da escura noute
> que a pura marca e açoute
> se encaminha. . . .
> Aqui onde o filho he fusco
> e quasi negro o neto,
> e tudo negro o bisneto,
> e tudo escuro. . . .[40]

We have seen that Cadornega claimed that in his day Luanda contained sufficient qualified white citizens to serve both the Camara and the Misericordia; but the correspondence of the Camara in the eighteenth century is full of complaints about the high mortality and the shortage of qualified persons. Physicians and surgeons were no longer-lived than were ordinary laymen, and there were years on end when none were available in the colony. The citizens then had no alternative but to resort to quack doctors or *curandeiros*. In 1728, the governor complained that there were not more than one hundred and fifty white men in Luanda, and that no slave-trader was good for a bill of exchange amounting to 50 milreis in Brazil, "so many bills having been returned protested that the trade is ruined and the Negro slaves have no value in America." [41] The governor was evidently exaggerating, but

39. I have a typed copy of the original in the municipal archives, Luanda.
40. Cadornego, *História Geral das Guerras Angolanas*, Vol. III, pp. 382–86, for full text.
41. Governor to Crown, 16 February 1728, in Arquivo Histórico, Luanda, "Governo, Ofícios para o Reino," No. 1, Gav. 1, Cod. 1, doc. no. 32.

eyewitness accounts of Luanda in the last quarter of the eighteenth century leave no doubt as to the depths of poverty and degradation to which the city so proudly described by Cadornega a century earlier had sunk.[42] The citizens of Luanda could certainly not at this period have organized such costly and elaborate festivities as those staged in honour of the beatification of Francis Xavier in July 1620.[43]

Although the splendour of the 1620 *festas* was probably never surpassed, the Camara contrived to celebrate as well as it could the three religious feasts which were its civic responsibility — St. Sebastian (20 January), Corpus Christi, and the Assumption (15 August), this last celebration being combined with that commemorating the recapture of the city from the Dutch. In fact, the Camara often devoted the larger part of its annual income to celebrating these three festivals. As elsewhere in the Portuguese world, attendance at these processions was compulsory, and citizens who failed to participate were fined unless they could give a convincing excuse for their absence.[44]

The surviving records of the Camara show that the municipal councilors usually took their duties seriously, though in some years they did not meet as often as the legal minimum of twice a week. In 1670, for example, the Camara met only on the following days: 4, 5, 8, 18, 22, 29 January; 5, 8, 12, 15, 20, 22, 26 February; 5 March; 9, 22, 26 April; twice in May; twice in June; thrice in July; twice in August; once in September; once in October; and twice in December, including the final meeting on Old Year's Day for the election of the new officeholders. Most of the business transacted on these occa-

42. Elias Alexandre da Silva Correia, *História de Angola, 1782–95;* J. Gentil da Silva, "En Afrique Portugaise: L'Angola au XVIIIe siècle," in *Annales,* Vol. XIV (Paris, 1959), pp. 571–80.

43. Delgado, *História de Angola,* Vol. II, pp. 72–78, for a documented description of the festivities of 1620.

44. "Livro de Posturas" in the municipal archives, Luanda.

sions was purely routine, "treating of the common weal and dealing with petitions and papers," as the stereotyped phrase in the *termos* read.[45] This routine business included, as with the other Camaras, the issue of licenses to shopkeepers, stall-holders, and street-vendors; the regulation of the retail prices of manufactured goods and food supplies; and the verification of all weights and measures in accordance with the official prototypes kept in the Town Hall.

The Camara of Luanda experienced the same difficulty in keeping the city clean, and in preventing streets and pavements from being washed away by the torrential rains, as did the Camara of Bahia. Similarly, the admonitions periodically promulgated by the Camara of Luanda concerning the danger of allowing filth to accumulate in the streets, and the desirability of keeping the slave-quarters clean, in order to prevent the spread of infectious disease, seem largely to have been ignored in practice. Though the enforcement of these sanitary regulations was supported by an ascending scale of fines for repeated offenses, they were usually only obeyed after an epidemic had already begun. The Camara complained repeatedly about this state of affairs, which endured for centuries. In this respect, the files of the official *Boletim de Angola* in the 1850's recall the admonitions of the Camara one and two centuries earlier.[46]

Like the Camara of Bahia, the municipal council of Luanda was jealous of its status and privileges to the extent that it sometimes adopted a dog-in-the-manger attitude to other civic bodies. Just as the Camara of Bahia displayed a certain

45. Original *termos dos assentos* (minutes of the municipal council meetings) for 1670 in the municipal archives, Luanda.
46. *Bandos* promulgated by the Camara, 3 November 1717, 4 February 1719, 11 February 1719, 29 April 1719, 13 January 1720, in municipal archives, Luanda. Cf. *Boletim Official do governo geral da provincia de Angola* (Luanda, 1857), *passim* for many complaints about the unhygienic condition of Luanda and the way in which sanitary regulations were ignored.

antagonism to the municipality of Cachoeira in the Reconcavo, so the Camara of Luanda tried to thwart that of Massangano. When the *moradores* of Massangano, led by Cadornega, set about instituting a local branch of the Holy House of Mercy, both the Camara and the Misericordia of Luanda strongly opposed this move. In this they were supported by the governor, João Fernandes Vieira, who in 1661 advised the Crown to reduce Massangano to a mere garrison post. He further advocated the enforced removal of the *moradores* of Massangano to Luanda, "in order to prevent them from being as unruly as they are, giving a bad example to the heathen, and despoiling them tyrannically." [47]

The Camara and Misericordia of Luanda further alleged that Angola was too poor and too sparsely colonized to bear the cost of two Misericordias. They claimed that the existing one at Luanda would suffice for both communities, and they insinuated that Massangano had no right to call itself a town and to possess a municipal council. The *moradores* of Massangano persisted in their claims to full autonomy, and most of the governors after 1661 supported them. After prolonged debates in the Overseas Council, the Crown eventually gave a decision in favour of Massangano, confirming the existence of the Camara and authorizing the institution of a Misericordia with the privileges of those at Luanda in 1676–77. A perusal of the arguments advanced by both sides in this dispute shows clearly that the petitioners of Massangano had the stronger case. But the fifteen-year paper battle at Lisbon

47. For the quarrel between Luanda and Massangano in 1661–76, cf. Cadornega, *História das Guerras Angolanas*, Vol. II, pp. 155–57, 205–6, 516, 518; Delgado, *História de Angola*, Vol. III, pp. 238–43, 249–50; Padre António Brasio, C.S.Sp., "As Misericórdias se Angola," in *Studia: Revista Semestral*, Vol. IV (1959), pp. 106–49, especially pp. 134–44. For the *má vontade* shown by the Camara of Bahia to that of Cachoeira in 1728–30, cf. the documents printed in Accioli-Amaral, *Memorias Históricas do Estado da Bahia*, Vol. II, pp. 359–62.

also shows that the views of the municipal councilors at Luanda carried considerable weight with the Crown and its advisers in this as in all other matters affecting what Cadornega called "this noble and populous city of St. Paul of the Assumption, also called by the old name of Loanda, head of these kingdoms and dominions of Angola." [48]

48. Cadornega, *História Geral das Guerras Angolanas*, Vol. III, p. 34.

Conclusion

From the foregoing it will, I hope, be clear that the colonial municipal councils played a more important role in the Portuguese empire than is indicated by the amount of space accorded them in the standard histories. The Crown on the one hand, and the colonial governors on the other, often relied on them to raise and administer funds for a wide variety of purposes, including the maintenance of naval and military establishments, which in other empires were not the responsibility of such civic bodies. The Camaras were also actively concerned with the economic sinews of the Portuguese empire such as the entrepôt trade of Goa, the silver and sandalwood trades of Macao, the sugar trade of Bahia, and the slave trade of Luanda. Although situated so far away from each other and from Portugal, these four maritime municipalities possessed certain other characteristics in common, which they maintained through the vicissitudes of several centuries. Among them may be enumerated the following.

First, the strongly conservative nature of Portuguese society, as shown by the tenacious way in which the colonial Camaras clung to their privileges, whether modelled on those of Lisbon, Evora, or Oporto, and the degree to which they succeeded in maintaining them. This conservatism was, of course, shared by the Crown and its advisers, which in its turn was a powerful factor in preserving the *status quo*. One typical instance will suffice to illustrate this point. When the Camara of Goa petitioned for a change in the municipal election system in 1651, Tomé Pinheiro da Veiga, the *Procurador da Coroa* at Lisbon, advised the Crown that, as a matter of principle, all innovations were to be deprecated, and that it was much better to adhere to the old time-honoured precedents.[1]

Secondly, these four colonial Camaras were not easily over-awed by autocratic viceroys and governors, despite the Camara of Luanda's allegations to the contrary in 1702. We have seen that the municipal councilors could hold their own with even such forceful characters as the Count of Linhares at Goa and the Count of Sabugosa at Bahia. In this connection, the Camaras also made full use of their cherished right to correspond directly with the Crown, and from time to time they were able to influence the Crown's colonial policy. Admittedly, the Camaras often complained that the Crown and the Overseas Council at Lisbon either ignored their representations or else left them unanswered for years on end; but these complaints should not be taken too seriously. The Portuguese bureaucratic machine was a slow-moving one at the best of times, and the fact that every matter of importance — and many of no importance whatsoever — had to be referred

---

1. ". . . toda a novidade afronta a experiencia com descobrir inconvenientes que agora se não vem . . . *et minime mutanda sunt quae certam semper habuerunt observationem*, guardandose a veneravel antiguidade." — Autograph *parecer* of Tomé Pinheiro da Veiga, Lisbon, 31 January 1652, in the writer's collection.

to the King himself for a final decision inevitably clogged the channels of communication. A further obstacle to the speedy dispatch of routine government business was formed by "the 145 holidays in the year, punctually observed by them," as the English envoy at Lisbon complained in 1669.[2] But we know from the records that the Overseas Council at Lisbon was often earnestly debating the problems about which the Camaras could get no speedy decision or reply. Another reason which helps to account for the Crown's procrastination was its reluctance, or, as often as not, its inability, to find the money needed to implement a particular proposal. This was something from which the municipal council at Lisbon suffered even more than did the colonial Camaras. To instance two examples out of many, I may cite the vain and frantic efforts of the Lisbon municipality to obtain from the Crown the payments it had been promised to help liquidate the enormous debt incurred (at the Crown's behest) in celebrating the Feast of Corpus Christi in 1719, and in paving the road to Mafra in 1730–50.[3]

Mention of the Feast of Corpus Christi brings us to our third point. The published and unpublished records of these four colonial Camaras show that a large proportion of their expenditure was incurred in celebrating the annual religious feasts of their respective patron saints, in accordance with their statutory obligations, and in particular the Feast of

2. Sir Robert Southwell's report of 29 April 1669, quoted in C. R. Boxer, *Salvador de Sá and the Struggle for Brazil and Angola* (London, 1952), pp. 372–73. Cf. the identical complaint of D. Luís da Cunha in 1736: "Já considerei que constando o anno de 366 dias [*sic*], só a terça parte delles erão de trabalho, se descontarmos os domingos, as quatro grandes festas, e as particulares de cada parrochia, e o orago do convento, e os dias das procissões." — *Instrucções inéditas de D. Luís da Cunha a Marco António de Azevedo Coutinho* (Coimbra, 1930), pp. 124–25. Cf. also *APO*, Fasc. I, Part 2 (1876), p. 90, for a similar complaint from Goa in 1601.

3. Eduardo Freire de Oliveira, *Elementos para a História do Município de Lisboa*, Vol. X, pp. 273, 350–52, Vol. XI, pp. 319 ff., Vol. XV, p. 550.

Corpus Christi. Moreover, if the Camaras showed any tendency to evade or to economize on these obligations, they were sharply reproved by the local governors, or even, on occasion, by the Crown. Here again, the Lisbon municipality was in the same boat; and the enormous debt which it incurred in financing the previously mentioned Feast of Corpus Christi in 1719 gave its finances a blow from which they never recovered. Another fiscal burden which the colonial and the metropolitan Camaras shared in common was their annual contribution to the dual indemnity of the *Dote de Inglaterra e paz de Holanda*. No sooner had the last installments of this indemnity been paid off, than the royal marriages between the ruling houses of Spain and Portugal in 1729 involved them in further heavy annual contributions which they could ill afford to pay, and from which the Camara of Luanda received exemption.[4] When these and the other financial impositions to which I have previously alluded are borne in mind, we can safely conclude that the expenditure of the Camaras usually outran their receipts. More especially, they could seldom find enough money for the upkeep of roads, bridges, pavements, and other public works, which had originally been the first charge upon their resources.

A fourth characteristic of those Camaras which we have studied was the jealousy which frequently existed between them and the local High Court (*Relação*), or with the Crown *ouvidor*, when there was one.[5] This rivalry with the Crown lawyers was not appreciably lessened by the fact that from 1606 onwards the majority of the municipal councilors at

4. For the royal marriages of 1729 and the *donativo* demanded from Brazil, cf. C. R. Boxer, *The Golden Age of Brazil, 1695–1750* (Berkeley, 1962), pp. 188–89, 318–20, 325. For the exemption received by Luanda, cf. *Arquivos de Angola*, 2d Series, Vol. XVI, p. 44.

5. There were, of course, exceptions. In 1688, the Camara of Luanda was forbidden by the Crown to place in the Town Hall the portraits of *ouvidores* who had functioned to the satisfaction of the Council (*Arquivos de Angola*, 1st Series, Vol. II, p. 17).

Lisbon were themselves lawyers, nor by the fact that the presidents of the Camaras of Bahia and Luanda were Crown lawyers from 1696 onwards. Rivalry between the Camaras and the governors was another noticeable feature of their history, particularly in the case of the Senate of Macao; but the rivalry with the Crown lawyers, though less publicized, seems to have been even more general. This mutual jealousy naturally hindered the smooth functioning of the administration at times, as the Crown was well aware. But the Crown was equally aware that this rivalry formed an essential part of the system of mutual checks and balances on which the Portuguese administration, like that of the Spanish, largely depended. As the Overseas Councilors observed to D. João V in 1728: "It has always been realized that it was not very convenient for Your Majesty's service that the governors and the senior officials who serve with them should be on very friendly terms, since it is very advantageous that they should be mistrustful of each other" — always provided, the Councilors added, that this mutual jealousy did not go too far.[6] Another advantage of the Camaras, from the Crown's point of view, was that they provided an element of stability and continuity in cities where the viceroys and governors were usually relieved every three years.

Fifthly, the respective attitudes of the Camaras of Goa, Macao, and Bahia to the establishment of a nunnery in each of those cities contained certain common features. In all three places, the prestige conferred by such an establishment, in which the unmarried daughters of the citizens (and especially of the municipal councilors) could be received, clashed with the arguments of those who maintained that such girls ought rather to be available for marriage with Portuguese citizens, settlers, or merchants, so as to strengthen white supremacy overseas.

6. *Consulta* of 12 November 1728, in *Documentos Históricos*, Vol. XC, p. 175.

Sixthly, the history of the colonial Camaras reflects something of the history of leading and lowly personalities in what Gilberto Freyre has christened (not altogether felicitously) the Luso-tropical world; their respective hopes and fears, friendships and feuds, achievements and failures. The quarrels and factions which formed such a feature of Portuguese colonial life doubtless owed much to the shortness of temper which was apt to afflict most Europeans in the tropics, as the history of the Dutch, English, and French colonial empires likewise shows. But the strongly individualistic nature of the Portuguese character may have had something to do with it, and this individualism lost nothing of its strength when transplanted overseas. It gave rise to that habit of *murmuração*, or fault-finding, which the Count of Castanheira defined in 1553 as being the oldest and most typical sin of the Portuguese, and of which there are innumerable examples.[7] The chronicler, João de Barros, observed of Affonso de Albuquerque's carping critics at Goa: "a Portuguese is more upset by praise of his neighbors than by the neglect of his own merit." Two centuries later, the Franciscan chronicler at Macao commented that it was an old disease (*achaque velho*) of the *moradores* of the City of the Name of God in China "never to let one's neighbour raise his head, but to keep him down."[8] Nothing would be easier than to multiply such quotations from contemporary chronicles and records; but the modern reader, like the old Portuguese monarchs, must make due allowance for this *murmuração* when assessing the truth or otherwise of the complaints which converged on Lisbon from all quarters of the Portuguese empire. This does not mean that such complaints were invariably exaggerated or unjustified, but only that we must be cautious about taking them at their face value. The records of the colonial municipal coun-

7. Pp. 86–87 above.
9. João de Barros, *Decada II*, Livro 5, cap. xi; Fr. José de Jesus Maria, *Azia Sinica e Japonica, 1745*, Vol. II, p. 195.

cils frequently reveal the human weaknesses of the *oficiais da Camara*; but they also show how often they could sink their personal differences and cooperate for the common good.

As regards working-class representation on the four municipal councils with which we are concerned, it will be recalled that this was strongest and most lasting at Goa, where the *mesteres* were directly represented for more than 250 years. They also formed an integral and important part of the Camara of Bahia between 1641 and 1713, but they were never included in those of Macao and Luanda. The extent to which the Camaras were self-perpetuating oligarchies is more difficult to assess in the present state of our knowledge, as only for Goa and Bahia do we possess fairly extensive published lists of their members. But it is obvious that the Portuguese colonial municipalities never became closed corporations like the *cabildos* of Spanish America, where the post of councilor or *regidor* could often be bought and filled for a lifetime.[9]

It is quite clear from the surviving records of these four Camaras that they were officered predominantly by men of European birth, or at any rate by men with a relatively small admixture of indigenous blood. In other words, if there was not always a rigid colour-bar, there was a definite, and, in the circumstances, a natural and inevitable prejudice in favour of white blood. The authors of the *Município de Luanda*, published in 1919, err egregiously, if in all honesty, when they make the following claim about the Portuguese lack of a colour-bar — a claim which many people who should know better still accept uncritically.

Portuguese legislation, even in the remotest periods of colonization and in days when popular representation was more limited than it is now, never made any distinction between the indigenous inhabitants and those who were European-born. The political and

9. J. H. Parry, "The Sale of Municipal Dignities," in *The Sale of Public Offices in the Spanish Indies under the Hapsburgs* (Berkeley, 1953), pp. 33–47.

juridical status of both categories was the same before the laws and in social customs. And thus the *moradores* of any city, irrespective of their race, were all electors of the administrative bodies and were eligible to serve thereon, so long as they satisfied the general principles of the law which regulated those rights.

The short answer to this is that the *moradores* entitled to vote in the elections for the Camara were either pure Portuguese or, more rarely, *mestiços*. Full-blooded natives never served in any colonial Camara before the belated enforcement of the anti-colour-bar edicts promulgated at the insistence of the Marquis of Pombal in 1761–74. The term *raças infectas*, which appears frequently in official documents prior to that date, included Jews, Moors (i.e., Muslims), and Negroes. Persons "contaminated" with their blood were certainly not legally eligible to hold municipal office, even though they may have occasionally done so in practice.

I have neither the time nor, in some respects, the competence to make a thorough comparison between the Portuguese colonial Camara and the Spanish-American (and Philippine) *Cabildo*, though such a comparative study would certainly be of considerable interest. I must limit myself here to a few passing and tentative observations. Whereas in Spanish-America by the beginning of the seventeenth century most municipal posts had become both proprietory and hereditary, through the sale of office, this transformation never occurred in the Portuguese colonial Camaras. Nor were the Portuguese colonial Camaras subjected to frequent inspections by visiting commissioners (*pesquisidores* and *jueces de comisión*), as were many of the Spanish colonial Cabildos. The Spanish-American *Audiencia*, or High Court, with its *Oidores* exercised a much closer financial and administrative supervision over the Cabildos than did the Portuguese colonial *Relação* over the Camaras.[10]

10. F. B. Pike, "Visitas and Pesquizas," and "Audiencia power over cabildos," in *The Americas*, Vol. XV (October, 1958), pp. 143–48.

On the other hand, there were some marked resemblances between the colonial Camaras and Cabildos. The seats of *vereador* and *regidor,* respectively, were valued chiefly for the social status which they conferred and for the patronage which their occupants could wield, rather than for the usually modest stipends which were attached to them, or even for their more considerable perquisites and pickings. Camaras and Cabildos alike, though often heavily indebted and with their public works unfinished or in disrepair, would borrow large sums to lavish on the celebration of their patron saint's feast-day. But if this was a fault, it was one which was shared by all classes, and one which received the emphatic endorsement of the Iberian monarchs.

Finally, I would suggest that perhaps the most interesting aspect of the overseas Senado da Camara, and one which deserves further investigation and research, was the part played by this institution in holding together the far-flung Portuguese empire. The role of the Church and the religious orders was also a vital one in this respect, as instanced by the seventeenth-century Goan jingle:

Vice-rei vá, Vice-rei vem,
Padre Paulista sempre tem.[11]

The *oficiais da Camara* were even more omnipresent than the Jesuit Fathers, since the municipal council was an older institution than the Society of Jesus, and it continued to function after the suppression of the latter. We have seen how common it was for *Reinóis* who married local girls to settle down in Goa, Macao, Bahia, or Luanda, as the case might be, and to become members of the municipal council. In this way, Portuguese predominance was assured in the local elite, and the ties which bound the colony to the mother country were continually renewed and strengthened.

11. "Viceroys come and go, but the Jesuit Fathers are always with us."

A KING FOR PORTUGAL
The Madrigal Conspiracy, 1594–95
by Mary Elizabeth Brooks

A historical and literary examination of a colorful pretender to th
throne of Portugal, Gabriel de Espinosa, the Pastrymaker of Madrid
whose short career became a legend which fired the imaginations o
romantic Spanish and Portuguese writers.
200 pages, 8 illus. $5.0(

SPAIN AND THE WESTERN TRADITION
The Castilian Mind in Literature from *El Cid* to Calderón
by Otis H. Green

A detailed examination of the patterns of thought that determined th
content of Spanish literature during the Medieval and Renaissanc
periods.

"Professor Green will enable us now to see and define more clearly
exactly what is and what is not new. Henceforth it will not be possible
to trace continuity and change in Spanish literature up to Calderó
without reference to this book." *Hispanic Review*

"Commands respect for its scope and its frequent penetration of a
vexed and elusive subject." *Bulletin of Hispanic Studies*

Volume I 342 pages $7.5(
Volume II 374 pages $7.5(
Volume III about 544 pages $10.0(

THE HISPANIZATION OF THE PHILIPPINES
Spanish Aims and Filipino Responses, 1565–1700
by John Leddy Phelan

"A balanced and well-documented account of how and why the Fili
pinos became the only Asian people profoundly and consistently in
fluenced by European culture in the last few centuries." *JRAS*

"A concise, pointed monograph based on original materials in Spain
the Philippines and the United States." *Journal of Asian Studies*
234 pages, 5 illus. $4.0(

THE UNIVERSITY OF WISCONSIN PRESS
P.O. Box 1379   Madison, Wisconsin 5370

REFERENCE MATTER

Appendix:
Selected Documents

1. SUMMONS TO A MEETING AT THE
TOWN HALL, GOA, 21 APRIL 1535 [1]

Hear the proclamation of the aldermen and officers of the Council
of this City of Goa, that every citizen and any other head of a household [*morador*] of any quality nation [2] who is Portuguese, should
come next Monday morning very early to the council chamber,
since this is needful for the good of the common weal of the city;
under penalty that anyone who does not turn up in the said council
chamber must accept whatever is decided there on the said day by
a majority vote of the people and leading men of the municipality,

1. Viriato A. C. B. de Albuquerque, *O Senado de Goa: Memoria Histórico-Archeologica*, p. 443.
2. The word *nação* was added above the line later. J. H. da Cunha Rivara,
who first printed this proclamation (in the *Imprensa* of Nova Goa, No. 13, in
1871), observed that it was originally intended on such occasions only to summon the citizens of Portuguese birth, but that after 1535 this privilege was
extended to others. It is possible that the word *nação* here implies *Christão-
novo*, as persons of Jewish origin were often called *gente da nação*. Theoretically, Indian converts to Christianity were granted the same privileges as
the Portuguese and Eurasian *moradores* by a *carta-régia* of 24 March 1542, but
this measure was not implemented in practice for over two centuries.

and he cannot plead that he was not informed that the meeting was to be held. In Goa, on the 21 April 1535. [Signatures of the city councilors.]

2. QUALIFICATIONS LAID DOWN
FOR MUNICIPAL OFFICEHOLDERS AT GOA
24 MARCH 1542 [3]

Dom João, by the grace of God, King of Portugal and of the Algarves on both sides of the sea in Africa, Lord of Guinea, and of the conquest, navigation, and commerce of Ethiopia, Arabia, Persia, and of India. I make known to all those who see this my edict that being desirous that my city of Goa in the regions of India should always be well governed and administered by qualified persons who fully understand how to govern and administer it as befits my service and its ennoblement, and wishing likewise to grant rewards to the fidalgos, knights, squires, leading men and the people thereof, it is my good pleasure that the offices of aldermen, judges, procurator, secretary of the council, almotacéls, procurators of the people, and the twenty-four representatives of the guilds, in whom the control and the administration of the city are vested, should always be drawn from among the married men and heads of households therein, who are Portuguese by nationality and birth [*forem portuguezes de nação e geração*], and not from among those of any other nationality, birth, and quality whatsoever. I therefore notify this accordingly to my captain-major and governor in those regions, as likewise to the captain of the said city, the Chief Justice, and Crown judges thereof, and to each and every one of my officers and people to whom this edict of mine may be shown, and who have to take cognizance of it; and I further command that they must obey and fulfill it entirely as it is written, without raising any doubts or reservation thereto, for this is my pleasure and royal service. Given in the city of Lisbon on the 24 March. Pero Fernandez wrote it in the year of our Lord Jesus Christ 1542. And I wish this edict to be evaluated and implemented even though it is not endorsed by the Chancery Court in despite of the ordinance to the contrary. [Signed] *The King.*

3. J. H. da Cunha Rivara (ed.), *Archivo Portuguez-Oriental* (hereafter cited as *APO*), Fasc. II, *Livro dos privilegios da Cidade de Goa* (Nova Goa, 1857), pp. 115–16.

3. THE SENATE OF GOA AND THE
WORKING-CLASS REPRESENTATIVES,
1595–1607

[A. EXTRACT FROM AN OFFICIAL LETTER OF THE
SENATE OF GOA TO THE CROWN, 1597 [4]]

Your predecessors the previous kings in the regulation which they made for the municipality of Lisbon, which is followed by this of Goa, added four procurators of the people to the other and noble officers of the municipality who administer it, so that the former might advocate whatever was required for the good of the common people in general. And in order that they should do this more willingly, they were honoured with some privileges, which, through the malice of the present time, are now very prejudicial to the good government of this city. For since these same procurators have equal voting rights with the aldermen and the other noble officers, both in bestowing offices which are in the gift of the city and in spending its revenues, those are the only things they concern themselves with when participating in council meetings, without advocating therein the matters which pertain to their sphere. This has caused great disorders in this city, which the aldermen have glossed over, because each one of them wants to have the workers' procurators on his side, on account of their votes. In addition to this defect, since they are people of limited intelligence, they have another and still graver fault, which is that they can seldom keep secrecy about matters which are discussed at the council table, and which are none of their concern, and likewise in those about which we write to Your Majesty.

Because of this, and for other drawbacks which we need not specify, it is necessary that Your Majesty should amend this regulation, and ordain that these representatives of the workers should not participate in the deliberation of the municipal council, save only when matters which directly concern them are tabled. They should no longer be allowed to vote in appointments made to municipal offices, and in other municipal affairs, nor should they be given copies of Your Majesty's letters,[5] save only those which are essen-

4. *APO, Cartas da Camara de Goa a Sua Magestade, 1595–1609* (ed. 1876), pp. 30–31.
5. Cf. *APO*, Fasc. I (1877), p. 34, for a *carta-régia* of 2 March 1551, which dealt with this problem, and *APO*, Fasc. II (1857), pp. 148–51, for the

tial to their proper functions, since their brains are not capable of coping with the others. The aldermen should be given authorization and discretion to make them demand what is good for the common people and their concerns, and to punish them when they are negligent therein, which we cannot do at present owing to their aforesaid privilege which has made them very upstart.

[B. EXTRACT FROM A LETTER OF THE SENATE OF GOA
TO THE CROWN, 1605 [6]]

This is also the opportunity to tell Your Majesty about a novelty which the Viceroy Dom Martim Affonso [de Castro] introduced in the protocol concerning the officers of this city, which, as it is unprecedented, and novelties always raise difficulties, Your Majesty should resolve in the way which is best for your service. It is a long-established custom, and one which has existed time out of mind, that when the municipality goes in corporation with all its officers to discuss with the viceroys matters concerning Your Majesty's service or the common weal, the four procurators of the workers likewise go with us, as persons who have voting rights in all municipal concerns, as do the other officers. When the municipality in corporation discusses such affairs with the viceroys, these procurators are also given seats; for since by the regulations of this city council they form an integral part of the government of this republic, it is not in our power to separate ourselves from them and go without them. In this way, they went with us on the three occasions when we went to meet the Viceroy after his arrival, the first time when he reached the fortress of the Kings,[7] the second time after his solemn entry and the third time to discuss concerns of the common weal on a day which he assigned for this purpose. And the Viceroy, not wishing to give seats to the Mesteres, remained standing as long as we were with him; and he afterwards sent to tell us through the Archbishop, that he was not disposed to allow the said Mesteres to be seated. And since this practice has been unchanged for so long, and these men have their part to play in the concerns of

right of the *procuradores dos mesteres* to see all the Senate's official correspondence.

6. *APO, Cartas da Camara de Goa, 1595–1609,* pp. 153–54.

7. The fortress of Reis Magos on the north bank of the river Mandovi, where the handing-over between the outgoing and the incoming viceroy usually took place.

this municipality, and they are officers coöpted thereto in order that they may advocate matters concerning the common weal, and as such they have the right to be present on all occasions when the viceroys have dealings with the city, in which they are entitled to give their views, and without which the other municipal officers can decide nothing by themselves, it seemed to us that we ought not to agree to this pretension without submitting the matter to Your Majesty. For this reason, we beg Your Majesty to have this matter deliberated in council, so that a decision may be reached on what Your Majesty should decide to order, instructing us on the way in which we should act when these men go with us on such occasions, or whether this council board can discuss and decide matters with the viceroys without asking their [the *mesteres'*] opinion, so as to avoid inconveniences which will always be a disservice to Your Majesty.

[C. EXTRACT FROM A LETTER OF THE SENATE OF GOA
TO THE CROWN, 1607 [8]]

Your Majesty sent to tell us that you were pleased to command that when the municipality went to see the Viceroy about matters concerning the common weal, he should hear it seated, and should give chairs to the aldermen and other officers, and stools to the Mesteres; [9] and by another letter, signed in Madrid, Your Majesty sent to tell us that everyone should be given seats as had always been the custom hitherto. And as up to now it has been the practice to give chairs without arms to the Mesteres, we remain doubtful as to whether we should give them chairs to sit on, as hitherto, or whether we should only give them stools, in accordance with the recent order. And as they have precedence on their side, they are asking Your Majesty to deal justly by them, for which purpose they are sending you their reasons in another letter, which goes with this. Your Majesty will do us a favour by ordering it to be deliberated on, and a decision reached in the way which is best for your service.

8. *APO, Cartas da Camara de Goa, 1595–1609*, p. 213.
9. Cf. the *carta-régia* of 18 January 1607, in R. Bulhão Pato (ed.), *Documentos Remettidos da India ou Livros das Monções*, Vol. I, p. 110.

4. THE MESTERES OF GOA AND THE
FEAST OF CORPUS CHRISTI IN 1618 [10]

Forasmuch as the Feasts which this municipality customarily cele-
brates with due solemnity, both by the ordinances and regulations
of the municipality of Lisbon as by the obligations which it owes
to Our Lord for the favours received, are not more than two, Corpus Christi and Saint Catherine, in which the working-class officers
are wont to carry their banners, castles, dragon, serpents, giants,
and carriages of the coopers and market-gardeners: We hereby
order and proclaim by statute that henceforward this said solemnity need only be exactly exercised on the said two feast-days,
and not on any other, however festive it may be; so that these two
feast-days may always be held in greater esteem than any others,
on account of what they represent in themselves and by way of
special devotion to this people. And in the Feasts of Saint Isabel,
the Guardian Angel, Saint Martin, and Saint Sebastian, there will
be no greater solemnities than the usual ones, viz., carrying the
staves and banners of the officers, without castles or any other insignia. And neither staves nor banners will be used on any other
feast-day, however solemn it may be, whether of those which are
customarily celebrated in the course of the year, or of those which
are spontaneously arranged in order to celebrate some happy
events, forasmuch as it is not right that any other feast-days should
be celebrated on a level with those above-mentioned. And it is also
needful that the working-class officers of this people should be relieved as far as possible of such impositions, which have become
burdensome, as we have been given to understand.

And on the said two feast-days, but on no other, the officers of
each and every craft will be obliged to carry their castles, etc., in
the traditional manner, as they are allotted by the judges and ma-
jordomos of their respective crafts. And the officer who does not
carry the castle, etc., which he has been assigned will pay a fine of
1,000 reis for the first offense, and two thousand for the second, half
for the council and the other half for the guild, under the same
penalty. And the [guild-]judge who compels any officer to carry a castle, etc., on any other day than the above two, or who orders
other insignia to be carried besides the banners and staves, will be

10. Albuquerque, *Senado de Goa*, p. 426. Cf. also *APO*, Fasc. II (1857),
pp. 38–39.

fined 10 pardaus for the first offense, and twenty for the second, half for the council, and the other half for the accuser. And the aldermen who are serving now, and those who may serve in the future, will not be allowed to alter this our statute save only by summoning the Twenty-Four. In Goa, 3 November 1618. I Bartholomeu Soares, Secretary of the Municipality had it written. [Signed] *Luis da Costa Lobato / Antonio de Tavora / Francisco Ferreira de Sá / Diogo da Cunha / Diogo Lobo Pereira / Domingos Vieira Soares / Bartholomeu Pereira / Domingos da Fonseca / Diogo Rodrigues / Ignacio Domingues.*

5. ELECTION OF THE MUNICIPAL COUNCILORS OF GOA FOR THE YEAR 1602 [11]

ACT OF THE ELECTION OF THE OFFICERS WHO WERE
BALLOTED FOR TO SERVE IN THE COUNCIL FOR THE
YEAR 1602, DATED GOA, 31 DECEMBER 1601

. . . and raising at the council table the matter of drawing lots for the officers who are to serve in the government of this city for this said year of 1602, it was resolved that it was necessary for the common weal of this Republic that they should go and ask the Viceroy not to act contrary to what is laid down in the royal ordinance concerning the drawing of lots by a little boy, and that he should not make a distinction between the first, second, and third year, as some previous viceroys had done. . . . [The Camara then went in deputation to interview the viceroy.] And the viceroy replied that although he had already made a distinction in the said lots [*pelouros*] between the first, second, and third years, yet he now agreed that the stipulations laid down in the Ordinance should be fulfilled and carried out accordingly, through drawing of lots by a little boy. And coming to the municipal council, the coffer was taken out of the cupboard, and being opened, a little Portuguese boy took a *pelouro* out of the aldermen's compartment, in which was written [three names] as aldermen, and [two names] as ordinary judges, and Salvador Ribeiro as procurator of the city, all

11. Historical Archive, Goa, Senado de Goa, "Livros dos Acordãos e Assentos," Vol. IV (1597–1603), fls. 145–46. Unfortunately, I neglected to copy out this *auto da eleição* in full, but this extract is sufficient to show the working of the system.

of whom were then called to the council chamber. [On arrival they were formerly inducted in their respective offices] taking an oath that they would well and truly serve the offices to which they had been elected, guarding in everything the service of God and of His Majesty, and dealing justly with all the plaintiffs and defendants and people, divesting themselves of all hatred and partiality, keeping secret all matters discussed at the council table for the sake of justice, doing their best endeavours to ensure that the honours, pre-eminencies, liberties and privileges of the said city should be kept inviolate just as they are laid down, the which they promised to do. . . .[12]

6. THE SENATE OF GOA AND THE ARMADA DA COLLECTA, 1623–68

[A. EXTRACT FROM A LETTER OF THE DESEMBARGADOR, DR. PEDRO ALVARES PEREIRA TO THE CROWN, GOA, 15 SEPTEMBER 1623 [13]]

The people of this city of Goa, reflecting on the defenselessness which it experienced in the previous year of 1623, when the great ships of the European enemies lay off the bar, placing this island in dire jeopardy had they tried to attack it, since it lacked everything necessary for its defense — the people resolved to carry out a plan that several citizens had discussed among themselves in the time of the Governor [Fernão de Albuquerque] before the arrival of the Count-Viceroy.[14] This plan was to impose a new and general tax which would as far as possible supply this want; and some of them wrote about this idea to the Count-Viceroy when he reached Cochin. He, grasping this opportunity, on his arrival at Goa sum-

12. Cf. also *APO*, Fasc. I, Part 2, *Cartas da Camara de Goa, 1595–1609*, p. 46, for a complaint in 1596 that "pervertem os Viso-Reis de alguns annos a esta parte [a *Ordenação* de Vossa Magestade] e destintamente nomeão as pessoas para o primeiro, segundo, terceiro anno, fundados em seus respeitos particulares."

13. Original MS, with autograph signature of Dr. Pedro Alvares Pereira, in the writer's collection.

14. For the blockade of Goa by the Anglo-Dutch "Fleet of Defense" in 1622–23, see A. Botelho de Sousa, *Subsídios para a História militar-marítima da India*, Vol. III, *1618–1635* (Lisbon, 1953), pp. 189–93, 230–36.

moned most of the leading citizens one by one, and asked them how this plan could best be carried out and achieved. This was so easily done that it was only necessary to assemble the Religious, Fidalgos, lawyers, citizens, and municipal councilors in the Senate House, when they agreed to levy this tax for the period of six years, although the Count-Viceroy had asked for it only during the period of his viceroyalty. And in order to decide how the money should be raised and how it should be spent, and how the contract should be drawn up in such a way that the viceroys should carry it out properly, and in order to avoid the confusion which would ensue if all the people gave their views about this, they decided to nominate a committee to handle the matter. This committee was composed of the ten municipal councilors, viz., three aldermen, two ordinary judges, a procurator of the city, four *Mesteres*, together with an additional twelve elected persons, viz., two Religious Theologians, one lawyer,[15] and nine citizens, thus forming a committee of twenty-two persons, as was convenient for Your Majesty's service and the good of this city and State. The idea of electing these twelve additional individuals was to overcome all difficulties which might arise, since everyone was certain that these elected persons were solely desirous of working for the common weal. This was not the case with the municipal councilors during the recent years, since they are apt to curry favour with the viceroys, who scrutinize the electoral lists and manipulate them to conform with their wishes.[16] And since the aldermen of this year were made by the Count-Viceroy with this intention, seeing that the joint-commissioners likewise numbered twelve, the municipal councilors resolved to make their own number up to twelve, for which purpose they summoned and coöpted in this committee the captain of the city and gave him two votes, like he has when he votes in the municipal council meetings, though this is only when the councilors elect persons to municipal posts in the gift of the city; and in this way the councilors received twelve votes just like the twelve joint-commissioners. Moreover, they secured another advantage, derived from a declaration (which might well be termed a falsification) which the Secretary of the Senate placed in the margin of the contract made by the people,

15. Dr. Pedro Alvares Pereira, the writer of this letter.

16. A long-standing complaint, but one which was not always well founded. Cf. *APO*, Fasc. II (1857), pp. 246–50.

in which he stated that the twelve joint-commissioners had been elected so that if any of them were absent the committee could still transact business with those who did turn up — which stipulation was not in the original contract that was drawn up and signed by the people.[17] On the strength of this marginal note, as soon as the aldermen see six or seven of the joint-commissioners in the committee, they try and push through what they want done, which, at the beginning, did not seem such a bad thing, since everybody from the viceroy to the lowest official of this committee was very anxious to carry out everything truly and exactly for the good of the common weal. However it is now clear that is quite unjustifiable for the captain of the city to have two votes, for no sooner were the conditions drawn up and the contract signed by the Count-Viceroy than he forthwith proceeded to try and break it in the same committee. The situation was saved because some of the joint-commissioners told the aldermen who put forward the Count's proposals that they would transact no business whatsoever until the viceroy had signed the provisions stipulated in the contract, and until all the other members of the committee had signed them as well; since they on their side did not wish to break any of the conditions. And if this had not been so clearly right and just, the matter would not have been satisfactorily settled, due to the attitude of the aldermen and the captain of the city. . . .[18]

[B. ROYAL LETTER FOR THE SENATE OF GOA,
25 JANUARY 1624 [19]]

Judges, Aldermen, and procurators of the Municipal Council of the City of Goa. I the King send you hearty greetings. Having seen what the Count of Vidigueira, my Viceroy in that State, wrote me concerning the impost which that City had placed on provisions in imitation of the *Real d'agua* levied in this city of Lisbon,[20] to run

17. "Treslado das condições com que esta cidade e povo de Goa concedeo a collecta a Sua Magestade." MS of 8 pp., enclosed with Dr. Pedro Alvares Pereira's letter of 15 September 1623.

18. The rest of this letter is mainly concerned with the Viceroy's alleged attempts to "pack" the Senate of Goa, and his support of the German-born pepper contractor, Fernão de Cron.

19. *APO*, Fasc. II (1857), pp. 243–44.

20. For the highly unpopular tax of the *real de agua* at Lisbon, cf. the references in the index volume of Eduardo Freire de Oliveira, *Elementos para a História do Município de Lisboa*, pp. 401–2, "Reais de Agua."

for the period of six years, and in the same way in all the other cities of the State, and the revenue derived therefrom was to be employed in the war against the rebels — I took particular pleasure in learning of the great service which the municipal council of Goa has done me in levying this tax, and the willingness which it displayed on this occasion, which I will remember (as is right) so I may gladly bestow on it all the favours and rewards which are just. And I have no doubt but that all the other cities have done the same, following the precedent set by that of Goa, in which I will be equally well served, as you may inform them on my behalf. And as regards the revenue from this tax being spent only on the purposes for which it was raised, I have been pleased to grant your request in this respect, as you will understand from the Count-Viceroy. Written at Lisbon on the 25 January 1624. [Signed] *King / The Duke of Villa Hermosa / Count of Ficalho / Nuno de Mendonça*.

[C. ROYAL LETTER FOR THE SENATE OF GOA, 17 AUGUST 1626 [21]]

Judges, Aldermen, and other officers of the Municipal Council of the City of Goa. I the King send you hearty greeting. I charge you to send me every year an account by several conveyances of how much was derived each year from the tax known as the *Collecta* in that city, and on what it has been spent; for I would like to see it and to know thereby that I have to thank your city still more. Written at Lisbon on the 17 August 1626. [Signed] *Dom Diogo da Silva / Dom Diogo do Castro*.

[D. ROYAL LETTER TO THE VICEROY OF INDIA, 4 APRIL 1644 [22]]

Count-Viceroy of India, friend. I the King send you hearty greeting, as to one that I love. It has been represented to me on behalf of the municipality of that city of Goa that whereas the revenue of the *Collecta* was intended to finance the upkeep of an armada which should guard the flotillas of boats carrying provisions to the said city, this money has been diverted to other purposes, to the great loss of that republic. And forasmuch as it is not right that

21. *APO*, Fasc. II (1857), p. 247.
22. *Ibid.*, pp. 255–56.

the armada should be employed in any other way, as the revenue which supplies and maintains it was raised expressly for this purpose, I hereby order that on no account should this armada be used for any purpose other than that of convoying the said provisions. I further order that for as long as this tax is imposed, the condition should be strictly kept which stipulates that if any citizens should die before the posts which they have been awarded become vacant, then those posts can be transmitted in order of seniority to their wives and children, and the same ruling applies to those who are killed fighting in my service in the war against the enemy. Written at Lisbon on the 4 April 1644. [Signed] *King*.

[E. PETITION OF THE SENATE OF GOA TO THE
GOVERNORS OF INDIA, DECEMBER 1668 [23]]

The Aldermen and other officers of the municipal council of this City of Goa, declare that His Majesty granted them the privilege that while the *Collecta* tax lasts, the citizens can renounce the posts which they have been awarded, when the time comes to take them up, and they can bequeath them to their wives or children, when vacancies occur, as can be seen from the royal orders, of which copies are submitted herewith. And forasmuch as the *Collecta* has been renewed and extended, with the consent of the people, on the express condition that they will enjoy the same privileges, and otherwise the said tax will be automatically discontinued, and the late Viceroy (may he be with God) promised to keep the said privileges and signed the contract made with the people, a copy of which is attached; and because His Majesty's grant is still in force, since it was made to last as long as the *Collecta* endures, as it does at present, to the great utility of the Republic and augmentation of the State — For all these reasons we ask Your Worships to do us the favour of ordering that the said privileges should be kept, and that the citizens can renounce and bequeath their posts, in accordance with the grant and faculty given by His Majesty, and the contract made with the people and confirmed by the signature of the said Viceroy. And your petitioners will ever pray, etc.

23. *Ibid.*, pp. 262–63. The Governors of the State of India, Antonio de Mello de Castro and Manuel Corte-Real de Sampaio, gave a favourable *despacho* to this petition on 13 December 1668.

7. THE SENATE OF GOA AND THE DECAY OF THE CITY IN 1680

COPY OF THE DECISION OF THE SENATE ON THE REPAIR OF THE HOUSES OF THE OLD CITY, 14 AUGUST 1680 [24]

On the 14 August 1680, in this city of Goa and in the council chamber of the Municipality, with the aldermen and other officers assembled at the council table together with me, Vicente Soares de Castelbranco, secretary of the municipal council, the presiding alderman [*vereador do meio*] moved that since one of the chief duties of this Senate was the repair and maintenance of the houses and buildings of the city, which form the adornment and beautification thereof, which in well-governed communities were and are carefully maintained, and whereas it was notorious to everyone that the sumptuous houses and buildings of this said city are sadly decayed and for the most part demolished and destroyed, and, what is even worse, this destruction is proceeding apace to the great detriment of the common and public weal, without the various attempts made by this Senate to remedy this grave evil and to repair and maintain the said houses and buildings having had any effect up to now, partly owing to the stubbornness of the owners and partly owing to the feeble way in which the decrees and orders of this Senate are enforced — and that for all these reasons it was urgent that some definite means should be taken to repair and maintain the houses and streets which still remained. And having duly considered and discussed the import of this motion, it was unanimously resolved by all those present that the foreman of works of this city should examine all the streets thereof from the Powder Magazine to Santa Lucia, São Thomé and Nossa Senhora da Luz, twice a week during the winter months, and every fifteen days in the summer, together with the Naik of his department. And he should enter all the houses which were in bad repair and in ruinous condition, and should estimate what repairs were needed for each one. He should further ascertain the names and surnames of the owners, occupants, and renters thereof, and submit an account of everything to this Senate. And the said Senate should send to notify the said owners and occupants, and in their absence their procurators, that within the space of one month without fail they should have them properly repaired, without their being able to al-

24. Albuquerque, *Senado de Goa*, pp. 376–77.

lege any excuse for non-compliance, on pain of being deprived of the ownership, occupancy, and any rights they might have in such houses. And if, after being thus notified, they did not have them restored and repaired within the said term of one month, then they would be automatically deprived of all ownership, occupational or other rights to the said houses, without it being necessary to pronounce any further judicial sentence against them. These houses would then revert to this Senate, which would have them repaired at the expense of the municipal treasury, and could freely keep, own, sell, or rent the said houses and dispose of them as its own property, on condition that it could not give away any of them to anybody, since this would be unlawful. And it was further resolved that henceforward nobody would be given a license to demolish, destroy, or change the old style of the houses of this city and rebuild them smaller, despite any reasons that anyone might allege. And if any of the serving aldermen, or those who may serve in future, should concede such a license, the secretary of the municipal council would be obliged to draw their attention to this prohibition, and if they should disregard this warning, then he would be obliged to inform the government of this matter so that these orders could be enforced. If he neglects to do this, he will be liable to a fine of 500 xerafines, payable to this municipality, and he will not be excused this fine unless he can produce a written certificate to prove that he has done his utmost to enforce these stipulations. And for the strengthening of this resolution, it was further resolved that the Senate should ask His Worship the Governor to promulgate an edict confirming this decision, and to explain it to His Majesty (whom God preserve) so that he could order it to be kept in due legal form, seeing that it is for the benefit of the common weal of this republic. And in order that this might come to the notice of everybody, and to prevent anyone from alleging ignorance thereof, this resolution should be promulgated in the usual public places of this city. Felicio da Cunha, the chief clerk wrote it. Vicente Soares de Castelbranco, Secretary of the Municipality had it written. [Signed] *João Ribeiro / Francisco de Abreu.*

8. ELECTION OF THE MUNICIPAL COUNCILORS OF MACAO FOR THE YEAR 1718 [25]

MINUTES OF THE MEETING ON 27 DECEMBER 1717

On the 27 day of the month of December 1717 in this City of Macao of the Name of God in China, in the council chamber of the municipality thereof, present the ministers and officers who serve in this Senate for this said year, with the presiding alderman Antonio de Aguiar, the following items of business were transacted.

A letter was written to His Majesty's Crown Judge [*Ouvidor*], Gaspar Franco da Silva, notifying him to come and organize the election since he enjoys the powers of a district judge [*corregedor da Comarca*].[26]

It was arranged to hold the said general election, for which purpose the following persons were chosen as electors: Francisco Rangel, Francisco de Mendonça Furtado, Antonio de Sousa Gayo, Joseph de Abreu de Sampaio, Francisco Barradas da Roza, and João Valente de Faria.

The Crown Judge placed the *pelouros* of the said election in the cabinet on the council table in the presence of the officers; and after it was locked, he handed the key to the alderman João da Gama Lobo; and this was the last item on the agenda of the meeting, in proof of which I entered these minutes which were signed by those present as above. [Signed] *Manuel Pires de Moura.*

MINUTES OF THE MEETING ON 31 DECEMBER 1717

On the 31 day of the month of December 1717 in this City of Macao of the Name of God in China, in the council chamber of the municipality thereof, present the ministers and officers who serve this said year in this Senate, with the presiding alderman Antonio de Aguiar, the following items of business were transacted.

The accounts, both of receipts and expenditure, were submitted by the Procurator and signed, since the ordinary judge to

25. Copied from the original "Livros das actas das Sessões do Leal Senado desde 24 de fevereiro de 1712 até junho de 1718," in the archives of the Macao municipality, by the kindness of Mr. J. M. Braga and Senhor Luís Gomes. This volume is badly wormed and some readings are conjectural.

26. As with most of the *ouvidores* at this period, Gaspar Franco da Silva was not a professional lawyer, but a trader settled at Macao who often served on the Senate.

whom they had been submitted for verification stated they were in order. The leading citizens [*homens bons*] were assembled and the *pelouro* was opened with the usual solemnities, and the following officers were found to be nominated therein: for ordinary judges, Manuel Leme da Silva and Francisco Barradas da Roza. For aldermen, Francisco Xaxier Doutel, Francisco de Mendonça Furtado, and Francisco Jorge Delgado. For procurator, Manuel Pires de Moura; and for Judge of the orphans, Diogo Lopes. And in the absence of Francisco Xavier Doutel and Francisco Jorge Delgado, there were elected to serve in their places, Pedro Ribeiro de Sousa and Antonio de Sousa Gayo. And Gaspar Barradas was elected to serve as procurator in the temporary absence of Manuel Vicente Roza. A letter was written to the Crown Judge notifying him that the *pelouro* had been opened, so that he could verify from the criminal record whether any of those elected were listed therein; and a reply was received that none of those elected had been involved in any crime. They were therefore all sworn in, with the usual formality, as is given at greater length in the minute-book of the *Homens Bons* on page [blank]. And this was the last item on the agenda, in proof of which I entered these minutes, which were signed by all the ministers and officers who were present as above. [Signed] *Manuel Pires de Moura.*

9. REFUSAL TO SERVE THE OFFICE OF ALMOTACÉL AT MACAO IN 1639

MINUTES OF THE DECISION REACHED AT THE MEETING
OF THE 24 DECEMBER 1639, CONCERNING THE REFUSAL
OF MANUEL DE VASCONCELLOS TO SERVE AS ALMOTACÉL [27]

On the 24 day of December of this present year of 1639 in this council chamber of the municipality of this city of the Name of God in China, present at the council table the officers who serve in the said year, the matter was raised that Manuel de Vasconcellos was under arrest in his house, on account of his disobedience in refusing to serve the office of *Almotacél*, and the rude and unmannerly way in which he made this refusal. And the said officers, considering that His Majesty neither wants nor permits that any of his vassals should excuse themselves from serving in

27. *Arquivos de Macau*, Vol. III, p. 59.

his cities and republics, and in view of other considerations they decided that the said Manuel de Vasconcellos could never again be elected to serve as *Almotacél* at any time, nor could he henceforth enjoy the privileges and status of a citizen. And furthermore, that he could never henceforth be elected to any office in this republic, nor could he serve any charge or post whatsoever. And in view of their having resolved and decided this, they ordered this minute to be entered, which they all signed, so that this record should endure for all time.

I, Simão Vaz de Paiva, Ensign and Secretary of the municipal council, wrote it. [Signed] *Diogo Henriques de Lousada / Francisco Botelho / Manuel de Siqueira / Innocencio Vieira de Campos.*

10. THE SENATE OF MACAO
AND THE SANDALWOOD TRADE WITH TIMOR,
1689

MINUTES OF THE MUNICIPAL COUNCIL MEETING OF THE
20 OCTOBER 1689, AT WHICH WAS DECIDED THE LADING
OF THE CARGO FOR THE SHIPS FOR TIMOR, TO BE
DIVIDED AMONG THE MORADORES AS FOLLOWS: [28]

On the 20 day of the month of October of the year 1689, in this city of the Name of God in China, in the council chamber of the municipality thereof, present at the council table the officers who serve in the said year, they agreed that in accordance with the estimate made by the pilots and the supercargo of the ships which are to fetch the sandalwood in this said year, and which are now ready to sail for Timor, as is declared in the foregoing minutes,[29] viz., that each of these ships can load 1,800 piculs of sandalwood cargo, above and below decks, and from these 1,800 piculs, after 622 piculs have been deducted for the liberties of all the crew, there remain 1,178 piculs in each ship, of which one third of the lading is allotted to the owners, in consideration of the great expenses which they incur with the ships, and the meas-

28. Archive of the Senate of Macao, "Livro de Termos dos Conselhos Gerais, 1685–1709," fl. 39. Typewritten copy kindly supplied by Mr. J. M. Braga.

29. "O barco *Sam Paullo* e o *Rozario Pequeno*," according to the *termo* of 10 October 1689, in *ibid.*, fl. 38v.

urement duties which they have to pay, which amount to 392 piculs, thus leaving to divide among the *moradores* 784 piculs in each one of the said ships, making a total of 1,578 piculs net, to divide among the said *moradores* in the manner stated in the lists compiled of the *Bague*. And in proof of this agreement, I Francisco Fragozo, Ensign and secretary of the Municipality entered and wrote these minutes, which the said officers signed. [Signed] *Francisco Nunes de Carvalho / Jozé da Cunha de Eça / João Correa de Liger / Gonçallo da Costa / Jozé Gomes.*

11. BRIBERY OF THE MANDARIN OF CH'IEN-SHAN BY THE SENATE OF MACAO, 1690

MINUTES OF THE MUNICIPAL COUNCIL MEETING ON THE 16 DECEMBER 1690, CONCERNING THE AMOUNT OF MONEY WHICH HAS TO BE GIVEN TO THE MANDARIN OF HIAN-XAN IN ORDER TO FINISH WITH VARIOUS LAWSUITS WHICH HE BROUGHT TO THE CITY [30]

On the 16 day of the month of December 1690, in this city of the Name of God in China, present at the council table the officers who serve in this year, they decided that since the Mandarin of Hian-xan [31] is now in this city, after having repeatedly threatened this government through various chops [32] concerning the embargo laid on the salt which came from India, and on the sulphur which another ship brought from Manila, and he further demanded that the captains of these two ships should appear to answer these charges in the Chinese courts, and he likewise threatened to sue the Crown Judge of this city and the Adjutant of the garrison about a Chinese who had been beaten up [by the soldiers], and all the foregoing demands were made solely so that he could come and blackmail this city, as the Chinese are wont to do in all their lawsuits, which will never be set-

30. Archive of the Senate of Macao, "Livro de Termos de 1685–1709." Translated from a typewritten copy kindly supplied by Mr. J. M. Braga.

31. Ch'ien-shan (Hueng-sham, in Cantonese), district capital of the island facing Macao.

32. This is *chapas* in the original, "chops" in pidgin-Chinese: official government orders and edicts.

tled in peace and quiet save only by satisfying the mandarins with a sum of money; and in view of all this, the said officers discussed how they could find out what sum the Mandarin would be contented with, both in order to desist from summoning the aforesaid captains to appear in the courts, and also to lift the embargo on the salt and obtain permanent leave to bring it from outside to help pay the expenses of this place and to avoid the Chinese salt-gabelle, and likewise to free the said surplus; and after full investigation it was found that the mandarin would not accept less than 400 taels, 300 for himself, and 100 for his subordinates; and he had further intimated that if this gift was not made with inviolable secrecy, he would accept nothing, and would prosecute all his demands through due process of law; and the said officers, seeing that if they did not finish the business in this way, much unpleasantness would ensue for the common people, who would likewise be subjected to the salt-gabelle, which would mean further expenditure for all concerned; and, moreover, seeing the great secrecy which the mandarin enjoined, they did not wish to summon the *homens bons*, for then the whole business would become public — In view of all this they therefore agreed to give him the said 400 taels, since this settlement was for the common good of all, and I, Francisco Fragozo, Ensign and Secretary of the Municipality, entered and wrote this minute, which the said officers signed. [Signed] *Jozé Vieira da Silva / Martim Afonço de Sousa / Domingos da Cunha Peixoto / Constantino Alvarez da Paz.*

12. THE SENATE OF MACAO AND THE PAYMENT OF GROUND-RENT TO THE CHINESE GOVERNMENT IN 1691

MINUTES OF THE GENERAL MEETING OF THE
HOMENS BONS CONCERNING THE INCREASE IN THE
PAYMENT OF GROUND-RENT, 14 JANUARY 1691 [33]

On the 14 day of the month of January of the year 1691, in this city of the Name of God in China, in the council chamber of the

33. Archive of the Senate of Macao, "Livro de Termos dos Conselhos Gerais, 1685–1709," fl. 51. Translated from a copy kindly supplied by Mr. J. M. Braga.

municipality thereof, present at the council table the officers who serve this year, all the *Homens Bons* were summoned to attend, and when they had arrived, they were told by the presiding alderman, Jozé da Cunha de Eça, that a chop had come demanding the payment of the ground-rent, with the addition of 100 taels to the 500 which have always been paid, since this addition had been decreed by the great Tribunals at the Court of Peking; and when Padre Francisco Xavier Filipuchi, ex-Visitor of the Company of Jesus, was asked as an expert in things Chinese whether any protest could be made against this increase in the ground-rent, the said Padre had replied that no protest or objection could be made in this matter, since it had been decreed by the Emperor; and in view of all this, their Worships might see what could best be done about it. The said *Homens Bons* having heard this, agreed unanimously that there was no alternative but to pay in full the ground-rent with the new increase, since this was the order of the Imperial Court. And I Francisco Fragozo, Ensign and Secretary of the Municipality of the said city, entered and wrote this minute, which was signed by all the officers and by the *Homens Bons.* [Signed] *Jozé da Cunha de Eça / Luís da Silva / Francisco Cabral da Costa / Manuel Fernandes Preto / Gonçallo da Costa / Jozé Vieira da Silva / Francisco Nunes de Carvalho / Domingos da Cunha Peixoto / Mathias Pereira / João Garcia de Luares / Manuel de Abreu / Luis de Araujo de Barros / Vicente de Moura e Bastos / Constantino Alvares da Paz / Jozé Gomes / Valentim da Costa de Lemos / Martim Afonço de Sousa / João Correa de Liger.*

13. THE SENATE OF MACAO AND THE MUNICIPAL BUDGET FOR 1691

MINUTES OF THE MEETING IN THIS COUNCIL CHAMBER
AT A GENERAL MEETING OF THE PEOPLE ON THE
22 JANUARY 1691 CONCERNING THE DUTIES
TO BE LEVIED IN THIS PRESENT YEAR [34]

On the 22 day of the month of January of the year 1691, in this city of the Name of God in China, in the council chamber thereof, present at the council table the officers who serve in this year,

34. *Ibid.,* fl. 51*v.*

the People were summoned to attend, and when they had arrived they were told by the presiding alderman, Jozé da Cunha de Eça, that they had been called to this council chamber so that they could be informed of the obligations which this city has incurred, both as regards the pay of the garrison and the other usual expenses, as likewise the excessive disbursements which continually have to be made to the Chinese for the peace and preservation of this place, and also the payment of the ground-rent which this year has been increased by 100 taels, and the repayment of the debt due to the King of Siam, and other debts which this city owes to some of its citizens, and to the Holy House of the Misericordia, and to the Mothers of Santa Clara with the customary one percent which is due to them. The people having heard this exposition, unanimously resolved that all the coarse [grossa] goods imported from outside should pay a duty of ten percent; and that all the fine [finas] goods which are weighed by dach-em [35] should pay five percent; and those which are weighed in the balancing-scales should pay two percent; on condition that out of the said ten percent should be taken the one percent due to the Holy House of the Misericordia, and the other one percent due to the Mothers of Santa Clara, on the supposition that if the said Mothers wished to enjoy the said one percent, they will be obliged to receive without a dowry, once in every five years, a daughter of a respectable citizen [morador grave], who should be chosen by a selection committee composed of the Senate with six joint-commissioners. And in order to inaugurate this agreement, the Reverend Mothers will receive in this present year the daughter of a morador who will be selected in the above-mentioned manner. And that this agreement should be notified forthwith to the aforesaid Mothers, and if they did not wish to accept it, then in that case the People would not be prepared to pay the said one percent to the Reverend Mothers. And the People further declared that the eight percent was intended to cover the ordinary expenses of the city, and there should be deducted therefrom the sum of 100 taels in alms for the Fathers of São Francisco; and if there was any surplus, then this should be applied to the payment of the debt due to the King of Siam. And

35. For this word and its derivatives (*datchin, dotchin, dachein,* etc.), a corruption of the Cantonese *tu'-ch'eng,* or hand-steelyard, cf. Yule and Burnell, *Hobson-Jobson* (ed. 1903), p. 298; S. R. Dalgado, *Glossário Luso-Asiático* (2 vols.; Coimbra, 1919–21), Vol. I, pp. 340–41.

that the cloths and textiles which were imported from outside for the *moradores*, should be tax-free only in so far as what would legitimately suffice for the use of their own households, according to the size of their respective families, and other petty items of ordinary household use should likewise be imported tax-free; and that anything which was destined for the religious brotherhoods [*confrarias*] and the Divine Cult should also be tax-free. And the people further declared that out of the said eight percent, one percent should be deducted for the payment of the debt to the King of Siam, and the remaining seven percent should be earmarked for the ordinary expenses of the city, and that anybody who should be found guilty of concealing silver which he owed, should be fined double the amount due. And I, Francisco Fragozo, Ensign and Secretary of the Municipality of the said city, entered and wrote this minute, which all the officers and people signed. [Signed] *Jozé da Cunha Eça / Luis da Silva / Manuel Fernandes Preto / Gonçallo da Costa / Jozé Vieira da Silva / Francisco Nunes de Carvalho / Martim Afonço de Souza / Gaspar Franco da Silva / Manuel Alvares / Jozé Gomes / Pedro Vaz da Fonseca Coutinho / Leonel de Sousa de Lima / Manuel Ferreira de Aragão / João Correa de Liger / Francisco Rodriguez Ribeiro / Manuel Moniz Correa / Niculão Homen da Cruz / Luis de Araujo de Barros / Vicente de Moura e Bastos / Constantino Alvares da Paz / Francisco Lourenço de Carvalho / Niculão Ribeiro / Manuel Simoens Pereira / Manuel Jozé de Medreiros / Francisco de Souza de Tavora / Paulo Pereira Dantas / Manuel Pereira Alpedrinha / Francisco Rodrigues / Manuel de Abreu / Manuel Caldeira de Gouvea.*

14. QUALIFICATIONS LAID DOWN FOR THE MUNICIPAL COUNCILORS OF MACAO, 1689–1709 [36]

I, the King, make known to all those who see this my confirmatory decree, that having regard to what Dom Rodrigo da Costa, when governing the State of India, promulgated at the request of the officers of the Municipality of the City of the Name of

36. Manuel Murias (ed.), *Instrução para o Bispo de Pequim e outros documentos para a história de Macau*, pp. 174–75.

God of Macao, concerning the qualifications required for the persons who serve therein as Aldermen, and other judges, and as officers of that republic, which decree runs as follows: Dom Rodrigo da Costa of the Council of His Majesty, Governor and Captain-General of India, etc., I make known to those who see this decree that the officers of the Municipality of the city of the Name of God of Macao submitted a petition to me representing that it was convenient for His Majesty's service and the authority of the said city that it should be governed by persons of pure blood [*pessoas limpas de sangue*], asking me to take the necessary measures to ensure this; and in accordance with what is laid down in the Laws of the Kingdom, and with what was agreed in the Council of State, I deem it good and order that the officers of the republic of the said city must be Old-Christians, Portuguese by nationality and birth [*Christaons Velhos Portuguezes de Nasção e Geração*], and if they turn out to be otherwise, then their elections and appointments will be regarded as null and void. I notify it thus to the said officers of the Municipality, to the Crown Judges, Justices, officials and all persons concerned, so that they should fulfill, keep, and carry it out entirely, and likewise ensure that this decree is strictly enforced in all its contents, without any doubt or objection being raised thereto. . . . and it will be registered in the municipal council of the said city, and it goes in duplicate. Francisco Gomes wrote it in Goa on the 30 April 1689. The Secretary, Luis Conçalves Cota had it written. *Dom Rodrigo da Costa.*

And considering that the basis of the said decree tends to the good of my service and the authority of the said municipality, and agreeing with what my Procurator opined about this matter, I am pleased to confirm (as by this I do confirm) the decree embodied therein, on condition, however, that the said posts of the municipal government of the city of Macao cannot be given to those who are not nobles [*os que não forem nobres*], irrespective of the other qualifications which are specified in the foregoing decree, which must be omitted. And subject to this declaration, I confirm and I want fulfilled and carried out entirely all the rest of it, for so long as I consider it for the good of my service and do not order the contrary. Wherefore I order my Viceroy or Governor of the State of India and the Comptroller of my Treasury there, that they should carry out and enforce it to the letter, without any query being raised . . . and it was issued in duplicate. Dionizio Cardozo Pereyra wrote it in Lisbon on the 30 of December 1709. The Secretary André Lopes de Laure had it written. [Signed] *King / Miguel Carlos.*

Confirmatory Decree by which Your Majesty is pleased to confirm what Dom Rodrigo da Costa, former Governor of the State of India, ordered to be promulgated at the request of the officers of the Municipality of the City of the Name of God of Macao, concerning the qualifications which the persons who serve therein must possess, whether they are aldermen, other judges, or officers of that republic, as is stated therein, and which goes in duplicate, and it does not pass through the Court of Chancery. For Your Majesty to see. By decision of His Majesty on the 14 March 1691 on a recommendation of the Overseas Council of the 9 December 1690. Registered on Fl. 395 *verso* in Book No. 4 of the Provisions of the Secretariat of the Overseas Council. Lisbon, 10 February 1710. [Signed] *André Lopes de Laure.* I, Antonio José Pereyra, Chief Ensign and Secretary of the Municipality who had it written and signed it. [Signed] *Antonio José Pereira.*

15. ELECTION OF THE MUNICIPAL COUNCILORS OF BAHIA FOR THE YEAR 1682

MINUTE OF HOW THE PELOURO WAS OPENED AND IN IT
WERE LISTED THE OFFICERS OF THE MUNICIPALITY
WHO ARE TO SERVE IN THIS YEAR OF 1682 [37]

On the first of January 1682, in this city of Salvador Bahia de Todos os Santos, and in the council chamber of the municipality thereof, present Dr. João de Goes de Araujo of the judiciary of His Highness, Chief Justice of the civil court with jurisdiction in the High Court of this State and who serves as District Magistrate, together with me, João de Couros Carneiro, Secretary of the municipal council of this city, he sent and had brought before him the cabinet containing the *pelouros*, of which cabinet he had one key and the alderman João Anriques Tourinho had a second, and I the secretary of the municipality had the third; all three of which were handed to me, and the said Chief Justice ordered me to open the said cabinet with them, which I did, in witness whereof I wrote and entered this minute, which was

37. *Atas de Câmara da Bahia,* Vol. V, *1669–1684,* pp. 316–17.

signed by the Said Chief Justice together with myself João de Couros Carneiro Secretary of the municipal council. [Signed] *João de Couros Carneiro.*

And after the said cabinet had been opened, the said Chief Justice ordered me the Secretary of the municipality to take out from it the bag in which were the said *pelouros,* which I did accordingly, the which bag is of green satin, and inside it was another little bag of white cloth, which the said Chief Justice likewise ordered to be opened after summoning before him a little boy who was found outside in the street, who was called João and who might be about four years old, son of Pedro Soares Peixoto. The said Chief Justice told him to put his hand in the bag which contained the *pelouros* and to take out one of them, which the little boy did, after first shuffling them round, and he took out with his hand one of the *pelouros* which were in the said bag, and when it was opened by me, the Secretary of the municipality, it was found that there were listed as ordinary judges Captain Francisco Freire de Andrade and Sebastião de Araujo de Goes, and as aldermen Miguel Munis Barreto, Manoel de Araujo de Aragão, and Francisco Dias Davilla, and as procurator Pedro Barboza Leal, which I the below-mentioned Secretary of the municipality duly testify, and I drew up this minute of everything which was signed by the said Chief Justice, together with me João de Couros Carneiro, Secretary of the municipal council. And I put back the bag containing the last *pelouro* into the said cabinet; and the Chief Justice retained one key and the Alderman João Anriques another, and the third was kept by me João de Couros Carneiro, Secretary of the municipal council who wrote and signed this. [Signed] *João de Couros Carneiro / João de Goes Araujo.*

16. NEW SYSTEM FOR THE ELECTION OF THE MUNICIPAL COUNCILORS AT BAHIA, 1697

MINUTES OF THE MEETING AT WHICH THE LIST OF THE ALDERMEN AND PROCURATORS FOR THE PRESENT YEAR OF 1697 WAS OPENED [38]

On the 27 day of the month of April of the year 1697, in this city of Salvador Bahia de Todos os Santos, in the council chamber of

38. *Ibid.,* Vol. VI, *1684–1700,* pp. 336–38.

the municipality thereof, present the *Juiz de Fora*, Dr. Joseph de Costa Correa, and the aldermen, Antonio Coelho Brandão, Francisco de Negreiros Corte-Real, and Manuel de Brito Lobo, and the procurator, João de Brito e Sousa, the president opened a letter of His Majesty from the Privy Council [*do dezembargo do Paço*], in which was enclosed the official decree listing the aldermen and procurator who are to serve in the present year, whose contents are as follows: Dom Pedro by the grace of God King of Portugal and of the Algarves on both sides of the sea in Africa, Lord of Guinea and of the conquest, navigation, commerce of Ethiopia, Arabia, Persia, and of India, I make known to the judge, aldermen, and procurator who are now serving in this city that it is my will and pleasure that in this year of 1697 there should serve as aldermen and procurator the following: as aldermen, Gaspar Masiel de Sáa, Antonio Machado, and Antonio de Brito Correa: as procurator, Domingo Afonço Sertão; all of whom you will straightway summon before you and will solemnly swear and induct them in office, that they will well and and truly serve their respective offices in accordance with the regulations, all of which will be duly entered in the minutes of the *Livro da Vereação*. Luis da Costa Sepulveda wrote it in this City of Salvador Bahia de Todos os Santos on the 26 day of the month of April in the year 1697. Bernardo Vieira Ravasco had it written. *Dom João Dalemcasro.* Decree by which Your Majesty's will and pleasure is that in this year of 1697, there should serve as aldermen, Gaspar Maciel de Sáa, Antonio Machado, Antonio de Brito Correa, and as procurator, Domingos Afonço Sertão; and Your Majesty further orders that the judge, aldermen, and procurators who are now serving in this City should induct and swear them in office on behalf of Your Majesty. And in view of the said decree which is filed in the archive of the municipal council by the officers thereof assembled at the council table, the *Juiz de Fora*, Dr. Joseph da Costa Correa, gave orders to Joseph da Costa, the archivist and doorkeeper of this Senate, that on behalf of the officers of the municipal council he should send word to the aldermen, Antonio Machado Velho and Antonio de Brito Correa, and to the procurator, Domingos Afonço Sertão, how they had been elected as aldermen and procurator. The said Joseph da Costa carried this message and in the same council meeting he returned with the answer, which was that the [newly appointed] procurator was ill and that he would come as soon as he was

better, and that the aldermen had said that they would come
some day soon [*que qualquer dia verião*] to the Municipal Council House to take the oath of office. And it was further resolved
at the same meeting that I, the Secretary of the municipality,
should notify in writing the alderman, Gaspar Maciel de Sáa,
who lives a long way off from this city, that he should come
forthwith and take up his office of alderman, which I accordingly did; and they ordered this minute of the foregoing business
to be drawn up, which they signed together with myself, João
de Couros Carneiro, who wrote it. [Signed] *Costa / Brandan /
Corte Real / Brito Lobo / Brito*.

17. DOWN-GRADING OF THE WORKERS'
REPRESENTATIVES BY THE ALDERMEN OF
BAHIA, 1650

MINUTE CONCERNING THE MOVING OF THE BENCH
OF THE MESTERES, 30 DECEMBER 1650 [39]

On the 30 day of December of the year 1650 in this city of Salvador Bahia de Todos os Santos, in the council chamber of the
municipality thereof, present the officers named below, I mean
who signed below, it was resolved by them that since experience
had shown the great disadvantages which resulted to the service
of God and of His Majesty and to the common weal of this People, from the *juiz do povo* and the *mesteres* being seated on the
same raised dais as the table where the said officers discuss and
deal with business of a secret and confidential nature and other
important concerns touching the general welfare, and whereas the
said *mesteres* are seated so close by that they can understand
the gist of the decisions taken, with the result that these are soon
made public, since they do not know how to keep the necessary
secrecy on which their effective implementation depends, and
whereas the said *mesteres* have no voting rights in these important matters which are none of their business — the officers wishing to avoid the drawbacks and the damages that result therefrom,
agreed that the said seating of the *mesteres* was not in a fit
and proper place for them, but should be removed and placed

39. *Ibid.*, Vol. III, *1649–1659*, pp. 111–12.

further away from the council table, just against the wall of the said council chamber, whence the said *mesteres* can raise the matters which pertain to their affairs, without their being able to hear the discussions at the council table. The officers further agreed that the bench on which the Secretary of the municipal council sits is now too far away from the council table and thus inconvenient for transacting written business, whereas secretaries should be seated near the middle of the council table so that they can better hear the secrets under discussion, as they do in all the other boards and tribunals; and in view of this, the officers ordered that the Secretary's bench should be divided into two equal halves, one of which would be placed opposite the middle of the council table, to serve as a seat for the said secretary of the municipality, and the other would remain at the end of the table where the secretary's bench was placed hitherto, so that the *procurador do conselho* [40] could be seated there, separating him from the aldermen, as is done in the municipality of Lisbon, where the seats of the aldermen and of the *procurador do conselho* are kept apart. And they added that this decision should be carried out forthwith, and should be minuted in this book, so as to be available for reference for all time, and to show the reasons why the officers felt impelled to take this resolution, which was disclosed to the persons eligible for municipal government, who were called for this purpose, and they approved unanimously thereof, regarding it as essential and well considered, and they ordered this resolution to be entered, which they then all signed, and I Rui de Carvalho Pinheiro, secretary of the municipality wrote it. [Signed] *Francisco de Araujo da Motta / Cosme de Saá Peixoto / João Leitão Arnozo / Gaspar de Araujo de Gois / Francisco Velho de Araujo / Balthazar Barreto / Francisco Gomes Aranha / Antonio Camello / João Jozé de Mesquita / Gaspar Leitão de Eça / Diogo Mendes Barradas / Simão de Oliveira.*

40. Presumably identical with the *procurador da cidade.*

18. THE MESTERES OF BAHIA AND THE
FEAST OF CORPUS CHRISTI, 1673

MINUTES OF THE AGREEMENT WHICH WAS MADE
WITH THE OFFICERS OF THE WORKERS' CORPORATIONS
OF THIS CITY CONCERNING THE INSIGNIA WHICH SHOULD
BE CHANGED FOR THE PROCESSIONS OF THIS
MUNICIPALITY, BAHIA, 22 NOVEMBER 1673 [41]

On the 22 day of November of the year 1673 in the council chamber of this City of Salvador Bahia de Todos os Santos, present the ordinary judge, Manuel de Brito Lobo, and the aldermen, and the *Procurador do concelho*, and the *Juiz do Povo*, and the *mesteres* who have signed below, as also the judges of the workers' corporations of this city, the said aldermen moved and proposed that forasmuch as there were badly wanting in the processions the time-honoured insignia of the past, such as the dragon, hobby horses, and other old-time curiosities, which greatly enhanced the splendour and festivity which Christian piety renders to God and to his Saints, and that whereas this city had grown greatly in all the arts and crafts, some of which made no contribution of any sort or kind to the said processions — in view of all this, the said officers of the municipality resolved and agreed that the carpenters would supply the banner as they usually do, and likewise the wooden frame for the dragon, sharing this responsibility with the joiners and the turners. And the tailors would be obliged to supply their usual banner, and the cloth which covers the serpent, painted and fitted, it being their responsibility to keep and look after it always; and the carpenters would provide the wood whenever this was necessary, and all these various corporations would provide Negroes who would carry it in the processions. And the cobblers would provide their usual banner, and the dragon as they always have done. And the stone-masons will supply a banner which they will make forthwith at their own cost. The dyers, the hatters, the harness-makers, the tinkers, and

---

41. *Atas da Câmara da Bahia*, Vol. V, *1669–1684*, pp. 114–15. Cf. also Carlos Ott, *Formação e Evolução da Cidade do Salvador*, Vol. II, pp. 32–33. It is interesting to compare this list with the equivalent "Regimento da maneira que os oficios mecanicos vam na procissão do dia do Corpo de Deus," at Lisbon and Goa in the early 16th century, in *APO*, Fasc. II (1857), pp. 38–39. Cf. also Document 4, on p. 158 above, for this procession at Goa in 1618.

the coopers will provide a banner and four hobbyhorses [*cavalinhos fuscos*]. And the male and female bakers and the pastry-cooks will provide two giants and a giantess, and a dwarf which the common people call "Father of the Giants." And the blacksmiths, the locksmiths, the barbers, the sword-cutlers, and the saddlers, who all belong to the religious brotherhood of São Jorge will be obliged to provide a banner or a pennant, as they usually do, and the statue of the Saint on his bier, and likewise the statue of the same Saint seated and arrayed on horseback, together with a Page and an Ensign, a trumpet, and drummers, and six sergeants of the guard, all properly dressed and equipped. And the itinerant women who sell from door to door, and the male and female tavern-keepers will contribute with four dances, including that of the rope-makers — And thus the said aldermen decided that this regulation concerning the form of the insignia in the said processions would be mandatory from this day forward, and that the corporations whose representatives were present should be notified forthwith that a fine of 6,000 reis paid from prison for the public works of this municipality and the new prison, would be inflicted on any which failed entirely to fulfill the obligations hereby imposed on them. And the officers further ordered that all this should be entered in these minutes which they signed, and I, João Peixoto Viegas, Secretary of the municipality, wrote it. [Signed] *Manoel de Brito / Pedro Borges Pacheco / Paulo Coelho de Vasconcellos / Sebastião de Araujo de Goes / João de Almeida Pinto / Sebastião de Lima.*

[A marginal entry reads as follows:] And the officers of the municipal council further decided that the cattle-traders will provide three little barren cows. João Peixoto Viegas wrote it on the same day and it was signed by *Lobo / Pacheco / Goes / Pinto.*

[Another marginal entry, in a later hand, reads:] At a council meeting on the 20 October 1713 we have to declare that the button-makers should be added to the banner of the coopers.

19. THE SENATE OF BAHIA AND THE
SALE OF RUM IN 1672

MINUTES OF THE GENERAL MEETING WHICH WAS CALLED
TO DECIDE THE CONDITIONS ON WHICH BRANDY AND
RUM SHOULD BE SOLD BY CONTRACT TO THE HIGHEST
BIDDER, IN ACCORDANCE WITH THE STIPULATIONS
READ TO THE PEOPLE AND WHICH ARE REPRODUCED BELOW [42]

On the 17 day of the month of February 1672, in this city of Salvador Bahia de Todos os Santos, in the council chamber of the municipality thereof, present at the council table the officers whose names are signed below, they sent to summon the people by ringing the bell, and when they were all present the judge, Joseph de Goes, stressed the lack of money in the Senate's funds wherewith to pay the infantry of the garrison, as this Senate is obliged to do; and further, that despite numerous proclamations and penalties which had been made against the sale of the strong drink called rum (*cachaça*), it had never been possible to abolish it, since it had only resulted in the rich making it and the poor perishing from it, and that for these and many other reasons it was convenient that the owners of each still that distilled rum should pay what was stipulated in the conditions which were read to the meeting and which are reproduced below, both for the distilling and the sale of rum in the way which is declared therein; and all those who were present unanimously gave their hearty consent to this proposal, which seemed very good to them, and that the conditions should be fulfilled and any infractions should be punished with the stipulated penalties. And the officers further ordered that this minute should be entered of how this had been agreed in the council meeting and approved by the assembled people who all signed it, and I, Rui de Carvalho Pinheiro, Secretary of the municipality, wrote it. [Signed] *Francisco Freire d'Andrade / Joseph de Gois Araujo / Nuno Damorim Cerqueira / Antonio Camello Pereira Daragão / Domingos Dias / João de Brito Cerqueira / Antonio Allures-Trosifal / Sebastião Lima / Antonio Francisco / Pantalião Rodriguez / Luis Cerqueira da Rocha / Domingos Martins Pereira / Lourenço da Rocha Mattos / João Pereira da Costa / Manoel Alvarez de Abreu / Manuel*

42. *Atas da Câmara da Bahia*, Vol. V, 1669–1684, pp. 60–63.

*Pereira Pinto / João Solinco de Carvalho / Francisco da Camara /
Francisco José de Carvalho / Manoel Dias Coimbra / Manuel Luis
Campos / Lourenço Freire Varela / Domingos Allures Barreto /
Domingos Pereira / Manoel Fernandez Ribeiro / Antonio Ribeiro /
Balthazar Ferreira Araujo / Antonio Anriques Soares / João de
Carvalho / Manoel Rodriguez Oliveira / Grabiel João / Francisco
Alures Roxo / Ilario Gonçalves / Domingos Gonçalves Ferreira /
Manoel de Almeida / João Rodrigues Reis / José da Silva /
Clemente Calheiros / Manoel Fernandez de Brito / Francisco de
Lima Bairros.*

REGISTER OF THE CONDITIONS ON WHICH
THIS MUNICIPALITY WILL AUCTION TO THE HIGHEST
BIDDER THE CONTRACT FOR BRANDIES AND RUMS
[AGOAS ARDENTES E CACHASAS], WHICH WERE
READ TO THE PEOPLE AND APPROVED BY THEM

Any person of whatever quality and condition he may be, who is
a householder in this Reconcavo, and in the Lower Towns,[43] and
in the captaincy of Sergipe del Rey, who wishes to distill the
local brandy [*agoardente da terra*] will pay to the contractor for
each still of one flue the sum of 50 milreis yearly, and for a still
of two flues 80 milreis, and if he distills without registering, he
will pay a fine of 100 milreis to the contractor for each time that
he is found guilty of not registering. All the sugar-planters [*senhores de engenho*] who distill with their own contraption will
pay to the contractor 40 milreis yearly for each still of one flue,
and if the said still has two flues then it will pay 60 milreis, and
unregistered stills will be fined the same penalty as above. And
these planters can claim a reduction of 10 milreis on a still of
one flue, and 20 milreis on one of two flues, owing to the expense
incurred in establishing the same, for each pipe of brandy which
is exported to Angola, the Lower Towns, the captaincy of Sergipe
del Rey, Rio Real, Rio de São Francisco, and the rest of the backlands [*certoins*]. And whoever sells it in this city will pay to the
contractor 1,000 reis per pipe, and for the quarter barrels in pipe
at the rate of 250 reis the barrel. And anyone who takes or sells

43. *Vilas de baixo.* The reference is to the townships of Cairú, Camamú,
and Boipebá in Ilhéus.

it without registering with the said contractor will have it confiscated and will pay 20 milreis from prison to the contractor each time that he is caught. And the same penalty will be inflicted on those who take it without registration. And the distillers can sell it on their own premises by retail as in a tavern, without paying anything extra. The contractor will issue a license to everyone who asks him for it, whether for distilling it, for exporting it, or for selling it retail in a tavern, on the conditions stipulated above, without their being charged anything extra on this account. And if the contractor declines to issue the said licenses then the aggrieved persons can appeal to the Senate to issue them. And the contractor will pay 1,000 reis fine to this Senate each time that it is proved he refused to issue any of the aforesaid licenses. No person will be allowed to make rum, nor to sell it in this city and its district without a license from the contractor, since the contractor must issue a license to all those who ask him for one to sell rum, insofar as this is just and reasonable; and the persons who sell brandy and rum without his license will pay a fine of 10 milreis from the prison for the contractor. And if the contractor should not wish to issue such a license, the aggrieved party can appeal to this Senate to give him one if he has a reasonable case. This Senate will be obliged to keep all these aforesaid conditions, and to order the issue of all the necessary executive instructions and other orders which may be necessary for the said contractor, so that he can recover and claim everything that is due to him as if it was for the Royal Treasury, on condition that the confiscations are quickly and summarily carried out, the contractor providing his independent witnesses and sworn evidence to be examined and tried summarily by the ordinary judge with whom the denunciation is lodged, and he will be allowed to carry the case on appeal to the High Court. And he will enjoy all the exemptions and privileges which the contractors of the Royal Treasury enjoy, which the governors and the captain-general will order to be proclaimed by public proclamation with the conditions of this contract and the penalties thereof, and they will give him all the help and favour which are necessary for it to be implemented. [Signed] *Francisco Freire d'Andrada / Joseph de Goes Araujo / Nuno Damorim Cerqueira / João de Brito Cerqueira / Pedro Camello Pereira d'Aragão.*

20. THE SENATE OF BAHIA AND THE
CRISIS IN THE SUGAR TRADE, 1687

LETTER FROM THE SENATE TO HIS MAJESTY
CONCERNING THE NEED TO FIND A MEANS TO ENCOURAGE
AN INCREASE IN THE EXPORTS OF THE PRODUCTS OF
THIS LAND, OWING TO THE WAY THEY HAVE
SLUMPED DUE TO THEIR DEARNESS AND
HIGH TAXATION, 12 AUGUST 1687 [44]

At the demand of the most eminent of the People of this city of
Bahia and impelled by our duty as the head thereof, We come to
the Royal Feet of Your Majesty in order to represent the universal
sorrow of us all at the slump in the products of Brazil — sugar
and tobacco. It is said that the foreigners no longer need them,
since there is a surplus from what they themselves cultivate in
the Indies, selling the refined sugar in Italy and the tobacco in
India. And exports of these commodities from Portugal are now
reduced to a very small quantity, which we still retain because
of the superior quality of our sugar over theirs, and because they
need some of every kind to drive a better business. This would
seem to be true, for the Customs Houses no longer clear these
commodities, and the people who went [to Portugal] in the fleet
of the last year of 1686, wrote and ordered their agents in Brazil
to send them their capital in money or in bills of exchange; for
sugar and tobacco are neither wanted nor bought by the foreigners, and for Portugal 8,000 or 10,000 chests of sugar and as
many more of tobacco suffice yearly. We are compelled to recognize the truth of this, since in this present fleet the merchants re-
frained more than ever before from buying these commodities,
and they only accepted sugar and tobacco in payment of their
goods when they were bound by previous contracts to do so.

Matters being in these straits, Sire, it seems that we can regard
the trade of Brazil as given over and lost, nor must Your Majesty's Council consider it in any other way. This is all the more
reason why every effort should be made to find a remedy before
it is too late, even though those who are in Portugal write us,
and those who come thence tell us, that this trade is already
lost, since there is no hope of making a profit therein, nor of ex-

44. *Cartas do Senado da Câmara da Bahia, 1638–1692* (3 vols.; Salvador,
1950–53), Vol. III, *1684–1692*, pp. 49–51.

porting these commodities from that kingdom. Those who discuss the cause thereof, state that both as regards Brazil and Portugal the collapse of the sugar was due to the duties which were laid on it on top of the old duties and the seven vintens per arroba for the convoy-tax when the Companhia Geral was founded, at a time when the emergency of the war justified this and when the sale price of sugar oscillated between 30,000 and 30,500 the arroba, thus enabling it to bear the new burden. And as regards the tobacco, the decline is due to the rigid monopoly thereof, and the heavy duty of one vintem per pound which was imposed on it, in addition to the other duties which had been levied on it at the same period of the war and of the convoy. That the English and the other peoples of the North, resentful of the high price of 30,500, resolved to go and cultivate these products in the Barbados and on the mainland of the Indies. That if it had been realized at the time what harm that diversion of this business boded for us, and the prices of our sugar and tobacco had been lowered to reasonable amounts, then it might well have happened that those nations would not have been so eager to grow those products for themselves, for despite everything their sugar is not of such fine quality and prestige as ours. But this was not done, and we now realize that this trade is lost to us:

Wherefore, Sire,

We beseech, prostrated at the Royal Feet of Your Majesty, that you would order to be considered in your [Overseas] Council some remedy to ensure that this State does not perish completely, nor that of Angola, nor the interests of Portugal and of Your Majesty, so important for both these two conquests; because if there is no longer any demand for field-labour in Brazil, then the slave trade of Angola will likewise perish. This much is obvious.

Considering how to find a remedy for this state of affairs, we can suggest no other than that the cause thereof should be removed — the high price of 30,500 which was current in the years from 1645 to 1655. It is true that this price has declined since many years ago, but this would not matter so much if the duties had been lowered as well. The same applies to tobacco and the rigidities of its monopoly, so that if greed of gain leads to some smuggling and evasions, the resulting profits should not be reaped by foreigners but by the native-born vassals. These were called sons by the Lord Kings, Your Majesty's ancestors, and it is only right that Your Majesty should hold us in equal regard, and more especially those of Brazil because of the willing generosity with which they serve Your Majesty, to a degree far beyond their resources, for there are very few who do not owe more than they are worth to the traders who come from Portugal, due to the excessively high prices which are charged for slaves, copper utensils, iron, pitch, *ireu* [?], and stuffs of silk and wool, as the ministers who serve and have served in this High Court can inform Your Majesty, since many bankruptcy and insolvency cases have passed through their hands. Furthermore, to this should be added the annual contribution of over 100,000 cruzados, comprising a levy of 40 percent on a total of 1,280,000 cruzados, which this city alone has to contribute towards the dowry of the Lady Queen of England and the peace with Holland. Not to mention another 600 added to the usual taxes to pay for the upkeep of the garrison (which is not the least important cause of our poverty) — so that if our products have no reliable export market, it must inevitably happen that we will not be able to carry these burdens and that Your Majesty's vassals in the whole state of Brazil will all be ruined. Moreover, it seems to us that this will be harmful to all the vassals in the kingdom of Portugal, since it follows that they, too, will then have fewer export markets for their own products. All this is very well known and understood by the fidalgos who have governed this State, and by the law officers of the Crown who have served here, for which reason we have ventured to expound it thus to Your Majesty, so that not only as our King and liege Lord, but also as our Father, you may rescue us all from the misery in which we lie. May God preserve the Royal Person of Your Majesty as these your vassals desire and need. Joam de Couros Carneiro wrote it in the municipal council at Bahia on the 12 August 1687. [Signed] *Antonio Guedes de Paiva / Manuel Pereira de Goes / Domingos Dias Machado / Francisco Pereira Ferraz / Domingos Pires de Carvalho.*

21. ELECTION OF THE MUNICIPAL COUNCILORS AT LUANDA FOR THE YEAR 1677

MINUTES OF THE ELECTION OF THE ELECTORS,
LUANDA, 26 DECEMBER 1676 [45]

On the 26 day of the month of December in the year 1676, in this city of São Paulo da Assumpção in the Kingdom of Angola, in the council chamber of the municipality thereof, present the judges Lourenço de Andrade Colaço and Luis da Silva da Motta, the aldermen Balthazar Van Dune,[46] Antonio de Buiça, and Henrique de Mendonça, and the procurator Francisco Barroso, together with the President of the Senate, Dr. Mathias de Almeida, Chief Justice and *Corregidor da Comarca*, as also the leading persons and all the respectable citizens of the republic, who had been summoned to attend by the Alcaide of the Municipal Council, Vasco Nunes, and in addition to being summoned by the said Alcaide they were also called by the sound of the bell which was rung many times. And when they were all assembled, the said Corregidor administered the oath to each of them individually on the holy gospels, charging them to name six of the most capable and qualified persons who could serve to elect the officers who are to serve in the three following years of 1677, 1678, and 1679; and when the votes were counted, the following were declared Electors by majority votes: Captain Balthazar Van Dune, Captain Diogo Vaz Camello, João de Araujo, Antonio Alvarez Correia, Antonio de Buiça, and Antonio de Oliveira Leite. Joseph Moreira de [torn] was elected instead of the said Antonio de Buiça, who is absent through illness. And the said Chief Justice summoned the said Electors and administered to them the oath on the holy gospels, charging them to elect the officers who are to serve in the next three years, both as judges, aldermen, and procurators, and the secretary, which they promised to do according to the best of their knowledge. And after they had all

45. Archive of the Senate of Luanda, "Livro de Termos de Vereações, 1676," fl. 252.

46. Balthazar Van Dune (or Van Dunen) was one of several Roman Catholic Dutchmen and Flemings, married to Portuguese women, who had been allowed to stay in Luanda after its recapture by Salvador Correia de Sá e Benavides in August 1648. Others included Paulo Escorel and Jorge Guterres Van Zil. All these three served as *oficiais da Camara* at various times during the second half of the 17th century.

drawn up the lists (*pautas*), which they signed, they handed them in. And these minutes of all the foregoing were entered and signed by them and by myself Antonio da Cunha, the Secretary of the municipality. [The signatures are omitted here.]

MINUTES OF THE OPENING OF THE PELOUROS,
1 JANUARY 1677 [47]

On the first day of the month of January of the year 1677, in this city of São Paulo da Assumpção, in the kingdom of Angola, in the council chamber of the municipality thereof, present the officers who served during the last year, and Dr. Mathias de Almeida, Chief Justice of this kingdom, *Corregidor da Comarca*, the said Chief Justice ordered the *pelouros* to be shuffled in the cabinet, and after they were shuffled he ordered a little boy [some words missing] to pick one out, and when it was opened there were found to be named as judges, captains João de Araujo and Mendo Pegado da Ponte, and as aldermen the captains João de Gouveia de Almeida, Diogo Vaz Camello, and the Ensign Manuel da Silva Claveiro; and as Procurator João Alvarez da Costa, and as Secretary the said Antonio da Cunha, who was already serving, to serve for another three years. And when they were all summoned to appear, the said Chief Justice administered to them the oath on the holy gospels, charging them with the duties of their posts, which they all promised to do according to the best of their knowledge. Dr. Mathias de Almeida, Chief Justice of this kingdom, ordered these minutes to be entered, which he signed, together with the new officers who are to serve during this present year of 1677, and I, Antonio da Cunha, Secretary of the municipality, wrote it. And it is hereby declared that the *pelouro* was opened after the bell had first been rung. [The signatures are omitted here.]

47. Archive of the Senate of Luanda, "Livro de Termos de Vereações, 1670–77," fl. 253.

22. TWO ROUTINE SESSIONS OF THE SENATE OF LUANDA, 1670 AND 1716

MINUTES OF THE COUNCIL MEETING OF THE
SENATE ON THE 4 JANUARY 1670. [48]

On the 4 day of the month of January of the year 1670, in this city of São Paulo da Assumpção in the kingdom of Angola, in the council chamber of the municipality thereof, present the Judges, Aldermen and Procurator, they discussed matters concerning the common weal, dealing with papers and petitions, of which they ordered this minute to be entered, which they all signed. Miguel Borges, Secretary of the municipality, wrote it. [The signatures are omitted here.]

MINUTES OF THE COUNCIL MEETING OF THE
SENATE ON THE 28 NOVEMBER 1716 [49]

On the 28 day of the month of November of the year 1716, in this city of São Paulo da Assumpção in the kingdom of Angola, in the council chamber of the municipality thereof, present in council the Judges and the other officers of the Senate of the municipality, they discussed matters concerning the common weal of this people, dealing with petitions and papers, and doing everything else as in duty bound. And in this way they finished the business of the meeting, and ordered me to enter this minute which they signed, and I, João Antunes Pereira, Secretary of the Municipality, wrote it. [The signatures are omitted here.]

23. THE SENATE OF LUANDA AND THE QUOTA FOR THE ANGLO-DUTCH INDEMNITY, 1672

MINUTE CONCERNING THE COLLECTION OF THE
DOWRY FOR ENGLAND AND THE PEACE WITH HOLLAND,
24 DECEMBER 1672 [50]

On the 24 day of the month of December of the year 1672, in this city of São Paulo da Assumpção in the kingdom of Angola, in the

48. Archive of the Senate of Luanda, "Livro de Termos de Vereações," Anno 1670.

49. *Ibid.*, Anno 1716.

50. Archive of the Senate of Luanda, "Livro dos Termos do ano de 1672," loose MS leaves.

council chamber thereof, present the Judges, Aldermen, Procurator, and the Chief Justice *Corregidor da Comarca*, it was moved that in view of the fact that the Procurators of this Senate have hitherto been responsible for the collection of the surtax in milreis on the slaves who are embarked from this port, paid to the account of the slippers of the Lady Queen of Great Britain and the Peace-treaty with Holland, which tax has proved a serious disability to this Municipality and Senate, because its collection hindered the dispatch of routine municipal business, since the Procurator was kept busy in collecting the said tax and giving clearance to the ships which had paid it, all this involving so much work that nobody was willing to serve the said office of Procurator, but virtually had to be compelled to do so by force, owing to the heavy work involved in collecting it and the notorious loss suffered thereby in the trade-goods which he does collect, apart from the additional reason that there are only a few householders in this republic, and fewer still who know how to cast accounts, and those persons charged with collecting this tax ought really to be cashiers, and those persons who do have some knowledge of the said function excuse themselves from serving on the plea that they are engaged in military service so that they cannot be compelled to act, which is gravely disadvantageous to the republic — the councilors, duly considering these and many other reasons, all of which militated against the service of His Highness, decided to appoint a cashier who was an expert in the said art, and that he would be responsible for the collection and the payment of the said voluntary tax, and that he should be paid an adequate salary for his maintenance and as compensation for his trouble and the losses he might sustain in trade-goods, as was notorious. And the said officers of the municipal council together with the Chief Justice resolved to engage a cashier who would be responsible for the collection and accounting of the said voluntary tax, so that the Procurator of the Municipality should be left free of this burden, so as to enable him to attend better to matters of the public weal, of all of which they ordered this minute to be made, which they duly signed.[51] [The signatures are omitted here.]

51. This was not the end of the matter, and in a council meeting on 14 January 1673, it was stated that great difficulty had been experienced in finding a suitable person to act as treasurer or cashier of this tax, since the post of treasurer of the Senate "era mechanico, e o de Procurador nobre, e quando

24. THE SENATE OF LUANDA AND THE SLAVE TRADE WITH BRAZIL IN 1711

[LETTER FROM THE SENATE OF LUANDA TO
KING DOM JOAO, V, 20 SEPTEMBER 1711 [52]]

Sire,

In this kingdom it always used to be customary that the ships which sail laden with slaves for Brazil were each given clearance for the ports which best suited them, whether Rio de Janeiro, Pernambuco, or Bahia; so that when any ship was ready to sail with its allotted number of slaves, the governor ordered it to be given clearance for any of the ports of Brazil which best suited the master of the ship. Subsequently, in the year 1703, His Majesty King Dom Pedro II (may he be with God in glory) ordained by a royal letter that thenceforward there should go each year from this port only 1,200 slaves for Rio de Janeiro, and 1,300 for Pernambuco and Paraiba, and that the remainder should be sent to Bahia, and this decision was taken at the instance of the *moradores* of Bahia, who have no justifiable reason to demand this; whereas the *moradores* of this kingdom have been so greatly prejudiced thereby that they have been reduced to the direst poverty, and we trust that Your Majesty's clemency will induce you to order some remedy to be taken, so as to prevent the final destruction of this wretched people.

The object, Sire, of the merchants and *moradores* of Bahia, is to ensure that the slaves who leave this port all go to that city, because if there are many of them then they can buy them at bargain prices, and for less than they cost in this city, as has happened these last few years. And they subsequently send them clandestinely from Bahia to Rio de Janeiro by sea, or else they send them by the best ways they can via the backlands [*sertão*] to the Mines of Gold, so that they may reap the benefit of the much higher prices which slaves fetch in Rio and in the Mines. Nor do they

---

os homens se escuzarão de Procurador muito mais se escuzarião deste de Thezureiro, sendo que de facto não avia homens mechanicos nesta republica moradores que se pudessem chamar para Thezoureiros da Camara." The difficulty was finally settled by the appointment of a wealthy *morador*, Captain Antonio Henriques da Fonseca, who consented to take the job in return for a salary on 21 January 1673.

52. Archive of the Senate of Luanda, Codex 483 (old numbering), "Livro 3 do Registo, 1674–1724."

lack slaves for agricultural work on their plantations, for apart from those they get from this port, they buy a large number along the Gold Coast [*Costa da Mina*],[53] and they even send to buy some in this city and along the coast of Loango with their trade-goods, and they order that these slaves should be sent direct to Rio de Janeiro, as is notorious everywhere. And by this it can be seen that there is no lack of slaves in that city of Bahia, but that the profit of embarking them for sale at Rio was the motive behind their petition. And the resultant prejudice to this city derives from the fact that if only 1,200 slaves are embarked annually from here for Rio de Janeiro, as is ordered, they are sent in three or four ships, and this number hardly suffices for the owners and crews of the said ships as their portion, leaving the *moradores* unable to embark a single slave from the profit of whose sale they may receive what they depend on for their trade and existence. For this reason they are suffering severely, since they cannot take advantage of the high prices which the slaves fetch at Rio, nor can they send to buy them at the slave markets [*Pumbos*] in the interior, for since the prices of the trade-goods have risen 100 percent above what they were in former years, and slaves are no longer bought for the old price, but for much more than double, the result is that nowadays in order to buy a Piece of the Indies (*peça de Indias*) [54] in the interior it is necessary to have as many trade-goods as would have sufficed for three Pieces a few years ago. And these trade-goods, besides being nowadays needed in greater quantity, have risen so much in price, that only a few *moradores* send to buy slaves in the *pumbos*, due to this fact that the slaves cost them more there than they can get for them at any port in Brazil, with the exception of Rio de Janeiro. Moreover, Sire, the foodstuffs of this land nowadays cost so much that few of the *moradores* can make two ends meet; for whereas a [illegible] of manioc-flour used to cost 400 reis, it is now worth 1,500 or 2,000, and everything else has increased in the same proportion, not to mention those goods which are imported from overseas. And since there is no other trade nor source of income in this land save only the trade in slaves, if this

53. For details of the revived Portuguese slave trade in Lower Guinea, see A. F. C. Ryder, "The re-establishment of Portuguese factories on the Costa da Mina to the mid-18th century," in *Journal of the Historical Society of Nigeria*, Vol. I (1958), pp. 157–83.

54. For a discussion of the term *peça de Indias*, cf. Frédéric Mauro, *Le Portugal et l'Atlantique au XVIIe siècle*, p. 173.

fails then the country will be completely ruined. Nor is it less prejudicial to the Royal Exchequer, for the revenue thereof is derived from the duties levied on the numerous slaves exported to Brazil; and if this slave trade in the interior declines, then far fewer slaves will be embarked from this port, as is already happening. For these reasons, we considered we ought to show Your Majesty the harm that is being done, begging you, prostrated at your Royal feet, in the name of all these your vassals, for the love of God and the preservation of this kingdom, to order that when ships are ready to clear from this port with cargoes of slaves for Brazil, the Governor should give clearance for the port of Rio de Janeiro to anyone who asks him for it; or at least that the Governor should be authorized to allow an annual export of 2,000 head for the port of Rio de Janeiro; and that the municipal councilors should be authorized to distribute a total of one-third of these in each of the ships among the *moradores*, up to the grand total of 2,000 head, and that the Governor should distribute the remainder among the owners and the crews of the ships and the traders that he sees fit. For otherwise the *moradores* will not be able to embark slaves for Rio de Janeiro, as experience has shown. For even before the limitation of embarking only 1,200 head for Rio de Janeiro was enforced, they were not able to do it, since the owners, officers, and crews of the ships monopolized all the slaves. And if the municipal councilors are authorized to allot the 2,000 head among the *moradores*, then it may well happen that these latter will thereby be encouraged to renew the slave trade in the interior, even if slaves cost a lot in the *pumbos*, in the hope that if they can send some to Rio de Janeiro they will get a better price for them, and the Royal Exchequer will likewise benefit from the larger revenue derived from the increase in slaves exported to Brazil. Your Majesty will decide what is best for your service. Luanda, 26 September 1711.[55] [The signatures are omitted here.]

55. As a result of this petition and further correspondence between Luanda and Lisbon, the Crown promulgated a decree on 24 March 1716, "concedendo aos Oficiais da Camara da cidade de São Paulo da Assumpção, Reino de Angola, a repartição da terça parte das praças de todos os navios que partirem deste reino para os portos do Estado do Brasil, à qual repartição assistirá o Ouvidor Geral para que se faça em boa igualdade e os negros não embarcarão sem primeiro constar se estão catequizados na forma da lei." Cf. *Arquivos de Angola*, 1st Series, Vol. III, pp. 21–22; Ralph Delgado, *História de Angola*, Vol. IV, pp. 301–5.

25. PAUCITY OF QUALIFIED CITIZENS AT LUANDA IN 1711

[LETTER FROM THE SENATE OF LUANDA TO KING DOM JOAO V, 20 SEPTEMBER 1711 [56]]

Sire,

There are nowadays in this kingdom so few respectable elderly householders and citizens [*moradores antigos e cidadoins*], that this has led to unqualified persons being elected to office as councilors and in other municipal posts, since they have been hastily married three days previously with girls who were not even the daughters of qualified officeholders, which practice is contrary to the laws of Your Majesty. For this reason, the most respectable persons excuse themselves from serving such offices, each one alleging the best reason that he can. All of this is harmful to the republic, because if it is not administered by the most respectable and best qualified householders, then this is often detrimental both to the good administration of justice and to the welfare of the community in general; and, moreover, since those posts are filled for only a year at a time, many people do not want to give themselves the trouble of holding public office. And since we are entitled to represent to Your Majesty anything, however trivial, which concerns the preservation of Your kingdoms and vassals, and reflecting that this harm will increase with the passage of time, we submit to Your Majesty that it will be advantageous for Your Majesty to order that the officers of the municipal council should serve for three consecutive years and not annually, making the *pelouro* for election to municipal office valid for three years instead of for one only as at present. Your Majesty should further order that nobody should be able to excuse himself from serving any municipal office to which he may be elected, whatever privilege he may plead, or whatever exemption he might claim for serving in military or militia posts without pay; for such persons have always been eligible to serve as aldermen and in other municipal offices in this kingdom; and if this regulation is enforced, then the republic may be better administered, and not reduced to such a wretched state as it is now. Furthermore, since the qualified householders and respectable citizens are so few, and they are nearly all related to

56. Archive of the Senate of Luanda, Codex 483 (old numbering), fl. 93. This request was repeated in a letter of the 7 May 1714 (*ibid.*, fl. 103).

each other, if the *pelouro* is made up to divide the annual offices of each triennial period between eighteen persons, as is the rule at present, it is inevitable that either individuals who are related to each other will serve on the council in the same year, or else unqualified individuals will have to be admitted into the municipal government; whereas if the period of office-holding was extended to three years, they would take better care of the common welfare than they have recently done. Finally, if Your Majesty doubts whether it is really advantageous for the municipal councilors to serve three consecutive years in this kingdom, Your Majesty can seek information on this matter from all of the ex-governors of Angola who are now living at Lisbon. [The signatures are omitted here.]

26. TYPICAL DEPORTEES FROM BRAZIL AND PORTUGAL TO ANGOLA, 1714–48

[SOME OF THE CONVICTS EXILED TO ANGOLA,
AND REGISTERED IN THE BOOKS OF THE SENATE
OF LUANDA, 1714–1748 [57]]

Pernambuco

Joseph Moniz, coloured man, 38 years old, round faced, round eyes, black beard, small mouth, thick lips, short body, many smallpox marks; banished for life to this kingdom as a vagrant and a player with loaded dice, which brought him in much money, which he divided with his accomplices in the same fraud, and with them he frequented the Northern districts, living on his thefts, all of which made him harmful to the common weal. (1714)

Bahia

Christovão Abram, a Swede by nationality, ex-servant of the Sergeant-Major Sebastião de Brito Bacellar, a bachelor youth of about

57. Archive of the Senate of Luanda, Codex 499, "Registo de Degredados condenados por varios crimes cometidos, que se desembarcaram nesta colónia, vindos de Portugal e Brazil, 1753 [alias 1663] a 1793." The first few folios are illegible.

20 years old, average height, narrow face, blue eyes, no beard, the hair of his head very blond and short; banished for life to the kingdom of Angola with a halter by public proclamation, and branded with the letter *P*, which sentence has been carried out, as likewise the flogging to which he was condemned, all for the crime of being a thief. He came from the city of Bahia in the ship *Nossa Senhora da Mãe de Deus Cinco Chagas e Almas*, master Antonio de Paiva, and owner Domingos da Costa Guimarães. He arrived on 9 February 1715.

Oporto

Luiza da Fonseca, spinster, native of the village of [illegible] in the precincts of the Town of Avo, District [*Comarca*] of Guarda, about 20 years old, average height, round face, chestnut-coloured eyes, long, sleek and black hair, and with one of her front teeth broken — banished for life to the kingdom of Angola by public proclamation with a halter, which sentence has already been carried out, by the High Court [*Relação*] of Oporto, for the crime of committing a theft, and transported to Bahia and thence to this kingdom. (1715)

São Tomé

Manuel Francisco de Araujo, a black man, householder in the island of São Tomé, who was transported from the said island to the city of Bahia, and thence transported to this kingdom in order to serve the life-sentence passed on him for the crime of rebelling against the Market-Inspector of the said island. (1715)

Lisbon

Pedro Gonsalves, a native of Braga, son of unknown parents, aged 22 years, sentenced for theft to five years' banishment in Angola. (1715)

Lisbon

Domingos João, native of São Pedro do Sul, in the bishopric of Viseu, son of Antonio João and an unknown mother, aged 21 years, sentenced to five years' banishment for theft. (1715)

Lisbon

Manuel de Sousa, native of Soure, son of Matheus Rodriguez and Maria Gomes, aged 20 years, sentenced for theft to ten years' banishment in Angola. (1715)

Lisbon

João Pereira, native of Guimarães, son of Antonio Pereira and of Catharina de Crasto, aged 18 years; sentenced for a theft to five years' banishment in Angola. (1715)

Lisbon

João Cosmé, gypsy, native of Loures, son of Rodrigo da Costa and Sabeanna Victoria, aged 20 years; sentenced for theft to five years' banishment in Angola. (1715)

Bahia

Domingos de São João, native of the city of Bahia and son of Anselmo da Trindade and Dorothea Anthunes, a cobbler by profession, aged 25 years; sentenced as a petty thief, without the length of the sentence being specified. (1715)

Bahia

Manuel Francisco [surname illegible], a coloured man, legitimate son of Jordam Vaz and his wife Dorothea de Mendonça, already deceased, native of the city of Bahia, 44 years old, thick, black curly hair, narrow swarthy face with pockmarks, black and not very bushy eyebrows, small chestnut-coloured eyes, thick nose and lips; sentenced to be paraded with a halter and flogged through the public streets of this city, and branded and banished for five years to Angola, for stealing a horse from Antonio Machado. The sentence of being publicly paraded with a halter and flogged through the streets, and branding, was carried out at Bahia by order of the High Court there, before his arrival here. (1716)

Lisbon

Antonio Fernandez, a coloured man, native of Borba, son of an unknown father and Francisca Rodriguez, aged 20 years, banished for life (after having been flogged) to the kingdom of Angola, for having raped and deflowered a girl. If he reappears in Portugal he is to be sentenced to death automatically and unavoidably. Sentenced by the High Court of Lisbon. (1717)

Lisbon

Padre Antonio da Silva Ordanhes, a clergyman of the habit of Saint Peter,[58] native of the Town of Santarem, aged 34 years, son of Fernando Bonuidessiam [*sic*] and of Maria da Encarnação, widow, banished for life to Angola by order of the Most Illustrious and Most Reverend Patriarch, for the crime of living scandalously and being sunk in vices. (1734)

Pernambuco

Simão de Freitas Vidal, native of the city of Olinda, son of Lourenço de Freitas Peixoto, aged about 30 years, a tall man, spare of body, like a mulatto [*amulatado*], round-faced, dark eyes, black and bushy eyebrows, two of his front teeth missing, disfigured by a sword-cut scar on the left side of his face, short and sleek black hair, jowl heavily bearded; banished for life to this kingdom to serve in the garrison posts of His Majesty whom God preserve, for the crimes of vagrancy, theft, turbulence, unemployment, and because when serving as a soldier he deserted and took to a gypsy's way of life, to the detriment of the justice, peace, and quiet of the common weal. (1714)

Pernambuco

Francisco da Silva, bachelor, vagrant, thief, rowdy, agitator, prejudicial to the common weal, banished for life to this kingdom by the Chief Justice's office at Pernambuco, without specifying any details other than the above. (1714)

Pernambuco

Clemente Pacheco, a free Negro, natural son of the Lieutenant General of the Regiment of Henrique Dias, banished for life for his contumacious and bad behaviour. (1714)

58. I.e., a secular priest.

Oporto

Maria, female slave of Antonio Nunes of this city, of average height, round face; banished for life to Benguela for the crime of procuring, for which she has already been flogged. (1734)

Rio de Janeiro

Manuel dos Santos, muleteer, 20 years old, average height, round face, chestnut-coloured eyes, black, sleek and short hair, beard of the same colour, native of the district of Viseu; banished for ten years to the kingdom of Angola, for the crime of being a thief, sentenced to be publicly flogged with a halter through the streets, and branded, which sentence has already been carried out. (1738)

Rio de Janeiro

Jozé Caetano de Aguillar, a free Negro, banished to this kingdom for the crime of being a vagabond, and without any trade or employment whatsoever, and so badly behaved that after living with a female slave of Salvador de Marenz [?] in the district of São Gonçalo in the termo of this city, he took away one of his daughters, called Catarina, and brought her to this city about two years ago, and placed her in the house of Escollastica [illegible] de Macedo, widow, and of Josefa de Jesus Sardinha, where he often went to see her, with the idea of marrying her to some youth who would take her to the Mines, committing the vile and abominable offense of [some words illegible] to the injury of her father and the notorious scandal of all who knew about this affair. He was sentenced to five years' banishment in this kingdom of Angola. (1734)

Minas Gerais

Custodio Brandão Sá Souto Maior, native of the Town of Ribeirão do Carmo, bachelor, a carpenter by profession, aged 20 years, has never been an enlisted man nor in holy orders, a white man. Banished for six years to Angola and prohibited from ever returning to any district of Minas Gerais, on penalty that if he does so and is found there, then he will be banished for life to the kingdom of Angola. Sentenced for participation in the mutinies and risings in the backlands of the River São Francisco, São Romão, and Brejo de

Salgado, with the object of preventing and hindering the agreed solution for the collection of the Royal Fifths. He was paraded through the streets with a halter and public proclamation of his crime and sentence. (1741)

Minas Gerais

Maria Gomes Pimentel, widow of Vicente Ferreira Jardim, native of Villa Nova da Rainha, a tall coloured woman; banished for 10 years to the kingdom of Angola, for being a willing accomplice in the murder of her husband in Villa Nova da Rainha, in the district of the Rio das Velhas, and she was publicly paraded through the streets with a halter and proclamation of her sentence. (1741)

Campo Maior

Joana de Salazar, gypsy, widow (so she says) of Francisco Romero, native of the city of Merida in the kingdom of Spain, aged 30 years; condemned by sentence of the High Court to perpetual banishment in the kingdom of Angola.

Maria, ten-year-old daughter of the above, sentenced to the same term of banishment as her mother.

Joana, a five-year-old daughter of the above, sentenced to the same term of banishment as her mother. (1741)

Campo Maior

Maria da Encarnação, gypsy, widow (so she says) of Manuel de Arede, native of the town of Albuquerque in the kingdom of Spain, aged 36 years, sentenced by the High Court to perpetual banishment in the kingdom of Angola. (1741)

Campo Maior

Manuel de Salazar, native of the place of Campanario in the kingdom of Spain, 14 years old, who came in a levy from the town of Campo Maior, for being one of a band which committed thefts. Sentenced by the High Court to be banished for life to the kingdom of Angola, according to the orders of His Majesty. This sentence was duly notified to him. (1741)

Ceará

Antonio Soares, Indian, native of Ceará, a married man, unemployed, illiterate, dressed in a cotton shirt and drawers, barefooted; banished for five years to the kingdom of Angola for the crime of vagrancy.

Bahia

Geraldo de Brito, son of Gregorio Ramos and Simoa de Aguiar, bachelor, native of the Town of Porto Calvo in the region of Pernambuco, aged 27 years, master of making sugar, not in holy orders, average height, round face, little beard, black eyes, small ears and mouth, flat nose. Sentenced to ten years' banishment in Angola for the murder of Ignacio Barbosa. (1742)

Bahia

Manuel da Silva Grassa, native of Lisbon, married with Isabel Vaz Cardoso of Sabará, a white man aged 44 years, unemployed; sentenced to five years' banishment in the kingdom of Angola for his share in the revolt along the River São Francisco. (1743)

Bahia

The Adjutant Manuel Correia de Mello, a white man, banished for eight years to the kingdom of Angola for the crime of being involved in a theft from Antonio Gomes de Sá in Pernambuco. (1743)

Bahia

Pedro Mendes Cardozo, a white man, banished for five years to the kingdom of Angola, for the crime of being involved in the murder of Jozé Cardoso who was killed with a musket-shot. (1743)

Bahia

Thomas Correia, native of the parish of Sapardos, *termo* of Villa Nova de Seveira, aged 33 years; sentenced to perpetual banishment in the kingdom of Angola, for the crime of being involved in the death of a little child. If he returns to Portugal, he will suffer the death penalty without remission. (1743)

Pernambuco

Amaro de Sousa, a coloured man, native of the parish of Nossa Senhora da Luz, a married man and a free man, aged 35 years, who was married with Luiza de Barros, by whom he had four sons, who was never in holy orders, and who was a cobbler by profession; fairly tall, dressed in a Hamburg shirt, with a waistcoat and drawers of dark camelot, barefooted and barelegged; deported to the kingdom of Angola to serve His Majesty as a soldier in the garrison posts of said kingdom, for the crime of being a vagrant and agitator, arrogant and haughty, and being found carrying a side arm and a sharp-pointed knife. (1743)

Bahia

João Correa Torres, native of Itaparica, cowboy, a white man; banished for five years to Angola for using side arms in the district of the Town of Cachoeira. (1743)

Vila Viçosa

João Vaz Semicas [?], who says he is married with Ignacia Maria, native of the place of the Freixados, *termo* of the Town of Pinhel, 42 years old, who came in a levy from Vila Viçosa for the crime of being one of a gang which stole chickens, beehives, and other things; sentenced by the High Court to be paraded through the streets with a halter and proclamation of his sentence, and banished to Angola for a period of five years. (1743)

Moura

Maria de Vargas, gypsy, married with Francisco Ximenez, the gypsy listed above [who had come in the levy from the town of Moura, aged 60 years, banished for five years to the kingdom of Angola, and fined in addition, for the crime of having stolen some pieces of gold and money, breaking down the doors to get in the house of Joam Goncalves Lages, who has pardoned him], native of Xares das Cavallarias, aged 54 years, who also came as a prisoner with her said husband, involved in the same crime, and likewise condemned to the same sentence. The following innocent children of the culprits came in their company: Diogo da Rocha, Luisa da Rocha, Miguel and Francisco, small children. (1743)

Bahia

Manuel Pereira, native of the parish of Santo Antonio do Rio de São Francisco, legitimate son of Pascoal Pereira and Joanna Cardoza, married with Rosa Maria, unemployed, has no ecclesiastical privilege, aged 26 years, a man of average height; banished for ten years to Benguela, for being involved in the murder of Joseph Cardozo by a musket-shot in the locality of Saio [or Caco?], *termo* of the town of Santo Amaro das Brotas, district of Sergipe. (1743)

Pernambuco

Hieronimo de Barros, a coloured man, native of the town of Goiana in this captaincy, sentenced as a vagrant and dissolute fellow, of no fixed abode and of bad behaviour, and involved in various thefts, a drunkard, molester of women, [some words illegible] scandalous and a swashbuckler; banished to the kingdom of Angola in order to serve His Majesty as a soldier in the garrison posts thereof. (1744)

Pernambuco

Manuel da Costa, a coloured man, corpulent, 22 years old, native of the parish of Santo Antonio de [illegible], sentenced for the crime of bad behaviour, committing thefts, molesting women, without following any way of life which would give him respectable and gainful employment, and as such he is prejudicial to all communities; banished to the kingdom of Angola, to serve His Majesty as a soldier in the garrison posts thereof, in accordance with his royal orders. (1745)

Ceará

Matthias da Fonseca Coresma, a white man, legitimate son of Lucas da Fonseca and his wife Tereza da Conceição, native of the town of Ceará, about 20 years old, bachelor and unemployed. He is a tall man, with a fair face, black and sleek hair, large ears, small forehead, black eyebrows, dark eyes, and body well proportioned. He is dressed in a shirt and drawers. Banished to the kingdom of Angola to serve His Majesty as a soldier in the garrison posts thereof. (1746)

Pernambuco

João de Paiva de Aguiar, a white man, legitimate son of João de Paiva de Aguiar and his wife Sebastiana de Lopes, native of the town of Aguiar, a bachelor of 23 years, unemployed. He is a man of average height, thick black hair, forehead well made, rather large ears, scant black beard, well-shaped nose, front upper and lower teeth missing, small mouth, thin lips, some hairs on his chest; dressed in an old green silk shirt and drawers. Banished to Angola to serve His Majesty as a soldier in the garrison posts thereof. (1746)

Pernambuco

Marcos da Costa Sallinas, a white man, native of the town of Porto Calvo, married, 33 years old, banished to the kingdom of Angola to serve His Majesty as a soldier in the garrison posts thereof in accordance with the royal orders, for the crime of being prejudicial to the common weal and living free of all restraint, ignoring all orders which were given him, as likewise threats of imprisonment, and for living in concubinage with married women, besides other instances of ill behaviour as recounted by eyewitnesses of his thefts and bully-boys. (1746)

Bahia

Manuel de Brito de Oliveira, banished for five years to Angola, and paraded through the streets with a halter, which last sentence has already been carried out, for the crime alleged in the suit brought against him by Francisco Cardozo da Fonseca, that he had carried off and committed adultery with the latter's wife, Ignacia Maria da Conceição, in the town of Jacobina, in addition to stealing some utensils from his house. (1746)

Lisbon

Francisco Miguel de Urguide, married with Maria Magdalena, son of João Miguel de Urguide and Anna Thomazia de Castro, both defunct, native of this city, baptized in the parish of Nossa Senhora de Alequerim, aged 35 years, arrested by order of the *Dezembargador* João Marques Bacalhão, for being involved with the gang which operated the Mint of false money at Paraopeba in the district of the Mines of Rio de Janeiro,[59] and sentenced by the High Court [of Lisbon] to ten years' banishment in the kingdom of Angola, and to be paraded through the streets with a halter and proclamation of his crime and sentence. He was further ordered never to return to Brazil, and he signed a certificate that he would not return from his banishment until he had paid the monetary fines imposed on him. (1746)

Pernambuco

Manuel Rodrigues Vassallar, a coloured man, 37 years old, he can read, is unemployed, some of his upper front teeth are missing, native of the city of Paraíba, deported to the kingdom of Angola in accordance with His Majesty's orders, for the crime of being a vagrant dissolute fellow, with no fixed abode, and living on the proceeds of stolen cattle and beasts, and carrying off married women with whom he lived in concubinage publicly, trusting in his prowesses. (1746)

Rio de Janeiro

Fernando Soares Navo, banished to the kingdom of Angola for the term of ten years, for the crime of breaking out of jail, and sleeping with Negresses in a shameless manner, and for inciting a riot to burn down the said jail, defying the magistrates. He was paraded through the streets with a halter and proclamation of his sentence, and was also flogged. (1746)

Pernambuco

João Gomes, *mestiço*, native of Piauhí, a bachelor, unemployed, illiterate, aged 30 years; deported to the kingdom of Angola to serve His Majesty as a soldier in the garrison posts thereof by His Majesty's orders, for the crime of being a vagrant and vagabond with no fixed abode, and very prejudicial to the common weal since he lived on the proceeds of stolen horses and cattle, able and willing to commit any crime and outrage, priding himself on being a

59. For the celebrated scandal of this clandestine mint and smeltery in Minas Gerais, see C. R. Boxer, *The Golden Age of Brazil, 1695–1750* (Berkeley, 1962), pp. 201–2, and the sources there quoted.

swashbuckling bravo, carrying defensive weapons prohibited by
the recently promulgated law. (1746)

Bahia

Vicente da Silva, nicknamed "the Turk," who was arrested by order of his excellency the viceroy Count of Galveas, for being an
impertinent vagrant and agitator, who was one of those involved in
the high crime of the jail-break in this city; he is sentenced to ten
years' banishment in the kingdom of Angola by decision of His Excellency. (1748)

I consider that the above selection represents a fair cross-section
of the several hundred entries which I examined in 1961. I obtained the impression that about as many *degredados* came from
Portugal as from Brazil, but I have deliberately given more Brazilian types here. The commonest crime seems to have been theft, but
vagrancy was also a very frequent offense, as may be seen from
these additional and equally typical entries: "pela culpa de mal
procedido e peralvilho, e sem officio algum de que viva mais do
que o de alcoviteiro"; "de ser prejudicial à Republica, vadio e sem
domicilio certo"; "mal procedido, sem ter officio de que viva, e uzeiro de furtar cavallos alheyos"; "revoltozo e prejudicial à Republica,
uzeiro a dar pancadas e motivador de brigas"; "temereiro, sem re-
speito às justiças, e vadio sem officio," etc.

Relatively few of these *degredados* came from the prisons of the
Inquisition, though these few included a "Padre Vigario" who had
figured in an *auto da fé* at Coimbra in August 1713. Murderers
seem to have got off comparatively lightly, as they were sometimes
sentenced to only five or ten years' banishment, whereas thieves,
gypsies, and vagrants often received life sentences. Many of the
deportees arrived dressed only in a shirt and drawers, but those
who were enlisted to serve in the garrison posts (*presidios*) presumably received a uniform of sorts.

It only remains to add that descriptions of the *degredados* vary
widely, as can be seen from the selections given above. Some are
described in great detail and others are dismissed in two or three
lines. The clerks who made the entries were often very careless,
and at times hardly literate. The entries for the years 1720–30 are
particularly hard to decipher, The spelling often verged on the in-

comprehensible, as instanced by one clerk who habitually wrote "sem do Mecillio serto" for "sem domicilio certo."

27. ACCOUNTS OF THE PROCURATOR
OF THE SENATE OF LUANDA FOR THE
YEAR 1699 [60]

1699 [fl. 7 verso]

Receita do que carrega sobre o procurador do Senado da Câmara que serve este presente ano de 1699, Alferes João Antunes Pereira — o seguinte:

Livro de Vereações fls. 240 verso. Em 12 de Dezembro carregam sobre o procurador do Senado da Câmara cento e trinta e sinco mil reis que em tantos foi arrematado o pêso da Cidade e de como carrega a sobredita quantia fiz este termo que assinou comigo visto de lhe não prejudicar enquanto não fizer a cobrança eu José da Roza Coutinho escrivão do Senado da Câmara o escrevi.   135,000

[Signed] *João Antunes Pereira*

Livros das entradas a fls. 55. Carrega sobre o dito procurador do Senado da Câmara em sete de Janeiro dois e mil e quinhentos reis que tantos renderam os subsídios de cinco pipas de aguardente de que deu entrada António Dias Cristelo, mestre do Navio *Sacramento e Almas* de que fiz este termo em que assinou, eu José da Roza Coutinho escrivão da Câmara que o escrevi.   2,500

[Signed] *João Antunes Pereira*

Livros das entradas a fls. 55 verso. Carrega sobre o dito procurador trinta e seis mil e quinhentos reis

60. A typewritten copy of the original in the archive of the municipality of Luanda was kindly made for me by Senhor Carlos Mendes Couto in 1961. It is interesting to compare these accounts with the similar ones of the Senate of Macao for the year 1644, printed in the *Arquivos de Macau*, 1st Series, Vol. I, pp. 387–93, Vol. II, pp. 7–15, 75–82, 183–86, 249–55, 305–9, Vol. III, pp. 161–64.

que tantos renderam os subsídios de sententa e tres pipas de aguardente de que deu entrada Domingos das Neves Geral Mestre do Navio *Nossa Senhora da Conçeição e. S. Gonçalo* vindo da Cidade da Baía de que fiz este termo eu José da Roza Coutinho, escrivão da Câmara o escrevi.   36,500

[Signed] *João Antunes Pereira*

Dito Livro a fls. 56. Carregou sobre o dito procurador vinte e cinco mil reis que tantos renderam os subsídios de cinquenta pipas de aguardente de que deu entrada Aurélio Roiz Mestre do Navio *Nossa Senhora do Monte do Carmo e Almas* vindo de Pernambuco de que fiz este termo que assinou eu José da Roza Coutinho escrivão da Câmara o escrevi.   25,000

[Signed] *João Antunes Pereira*   199,000

1699 [fl. 8 recto]

Despeza que se leva em conta ao procurador do presente ano João Antunes Pereira que faz com as festas anuais e o mais pelos oficiais do Senado da Câmara lhe é mandado.

Festa de S. Sebastião

Por os oficiais do Senado da Câmara foi visto uma conta que o procurador do dito Senado lhes apresentou do gasto que havia feito com a festa da procissão que se fez a S. Sebastião que importa conforme a dita conta que apresenta o procurador João Antunes Pereira cinquenta e seis mil novecentos e setenta reais a saber.

Por noventa e seis libras de cera em pau compradas a José Alves Pinheiro a duzentos e
seis libras 21,120
Por seis fuzos de algodão para pavios 300
Por lenha para cozer a cêra 200
Pelo feitio da cêra para o cerieiro 1,200
Por meia libra de incenso a João Roiz Carneiro 500

Por um libro de vinho para as missas   200
Pelo que pagou a quem armou a capella do
    santo   1,200
Por . . . para armar   150
Por carvão para o turibulo   100
Pelo que pagou aos Clerigos que fôram ao altar 10,000
Por mim que se deu ao padre pregador   12,000
Pelo que pagou ao mestre da Capela da música   10,000
                                              _____
                                              56,970   56,970

Importa o gasto que se fez com a dita festa como da
conta parece os ditos cinquenta e seis mil novecentos
e setenta reis que se levaram em conta ao dito procurador em Vereação de vinte e cinco de Fevereiro do
dito ano de seiscentos e noventa e nove de que man-
davam fazer este termo que assinaram eu José da Rosa
Coutinho escrivão da Câmara o escrevi.
        [Followed by six illegible signatures]

                    1699 [fl. 8 verso]

Vale a lauda atraz da receita que carrega o procura-
dor deste presente ano João Antunes Pereira   199,000

Livros das entradas a fls. 56 verso. Carrega sobre o
dito procurador vinte e cinco mil reis que tanto renderam os subsídios de cinquenta pipas de que deu entrada Domingos Braz mestre do Navio digo Sumaqua
Santa Roza e Santo António vindo da Baía de que fiz
este termo eu José da Roza Coutinho escrivão da
Câmara o escrevi.   25,000
                    [Signed] *João Antunes Pereira*

Livros das entradas a fls. 57. Carrega sobre o dito
procurador vinte e quatro mil reis que tantos renderam
os subsídios de quarenta e oito pipas de aguardente de
que deu entrada José da Silva mestre do Navio *Es-
pírito Santo e Nossa Senhora da Conceição* vindo do
Rio de Janeiro de que fiz este termo que assinou eu José
da Roza Coutinho escrivão da Câmara o escrevi.   24,000
                    [Signed] *João Antunes Pereira*

Livros das entradas a fls. 57 verso. Carrega mais
sobre o dito procurador da Câmara trinta e sete mil
reis que tantos renderam os subsídios de setenta e
quatro pipas de aguardente de que deu entrada Manuel Lopes da Silva, mestre de sumaca *São Lourenço e
São Domingos* vindo de Pernambuco que fiz este termo
que assinou eu José da Roza Coutinho escrivão da
Câmara que o escrevi.   37,000

[Signed] *João Antunes Pereira*

Livros das entradas a fls. 58. Carrega sobre o dito
procurador da Câmara onze mil e quinhentos reis que
tantos renderam os subsídios de vinte e três pipas de
vinho e aguardente de que deu entrada António Gonçalves dos Santos, mestre do Navio *Santo António e
Almas* vindo de Lisboa de que fiz este termo que assinou que José da Roza Coutinho, escrivão da Câmara
o escrevi.   11,500

[Signed] *João Antunes Pereira*   296,500

1699 [fl. 9 recto]

*Vale a lauda atraz da despeza do procurador do
presente ano João Antunes Pereira*   56,970

Festa do Corpo de Deus

Por 125 libras de cêra em pão compradas a José
  Alves Pinheiro a 220 reis a libra 27,500
Por algodão para pavios e lenha para se cozer   500
Pelo que pagou a quem fez a cêra   1,200
Por uma libra de incenso   1,000
Por vinho para missas e carvão para o turibulo   400
Pelo que pagou os charameleiros   800
Pelo que pagou aos Padres que foram ao Altar 10,000
Pelo que pagou ao Mestre da Capela 10,000
                                                   51,400   51,400

Importa o gasto que se fez cm a dita festa como da
conta acima parece que o dito procurador apresentou
em Veração de vinte de Junho deste presente ano de

seiscentos e noventa e nove cinquenta e um mil e quatrocentos reis que os ditos oficiais da Câmara lhe levaram em conta em dita Vereação ao dito procurador
de que mandaram fazer este termo que assinaram
eu José da Roza Coutinho, escrivão da Câmara que o
escrevi.

[Followed by four signatures]

108,370

Em Vereação de vinte e seis de Agosto deste ano de
1699 foi pelo procurador do Senado João Antunes Pereira apresentada aos oficiais da Câmara a conta dos
gastos que se fizeram com a festa de Nossa Senhora da
Assunção que é a seguinte:

Por 119 libras de cêra a 220 reis a libra	26,180	
Por algodão para pavios e lenha para cosêr a cêra	500	
Pelo que pagou a quem fêz a cera	1,200	
Por meia libra de incenso	500	
Por um libro de vinho para as missas	300	
Por carvão para o turibull	100	
Pello que pagou aos charameleiros	800	
	29,580	29,580

1699 [fl. 9 verso]

*Vale a lauda atraz da receita que carrega sobre o
procurador deste presente ano João Antunes Pereira*   296,500

Livros das entradas a fls. 58 verso. Carrega sobre o
dito procurador onze mil duzentos e cinquenta reis
que tantos renderam os subsídios de vinte e duas pipas
e dois barris de que deu entrada Afonso de Lima Calheiros, mestre da nau *Nossa Senhora de Roque* Ama-
dor vinda de Lisboa de que fiz este termo que assinou
e eu José da Roza Coutinho escrivão do Senado da
Câmara o escrevi.   11,250

[Signed] *João Antunes Pereira*

Livros das entradas a fls. 59. Carrega sobre o dito
procurador quinze e mil e duzentos e cinquenta que

tantos renderam os subsídios de trinta pipas e dois
barris de que deu entrada António Correia de Oliveira,
mestre do Navio *Nossa Senhora da Conçeição* vindo
de Rio de Janeiro de que fiz este termo que assinou eu
José da Roza Coutinho escrivão da Câmara o escrevi.　　15,250
[Signed] *João Antunes Pereira*

Livros das entradas a fls. 59 verso. Carrega sobre o
dito procurador sessenta mil reis que tantos renderam
os subsídios de cento e vinte pipas de aguardente de
que deu entrada António Gonçalves Roza, mestre da
nau *S. José Sol Doirado* vindo da cidade da Baía de
que fiz este termo que assinou eu José da Roza Coutinho escrivão da Câmara o escrevi.　　　　　　　　　60,000
[Signed] *João Antunes Pereira*

Livros das entradas a fls. 60. Carrega mais sobre o
dito procurador quinze mil reis que tantos renderam
os subsídios de trinta pipas de que deu entrada
Manuel Lopes da Silva, mestre do Navio *Nossa Senhora da Conceição* vindo da Baía de que fiz este termo
que assinou eu José da Roza Coutinho escrivão da
Câmara o subscrevi.　　　　　　　　　　　　　　　 15,000
[Signed] *João Antunes Pereira*　　 398,000

1699 [fl. 10 recto]

*Vale a lauda atraz da despeza do procurador do pre-
sente ano João Antunes Pereira*　　　　　　　　　　 108,370

Vale a lauda atraz da conta da procissão da
Nossa Senhora da Assunção 29,580
Pelo que pagou aos padres da missa 10,000
Pelo que pagou ao Padre prégador 12,000
Pelo que pagou ao Mestre da Capela 10,000
　　　　　　　　　　　　　　　　　　　　　　61,580　　 61,580

Importa o gasto que se fez com a dita festa como
da conta parece os ditos sessenta e um mil quinhentos
e oitenta reis que se levaram em conta ao dito procura-

dor em Vereação em vinte e seis de Agosto do dito ano
de 1699 de que os oficiais da Câmara mandaram fazer
este termo que assinaram eu José da Roza Coutinho
escrivão da Câmara o escrevi.   169,950
[Followed by five signatures]

Em Vereação de 12 de Dezembro deste presente
ano de seiscentos e noventa e nove que os oficiais da
Câmara faziam ali pelo procurador deste presente
ano foi apresentada uma conta dos gastos meudos que
por ordem do dito Senador havia feito requerendo-
lhes se levasse em conta da qual era o seguinte.

Gasto que fez com o Poço da Maianga

Por dez quindas para limpar o poço	500
Pelo que gastou com a gente do trabalho três dias	3,000
Por seis baldes a duzentos reiss cada um	1,200
Por seis cordas para os ditos	300
Por meio moio de cal que se gastou no concerto	1,100
	6,400

1699 [fl. 10 verso]

*Vale a lauda atraz de Receita que carrega sobre o
procurador deste presente ano João Antunes Pereira*   398,000

Livros das entradas a fls. 60 verso. Carrega sobre o
dito procurador vinte e cinco mil reis que tantos renderam os subsídios de cinquenta pipas de aguardente
de que deu entrada Lourenço Pinto, mestre do Navio
Nossa Senhora dos Mártires vindo da Baía de que fiz
este termo que assinou e eu José da Roza Coutinho,
escrivão do Senado da Câmara o escrevi.   25,000
[Signed] *João Antunes Pereira*

Livros das entradas a fls. 61. Carrega sobre o procurador dezanove mil e quinhentos reis que tantos
renderam os subsídios de trinta e nove pipas de aguardente de que deu entrada António Dias Cristelo mes-

tre do Navio *Sacramento e Almas* vindo de Pernambuco de que fiz este termo que assinou e eu José da Roza Coutinho escrivão do Senado da Câmara que o escrevi.   19,500

[Signed] *João Antunes Pereira*

Livros das entradas a fls. 61 verso. Carrega sobre o dito procurador vinte mil reis que tantos importavam os subsídios de quarenta pipas de aguardente de que deu entrada Domingos Trigo mestre do Navio *Corpo Santo e Almas* vindo da Baía de que fiz este termo que assinou e eu João da Roza Coutinho escrivão do Senado da Câmara que o escrevi.   20,000

[Signed] *João Antunes Pereira* ─────────
                                                  462,500

1699 [fl. 11 recto]

Vale a lauda atraz da despeza do procurador do presente ano João Antunes Pereira   169,950

Vale a soma da lauda atraz do gasto do Poço da Maianga como parece a fls. 10   6,400

Gastos Meudos

Pelo que pagou ao porteiro Amaro de Leão . . 1,800
Pelo que pagou ao charameleiros do bando
    dos porcos   600
Por um cêpo que comprou para o açougue . . . 1,500
Pelo carreto a quem o trouxe   200
Por um saco feito que comprou para uma carta
    que foi para Sua Magestade 3,000
Por duas terças de sêda verde para outro saco 1,000
Pelo que pagou a Matias Carvalho de lhe pôr
    as letras 2,000
Por feitio do saco a quem o fez   100
Por uma vara para o Juiz Manuel da Silva
    Claveiro 1,400
Por duas varas para os Juizes que hão-de en-
    trar 2,800
Por uma vara grossa para o Almotacé 1,600

Pelo que pagou ao Alcaide pelo seu trabalho
que sempre se lhe dão os foros 11,000
Pelo que pagou ao Ouvidor Geral o Dr. João
de Puga de Vasconcelos da Correição deste
presente ano 30,000
Pelo que pagou ao escrivão da Câmara do
Senado 60,000
Pelo que-ha-de pagar ao Reverendo Conego
João Roiz da Rocha por conta que se lhe
deve o Senado 38,787
Pelo que ha-de pagar a D. João Teixeira Lei-
tão pelo que se lhe deve o Senado 38,787
Pelo que se ha-de pagar a Manuel Frz Sar-
dinha por conta do que se lhe deve 38,787
Pelo que ha-de pagar a António Teixeira pelo
que se deve ao defunto seu sogro Domingos
Lobo de Mesquita 38,789
Pelo que ha-de pagar ao Dr. Ouvidor Geral
pelo Salario ou propina que se paga ao sec-
retario André Lopes 40,000

318,550	318,550
	488,500

1699 [fl. 11 verso]

*Vale a lauda atraz da Receita que carrega sobre o
procurador deste presente ano João Antunes Pereira* 462,500

Carrega sobre o procurador onze mil e quinhentos
reis que tantos renderam os subsídios de vinte e três
pipas de aguardente de que deu entrada António
Martins de Carvalho mestre de Navio *Santo António
e São Francisco* vindo da Baía de que fiz este termo
que assinou eu José da Roza Coutinho escrivão do
Senado da Câmara o escrevi. 11,500

[Signed] *João Antunes Pereira* 474,000

Carrega sobre o dito procurador onze mil reis que
tantos importaram os foros que se pagaram ao dito
Senado este presente ano de que fiz este termo eu
João da Roza Coutinho escrivão da Câmara que o

escrevi e o dito procurador assinou dito escrivão o
escrevi.   11,000

[Signed] *João Antunes Pereira*

Carrega sobre o dito procurador três e mil e quinhentos reis que tantos renderam os subsídios de aguardente de que deu entrada António Lourenço de Araujo
mestre do Navio *Santo António* vindo da cidade da
Baía de que fiz este termo que assinou e eu José da
Roza Coutinho escrivão da Câmara o escrevi.   3,500

[Signed] *João Antunes Pereira*   488,500

1699 [fl. 12 recto]

Importa a despeza do procurador do Senado da
Câmara este presente ano Alferes João Antunes Pereira
como parece da Lauda atraz a fls. 11, quatrocentos
oitenta e oito mil e quinhentos reis com que fica
ajustada com a sua receita em fronte.   488,500

Importa a conta da despeza acima como parece quatrocentos
e oitenta e oito mil e quinhentos reis que é a que fez o procurador
do Senado da Câmara deste presente ano de seiscentos e noventa
e nove João Antunes Pereira que tantos constou pela conta que
apresentou, haver despendido com as festas anuais a que este
Senado é obrigado assistir e mais gastos necessários como tudo
parece da dita conta que se mandou lançar neste livro a qual
quantia justa com a da Receita que carregava sobre o dito procurador ao qual pelos Juizes e mais oficiais da Câmara lhe houveram
de sobre ditas contas por tomadas e ajustadas e hão por deso-
brigar delas mandando que eu escrivão as lançasse em livro e que
pedindo o dito procurador certidão para sua claresa se lhe passasse
com o teor deste termo que mandaram fazer e assinaram nesta
Cidade de São Paulo da Assuncão Reino de Angola em Vereação
de vinte e dois de Dezembro de mil seiscentos e noventa e nove eu
José da Roza Coutinho escrivão do Senado da Câmara que o
escrevi.

[Signed] *A. João Soares*
[Signed] *João de Cunha Azevedo*
[Followed by three other illegible signatures]

Bibliography

A. THE MUNICIPAL ARCHIVES AND THEIR CONTENTS

GOA

For a list of the codices of the Senado da Camara of Goa, for the sixteenth through the eighteenth centuries, which are available in the Historical Archives (formerly Arquivo Histórico do Estado da India) at Goa-Pangim, see Panduronga Pissurlencar, *Roteiro dos Arquivos da India Portuguesa* (Bastorá-Goa, 1955), pp. 3, 15, 163–65, 199, 204–12, 215, 247.

MACAO

There is a full and detailed catalogue of the codices available in the Arquivo do Leal Senado da Camara of Macao by Luís Gonzaga Gomes in the *Boletim da Filmoteca Ultramarina Portuguesa*, No. 19 (Lisbon, 1961), pp. 339–446; *ibid.*, No. 25 (Lisbon, 1963), pp. 373–758. It is also available in a separate edition, *Catálogo dos manuscritos de Macau* (Lisbon, 1963).

BAHIA

There is no printed catalogue of the Arquivo Municipal da Cidade do Salvador, Bahia, that I know of; but some of the codices relevant to the history of the Camara of Bahia in the seventeenth and eighteenth centuries are listed in Thales de Azevedo, *Povoamento da Cidade do Salvador* (2d ed., São Paulo, 1955), p. 471. See also the published series of the *Atas da Câmara, 1625–1700*, and the *Cartas do Senado, 1638–1692*, listed in Section B below.

LUANDA

There was no printed catalogue of the Arquivo Municipal de Luanda when I worked there in 1955 and 1961. The codices and documents of the seventeenth and eighteenth centuries are now being sorted, classified, and repaired. It is to be hoped that a catalogue or hand-list will soon be available. Meantime, I append a note on those which I examined, in order to give some indication of their scope and contents, as of March 1961.

An historical account of the vicissitudes of the archives at Luanda, and an inventory of the surviving documents formerly in the archive of the provincial secretariat, and now in the Museu e Arquivo Histórico de Angola, compiled by the late Dr. Carlos Dias Coimbra, will be found in the *Arquivos de Angola*, 2d series, Vol. XVI, Nos. 66, 67 (July, December 1959), pp. 1–38. There does not exist, so far as I am aware, a similar inventory of the surviving seventeenth- and eighteenth-century documents in the archive of the Senado da Camara of Luanda. A five-week stay in Angola in February and March, 1961, enabled me to make a preliminary survey of the documents of the period 1650–1750, thanks to the courtesy of the President of the Municipal Council and the officials in charge of its library and archive, among whom I am particularly beholden to Senhor Engenheiro José de Almeida Santos Junior and Senhor Carlos Mendes Couto. As related by the seventeenth-century chronicler of Angola, António de Oliveira Cadornega, in his *História Geral das Guerras Angolanas* (Vol. I, pp. 73, 272, of the 1940 edition), the archives of the Senado da Camara were thrown into the River Bengo by the Dutch invaders who captured Luanda in August 1641. The Portuguese recaptured the place seven years later; but for practical purposes the existing archive may be said to date from 1650, since a few fragments are all that survive from 1649. I made a cursory examination of some of these documents during my first visit to Luanda in 1955. In 1961 I was enabled to study them more closely, but time did not permit of my noting more than a very few of those dating from after 1750.

We meet with several complaints in the second half of the eighteenth century that the archives at Luanda were suffering severely from the jaws of the larvae of the white ant (*salalé*, as this destructive insect was called locally), "from whose ravages only marble and bronze are exempt." The passage of another century and a half has not improved matters in this respect, to say nothing of the deterioration caused by damp, by corrosive ink, and by culpable neglect at certain periods. Many codices have disappeared entirely; others are so damaged that they are quite unreadable; but enough remains to be worth preserving from further deterioration, as will perhaps be evidenced from the short list below. I hope to describe some of these codices more fully in due course; but meanwhile it is clear that the archives of Angola, severely as they have suffered from both unavoidable and preventable causes, have weathered the vicissitudes of centuries better than those on the opposite coast of Moçambique, where the earliest surviving document is dated 1753. (Cf. Caetano Montez, *Inventário do fundo do seculo XVIII*, Lourenço Marques, 1958, pp. 3–7.)

Historians and students of African history may be disappointed to learn that the municipal archives of Luanda contain very little information about tribal life in the interior of Angola during the period covered here, but this is not surprising. As several of the more intelligent officials and missionaries repeatedly deplored, the whole existence of the colony was geared to the slave trade with Brazil, and everything else was subordinated to this overriding consideration. These documents do, however, tell us a good deal about the social and economic conditions prevailing in Luanda, and the reactions of its white and half-caste inhabitants to their tropical environment. I may add that some of the documents in the Municipal Archive are duplicated by others in the Arquivo Histórico Ultramarino at Lisbon, and others in the series entitled "Oficios para o Reino, 1726–1801," catalogued by the late Dr. Carlos Dias Coimbra in the *Arquivos de Angola*, 2d series, Vol. XVI, pp. 39–183, but the bulk of them are unpublished.

List of surviving documents for the period 1650–1750

Livro 496. Original minute-book of the Luanda Municipal Council meetings (*vereações*), 1650–59. It originally consisted of 238 numbered leaves but several are missing, and the remainder are illegible in whole or in part due to the action of the white ant.

Uncatalogued bundle (*maço*) of loose leaves comprising some of the original minutes of the Municipal Council meetings for the years 1663–1702. Incomplete and badly damaged by white ants in parts, but much of it still readable. I rearranged these documents in three separate files in chronological order: (1) 1663–69, (2) 1682–99, (3) 1700–1702. Gaps partly filled by the next three items.

Uncatalogued bundle (*maço*) of similar loose leaves with minutes of the council meetings for the years 1669–81, thus complementing the foregoing item. Inaccurately described on the outer cover as: "Livro de Termos de Vereaçoes da Camara. Incompleto, 1672." At one time belonging to No. 528 of an earlier *Registo Geral* or General Inventory. Incomplete and illegible in parts through the action of the white ant, corrosive ink, and damp, but the bulk still readable.

Uncatalogued bundle (*maço*) of the minutes of the council meetings beginning in 1685, and ending (apparently) in 1691. Too badly damaged by white ants to be readable save in a few places. The opening *Termo de abertura* is written and signed by António de Oliveira Cadornega.

Minute-book of the council meetings, lettered on the spine in nineteenth-century handwriting "No. 2. 1674–1755." In very bad condition and legible only in a few places. The earliest legible entry is dated 1692, but most of the few entries which are partly legible seem to be of the period 1700–1716.

Livro de Termos de Vereação, 1714–1715. Original minute-book of the council meetings from 27 June 1714 to 13 November 1715. Incomplete and badly damaged by white ants, but readable in parts.

Registo de determinações e providencias tomadas em sessão da Camara, 1721–1751. Original minute-book of council meetings, but very badly damaged (and very badly written in parts), the bulk of it being illegible. First entry dated 14 May 1721.

Livro de termos de Vereação, 1726. Original minute-book of council meetings for 1726. So badly damaged and so badly written as to be virtually illegible and completely useless.

Account-book of the Procurator of the Municipal Council, 1698–1714. Old numeration, Codex 42. Comprises 104 leaves. An earlier investigator has typed out the entries for 1699–1702, and transcribed in ink or pencil those for 1698. I have copied those for 1699, and reproduce them in Appendix 27 of this book. In pretty fair condition for the most part.

Livro 483 (old numbering). Letter-book of the correspondence of the Municipal Council of Luanda with the Crown and various authorities in Portugal, 1674–1724; 124 leaves plus 14 or 15 blank. Legibility varies greatly, but the bulk is readable. Covers a wide range of topics and is one of the most interesting codices extant.

Livro 482 (old numbering). Letter-book of the correspondence of the Municipal Council with the Crown and other authorities, and miscellaneous official documents. Originally consisted of two codices which were joined together in 1928, one of them being dated 22 July 1776. Incomplete and in poor condition but legible in parts. Contains many documents which are duplicates of those copied in Codex 483 above.

Registo de Termos de Posse, Arrematações, escrituras, etc., 1650–1848. In point of fact the first entry is dated 17 October 1679, and the last in 1848. Apparently a record of sales and leases of land and property belonging to the Municipal Council, and as such of considerable interest.

Registo de Fianças e auto de arrematações, 1688–1722. Some leaves badly damaged, but the bulk of the codex is readable. Contains a wide variety of municipal orders and instructions concerning the slave trade, schedules of prices, local taxation, sanitary and health regulations, besides the registration of the letters-patent of governors, judges, surgeons, and crown officials. In some ways the most interesting and valuable codex in the archive.

Registo de Ordenações Régias, 1649–1670. (Nineteenth-century lettering: "Livro I de Registo desde 1649 até 1654.") A mixture of original documents and transcripts in poor condition. Incomplete and many leaves bound in the wrong order. Includes some price-lists of tradesmen, salary scales of local officials, land grants and leases, besides royal orders for the governors and crown officials.

Livro 481. Eighteenth-century transcripts of various official documents and correspondence of the Municipal Council with the Crown, governors, etc. Incomplete and many leaves bound in wrong order. Chiefly documents of 1650–84, but contains two or three of 1623. In poor condition.

Registo de Cartas Régias e Alvarás 1741–1768. Comprises about 250 numbered leaves. Letter-book of correspondence between the Crown and the governors. The bulk of the codex is easily readable despite a fair amount of deterioration.

Bundle of papers listing the arrival of shipping from Portuguese and Brazilian ports, with names of ship, master, and manifest of cargoes on which the council levied a duty (chiefly wine, rum, and

brandy), 1735–71. Most of the entries before 1738 are illegible
through worming, but most of the remainder are readable. Another
codex, in remarkably good condition, contains similar entries from
1774 to 1816.

*Registo de disposições régias e manifestos de Navios vindos
com dinheiro dos Portos do Brazil 1742–1774.* In point of fact only
the first four leaves (containing a total of eight entries) contain
shipping *manifestos* for the years 1742–47, the remainder of the
codex (240 leaves) containing copies of official decrees (*alvarás,
provizões, leis*) and laws of the period 1750–80. In fair condition.

Livro 499. "Registo de Degredados, condenados por varias
crimes cometidos que se desembarcaram nesta colónia, vindos de
Portugal e Brazil, 1753 a 1793." The dates are wrong, as this codex
contains the names and physical description, together with the respective crimes and sentences, of convicts disembarked at Luanda
from 1714 to 1753. It is of great interest for the social history of
Brazil and Angola, and I publish some typical extracts in Appendix
26. The entries from 1750 onwards are mostly illegible, but the bulk
of the others are readable.

Livro 706. An eighteenth-century (*circa* 1780) alphabetical
inventory of the *Livros de Registo* then existing in the archive,
and as such extremely valuable, since the entries are given in some
detail; 113 numbered leaves, including a few blank. Ends with
the letter S. Legible for the most part, though some leaves are
badly worm-eaten and corroded.

B. PUBLISHED WORKS: A GUIDE
TO FURTHER READING.

This list is limited to giving the fuller titles of works which are
cited in the footnotes and which are relevant for the comparative
study of the four Portuguese colonial municipal councils with
which we are concerned. Short critical or explanatory comments
have been added where necessary, as a bibliography unprovided
with these indications is often virtually useless.

Abranches Garcia, José Ignacio de (ed.). *Archivo da Relação de
Goa, contendo varios documentos dos seculos XVII, XVIII, e
XIX.* 2 vols. Nova Goa, 1872–74. Despite the title, all the documents published are of the 17th century. Some of them illustrate
the rivalry between the Camara and the Relação of Goa.

Accioli-Amaral. *Memorias Historicas e Politicas da Provincia da Bahia. Do Coronel Ignacio Accioli de Cerqueira e Silva. Annotador, Dr. Braz do Amaral.* 6 vols. Salvador, 1919–40. Chiefly valuable for the numerous documents from the Bahia archives (including that of the Camara) inserted by Braz do Amaral.

Agostinho de Santa Maria, O.E.S.A. *História da Fundação do Real Convento de Santa Monica da Cidade de Goa, Corte do Estado da India, e do Imperio Lusitano do Oriente.* Lisbon, 1699. The author was never in India, but he quotes freely from contemporary letters and documents originating in Goa. A primary source for the dispute between the Camara of Goa and the Convent of Santa Monica.

Albuquerque, Viriato Antonio Caetano Brás de. *O Senado de Goa: Memoria Histórico-Archeologica. Escripta por incumbencia da referida Municipalidade.* Nova Goa, 1909. The author was archivist of the Goa Senate, but died while his book was in the press. Chiefly valuable for the documents printed in the second part, pp. 105–482. On pp. 7–28 is a list of the *vereadores* who served in the Camara of Goa from 1517 to 1895. There are many gaps before the year 1674, and in the period 1725–47. Moreover, not all of those listed seem in point of fact to have been *vereadores.*

Anais do Primeiro Congresso de História da Bahia. Vol. II. Salvador, 1950. Published by the Instituto Geográfico e Histórico da Bahia. Particularly valuable for the elaborate "Indice abreviado dos documentos do século XVII do Arquivo Histórico Colonial de Lisboa," pp. 7–353, by Luiza da Fonseca.

Archivo Portuguez-Oriental. Ed. J. H. da Cunha Rivara. 6 fascicles in 8 or 9 vols. Nova Goa, 1857–76. Cited as *APO.* Vol. I. (Fascicles I–II) consists entirely of documents relating to the Camara of Goa.

Arquivo das Colónias. Publicação oficial. 5 vols. Lisbon, 1917–33. Published by the Ministério das Colónias. Publication was interrupted 1920–21 and 1923–28.

Arquivos de Angola. 19 vols. Luanda, 1933–59. In progress. 1st series comprising 5 vols., including a slim index-volume, published in 1933–39; 2d series, 16 vols., 1943–59.

Arquivos de Macau. Publicação oficial. 4 vols. Macao, 1929–42. 1st series, 3 vols., 1929–31; 2d series, 1 vol., 1941–42. Publication has been resumed with a third series in 1946. Published by the government of Macao.

Atas [do Senado] da Câmara da Bahia, 1625–1700. 6 vols. Salvador, 1949–5?. Published by the Prefeitura do Município do Salvador, Bahia. The 6th vol., covering the years 1684–1700, has no date of publication.

Azevedo, Thales de. *Povoamento da Cidade do Salvador.* São Paulo, 1955. 2d (revised) edition of a standard work on 16th–18th century Salvador which draws heavily on the local archives, including that of the Camara.

Boletim da Filmoteca Ultramarina Portuguesa. 9 vols. Lisbon, 1954–64. In progress. Edited by Padre António da Silva Rego, Director of the Centro de Estudos Históricos Ultramarinos, Lisbon. Every volume is adequately indexed.

Cadornega, António de Oliveira. *História Geral das Guerras Angolanas.* 3 vols. Lisbon, 1940–42. Written at Luanda, in 1681–83, by a man who served in the Camaras of Luanda and Massangano. The first two volumes are edited by José Matias Delgado, and the third by Manuel Alves da Cunha. A most valuable primary source for the history of Angola, where the author lived from 1639 to 1685, the date and place of his death being uncertain.

Caldas, José Antonio. *Noticia Geral de toda esta capitania da Bahia desde o seu descobrimento até o presente ano de 1759. Edição facsimilar.* Salvador, 1951. An invaluable survey by a Bahian-born military engineer, who was also *procurador* of the Camara of Bahia in 1763.

Calmon, Pedro. *História do Brasil.* 7 vols. Rio de Janeiro, 1961. Vols. I–IV of this standard (and admirably indexed) work cover the colonial period.

Delgado, Ralph. *História de Angola, 1482–1836.* 4 vols. Benguela and Lobito, 1948–55. In progress. The 4 volumes published cover the period 1482–1737, and are based largely on the documents in the Arquivo Histórico Ultramarino at Lisbon. The best history of Angola to date.

Diário do 3º Conde de Linhares, Vice-Rei da Índia. Lisbon, 1937. Covers the period 6 Feb. 1634 to 16 Feb. 1635, and gives the other side to the dispute between the Camara of Goa and the Convent of Santa Monica as related by Fr. Agostinho de Santa Maria, *q.v.* Published by the Biblioteca Nacional, Lisbon. Title should read 4º and not 3º Count of Linhares.

Documentos Históricos da Biblioteca Nacional do Rio de Janeiro. 120 vols. Rio de Janeiro, 1928 to date. In progress. Vols.

LXXXVI–XCII and XCV–XCVIII are wholly or largely concerned with the Camara of Bahia in the 17th and 18th centuries.

Ferreira Martins, José Frederico. *História da Misericordia de Goa, 1520–1910.* 3 vols. Nova Goa, 1910–14. Diffuse and rambling, but useful for the documents which it prints, many of which concern the relations between the Camara and the Misericordia.

Freire de Oliveira, Eduardo. *Elementos para a História do Município de Lisboa. Publicação mandada fazer a expensas da Camara Municipal de Lisboa para commemorar o centenario do Marquez de Pombal em 8 de Maio de 1882.* 19 vols. Lisbon, 1882–1943. A truly monumental compilation of documents from the Lisbon Municipality's exceedingly rich archive. Consultation is greatly facilitated by the two admirable index volumes which comprise the last of the series.

Instrucção do Exmo. Vice-Rei Marquez de Alorna ao seu successor o Exmo. Vice-Rei Marquez de Tavora. Segunda edição, rectificada e enriquecida com novas peças do mesmo autor e 380 notas historicas por Felippe Nery Xavier. Nova Goa, 1856. The first part of this *Instrucção* is available in an annotated English translation by Surendranath Sen, *Studies in Indian History* (Calcutta, 1930), pp. 185–244.

Instrucções com que El-Rei D. José I mandou passar ao Estado da India o Governador e Capitão General e o Arcebispo Primaz do Oriente no anno de 1774, publicadas e annotadas por Claudio Lagrange Monteiro de Barbuda. Pangim, 1841. These *Instrucções*, signed by D. José I, were drafted by the Marquis of Pombal and reflect his realization of the need for colonial reforms as well as his fanatical anti-Jesuit obsession.

José de Jesus Maria, O.F.M., *Azia Sinica e Japonica. Obra postúma e inédita do frade Arrabido J. de J. M.* Ed. C. R. Boxer. 2 vols. Macao, 1941–50. The friar was in Macao, 1742–45, where he wrote this work in the archives of the Senate, expressly for the Academia Real da História Portuguesa, as recently shown by Josef Schütte, S.J., *Archivum Historicum Societatis Iesu*, Vol. XXXI (Rome, 1962), pp. 226, 251–54.

Lahmeyer Lobo, Eulália Maria. *Processo Administrativo Ibero-Americano: Aspectos sócio-econômicos. Período colonial.* Rio de Janeiro, 1962. Revised edition of a work published under a different title in 1952.

Livro do Tombo da Prefeitura Municipal da Cidade do Salvador. Vol. I [all published]. Salvador, 1953. Preface by Waldemar

Mattos. Published by the Prefeitura Municipal of Salvador, Bahia. Prints documents of 1653–1771.

Marques Pereira, António Feliciano. *Relatorio acerca das attribuições da Procuratura dos Negocios Sinicos da Cidade de Macau.* Macao, 1867. A. F. Marques Pereira was for some years the "Procurador dos Negocios Sinicos da Cidade de Macau."

———. *Ephemerides commemorativas da História de Macau e das relações da China com os povos christãos.* Macao, 1868.

———. *As Alfandegas Chinesas de Macau.* Macao, 1870.

Marques Pereira, José Feliciano. *Ta-Ssi-Yang-Kuo: Archivos e annaes do Extremo Oriente Portuguez.* 4 vols. Lisbon, 1899–1904. Particularly valuable for the reproduction of the diary of Padre Luis da Gama, S.J., Jesuit Visitor at Macao during a very critical period of the city's relations with the Chinese, 1664–70. J. F. Marques Pereira was the son of A. F. Marques Pereira.

Mauro, Frédéric. *Le Portugal et l'Atlantique au XVIIe siècle, 1570–1670: Étude économique.* Paris, 1960. An admirable work, with a critical bibliography (pp. xi–liv) which is required reading for anyone doing research in 17th-century Luso-Brazilian history.

———. *Le Brésil au XVIIe siècle: Documents inédits relatifs à l'Atlantique Portugais.* Coimbra, 1963. Not all the documents are "inédits," those on pp. 261–307 having been published previously elsewhere.

Mello Moraes, A. J. de *Brasil Histórico.* Rio de Janeiro, 1864–68. 1st series, 2 vols., 1864–65; 2d series, 3 vols., 1866–68. Began as a weekly periodical in January 1864, with the title of *O Medico do Povo,* changed to *Brasil Histórico* in May/June of the same year. An unsystematic repository, but including many 17th and 18th century documents from the archives at Bahia which are no longer extant.

Mendes da Luz, Francisco Paulo. *O Conselho da India: Contributo ao estudo da história da administração e do comercio do Ultramar Português nos Princípios do século XVII.* Lisbon, 1952. About half the work, pp. 357–616, comprises an "Apêndice Documental," reproducing documents of the period 1600–1623, with a few earlier ones.

Montalto de Jesus, C. A. *Historic Macao.* Hong Kong, 1902. A second (slightly revised and enlarged) edition published at Shanghai in 1926 was suppressed by the government of Macao.

Monteiro da Costa, Luiz. *Na Bahia Colonial: Apontamentos para a história militar da Cidade do Salvador.* Salvador, 1958. The documents printed herein about the mutinies of the Bahia garrison in 1688 and 1728 should be completed by those published in the *Documentos Históricos (q. v.)*, Vol. XXXIII, pp. 335–37, 442, and Vol. XC, pp. 176–96.

Murias, Manuel (ed.). *Instrução para o Bispo de Pequim [1784] e outros documentos para a história de Macau*. Lisbon, 1943. Contains *inter alia* the text of 28 viceregal *alvarás* of 1689, with royal confirmation of 1710, concerning various privileges awarded to the municipality of Macao (pp. 142–208).

O Município de Loanda. Luanda, 1919. Edited by the Camara Municipal. A typewritten copy of Chap. IV, "Anais do Município," was kindly given me by Senhor Carlos Mendes Couto, of Luanda.

O Oriente Portuguez: Revista da Commissão Archeologica da Índia Portugueza. 17 vols. Nova Goa, 1904–20. There are many relevant entries in the "Index alfabetico, chronologico e remissivo das reaes ordens espedidas para o governo do Estado da India, 1568–1811, e de muitos partes dadas pelo mesmo governo á corte," compiled by Diogo Vieira de Tovar e Albuquerque in 1811, and printed serially in Vols. VI–XV.

Ott, Carlos. *Formação e evolução étnica da Cidade do Salvador: O Folklore Bahiano*. 2 vols. Salvador, 1955–57. Excellent work, complementing that of Thales de Azevedo, *Provoamento, q.v.*

Pinheiro da Silva, José. "A Capitania da Baía. Subsídios para a história da sua colonização na segunda metade do século XVII," in the *Revista Portuguesa de História*. Vol. VIII, pp. 45–276. Vol. IX, pp. 211–45. Coimbra, 1959–60. Based chiefly on the original documents in the Arquivo Histórico Ultramarino at Lisbon, and on those published in the *Documentos Históricos, q.v.*

Pissurlencar, Panduronga. *Assentos do Conselho do Estado da India, 1618–1750*. 5 vols. Goa-Bastorá, 1953–57. Contains a good selection of correspondence at the end of each volume in addition to the minutes of the council meetings.

Privilegios dos Cidadãos da Cidade do Porto. Concedidos, e confirmados pellos Reys destes Reynos, e agora novamente por el Rey dom Phelippe II nosso senhor. Sendo Iuiz de fora o Lecenceado Rodrigo de Camera. Vereadores. Manoel Tavares Pereira. Diogo Leite de Azevedo. Afonso Correa de Azevedo. Alvaro Ferreira Pereira. Procurador da Cidade Baptista da Costa de Saa.

Oporto, 1611. Shows that the privileges of the municipality of Oporto were copied from those of Lisbon.

Rau, Virginia (ed.). *O "Livro de Rezão" de António Coelho Guerreiro.* Lisbon, 1956. Scholarly edition of the MS account-book of a man trading with Lisbon, Luanda, Bahia, and Goa, 1683–93.

Regimento dos ofiçiaaes das çidades villas e lugares destes Regnos. Cõ preuilegio del Rey nosso senhor. Edição facsimilada do texto impresso por Valentim Fernandes em 1504. Lisbon, 1955. With preface by Marcello Caetano.

Rocha Pitta, Sebastião da. *História da America Portugueza desde o anno de 1500 até o de 1724.* Lisbon, 1730. Though criticized by one of its original censors, António Rodrigues da Costa, as being more of a panegyric than a true history, and though unfairly denigrated by Robert Southey, this work contains some valuable information on various topics, including the Camara of Bahia, of which the author was a member in 1698, 1704, 1708, 1721, and 1727.

Ruy, Affonso. *História da Câmara Municipal da Cidade do Salvador.* Salvador, 1953. The list of municipal councilors and office-holders, 1550–1951 (pp. 347–74), seems to be pretty well complete from 1624 onwards.

Saldanha, Gabriel de. *História de Goa: Politica e arqueológica,* 2d ed. 2 vols. Nova Goa, 1925–26.

Silva Correia, Elias Alexandre da. *História de Angola, 1782–1795.* 2 vols. Lisbon, 1937. It is very interesting to compare this eye-witness account of Luanda and Angola in the late 18th century with Cadornega's account of a hundred years earlier.

Silva Correia, Germano da. *História da colonização portuguesa na India.* 6 vols. Lisbon, 1948–56. Contains a great deal of biographical information about the leading citizens of Goa in the 16th–18th centuries, and their families; but some of the material is rather uncritically presented, and the work suffers severely from the lack of an index (in the Anglo-Saxon as opposed to the Luso-Brazilian sense of the term).

Silva Rego, António da (ed.). *Documentação para a história das missões do padroado português do Oriente: India.* 12 vols. Lisbon, 1947–58. In progress. Contains many documents of more than merely missionary interest.

Soares, José Caetano. *Macau e a Assistência: Panorama médico-social.* Lisbon, 1950. The author was "Médico do Leal Senado e da Misericordia" of Macao in 1916–37.

Sousa, Francisco de. *Oriente Conquistado a Jesu Christo pelos Padres da Companhia de Jesus da Provincia de Goa.* 2 vols. Lisbon, 1710. The author, a Brazilian-born Jesuit, lived for most of his life at Goa, where he died in 1713. He gives us many interesting glimpses of life in "Golden Goa" during its decline.

Studia: Revista Semestral. 13 vols. Lisbon, 1958–64. In progress. Edited by Padre António da Silva Rego, Director of the Centro de Estudos Históricos Ultramarinos, Lisbon. Though no indication of the scope of this journal is given in the title, which recalls that of a magazine concerned with medieval studies, this valuable periodical is devoted to the history of Portugal's overseas possessions.

Taunay, Affonso de E. *Subsídios para a história do trafico Africano no Brasil.* São Paulo, 1941. One of the best-documented surveys of the slave trade between West Africa and Brazil in the 17th and 18th centuries, with which the Camaras of Luanda and Bahia were closely connected.

Teixeira, Padre Manuel. *Macau e a sua diocese no ano dos centenários da fundação e restauração.* Vol. I, *Macau e as suas Ilhas.* Vol. II, *Bispos e Governadores do Bispado de Macau.* Macao, 1940.

Vilhena, Luis dos Santos. *Recopilação de Noticias Soteropolitanas e Brasilicas contidas em vinte cartas que da Cidade do Salvador Bahia de Todos os Santos escreve hum a outro amigo em Lisboa, noticiando-o do estado daquella Cidade, sua Capitania, e algumas outras do Brasil.* Ed. Braz do Amaral. 2 vols. Bahia, 1922. Classic account of Bahia at the end of the 18th century by the Portuguese Professor of Greek at Salvador, 1787–98.

Wanderley [de Araujo] Pinho, José de. *História de um engenho do Recôncavo, 1552–1944: Matoim-Novo-Caboto-Freguezia.* Rio de Janeiro, 1946. A richly illustrated and documented work by a descendant of the old planter-aristocracy of Bahia.

Zenha, Edmundo. *O Município no Brasil, 1532–1700.* São Paulo, 1948. A useful survey, though relying mainly on the published records of the Camara of São Paulo.

Index

Aguardente [brandy], 113

Aguardente de terra [sugar-cane brandy, rum], 121–25, 183–85

Albuquerque, Affonso de, 12, 13, 28, 146

Albuquerque, Fernão de, 160

Albuquerque, Matthias de, 18

Albuquerque, Paulo Caetano de, 115

Alferes [ensign or standard bearer], 5; special position at Macao, 45

Almeida, D. Francisco de, 115

Almeida, D. Jeronimo de, 115

Almotacél [market-inspector], 5; status of, 7, 69; refusal to serve as, 46, 168–69

Almotacél de limpeza [sanitary inspector], 101

Alorna, Marquis of: criticizes Camara of Goa, 20–21

Antilles: sugar from, 80–81, 186, 187

Anti-Semitism: in Lisbon Camara, 8; at Goa, 30; at Macao, 68; at Luanda, 112; in general, 147–48

Arimos [Angolan farms], 121

Armada da collecta [coastguard or convoy fleet], 19, 160–64

Atouguia, Count of, 122

Audiencia [Spanish-American High Court]: compared with *Relação*, 148

Augustinian nuns at Goa, 35–39 *passim*

Bacalhau [dried codfish], 83

Bague [from Konkani *bhāg*; share-ticket in a joint enterprise]: system at Macao, 58–59, 169–70

Bahia: city and captaincy, 72n; Mint, 82–83, 85; connection with Reconcavo, 98–99; connection with Ilhéus, 103–4; dependence on sugar trade, 105

Bandeira [flag or banner], 8

Bandeira [guild, craft, or trade association], 8; at Bahia, 91, 181–82

Bando [proclamation], 69

Baneanes [Hindu merchants], 30

Banha Cardoso, Bento, 120

Barboza Leal, Pedro, 177

Barreto, Francisco: reprimands Camara of Bahia, 85; criticizes religious orders for tax evasion, 89; orders festivities, 92

Barros, João de, 12, 86n, 146

Batavia: trade with Macao, 57

Bocage, Manuel Maria Barbosa de: satirical sonnet on Macao by, 63–64

Bocarro, António: account of Macao by, 53, 66

Boipebá, 103, 184n

Boleta [ticket or certificate], 58

Botelho, Nuno Alvarez, 19

Braga, J. M., 68n

Brandy: in Bahia-Luanda trade, 113, 121–25, 183–85

Brazil Company: criticized by Camara of Bahia, 83–84

Bulhões, Luís Gomes de, 105

Cabeça [head], 8

Cabildo [Spanish-American municipal council]: compared and contrasted with Camara, 77, 147, 148–49

Cachaça [rum], 121–25, 183–85

Cachoeira, 106, 139

Cadornega, António de Oliveira: on miscegenation, 128; account of Luanda by, 128–30, 136, 140; on rivalry between Luanda and Massangano, 139

Cairatto, Giovanni Battista, 21

Cairú, 103, 185

Caldas, José António, 75n, 95

Caldeirão ["cauldron" tax]: at Macao, 54

Camamú, 103, 185n

Camara, Senado da [municipal council]: Portuguese prototype of, 5–10; at Lisbon, 7–9; compared with Spanish-American Cabildo, 148–49

—, at Bahia: composition of, 73–74; and privileges of Oporto, 74; changes in, 74–75; how financed, 78–79; represented in Cortes, 108–9

—, at Goa: composition of, 12–14; changes in, 14–16, 30, 49–50, 67; how financed, 21, 25; obtains seat in Cortes, 24; attitude toward Church, 40–41

—, at Luanda: composition of, 112–13; and privileges of Oporto, 112, 118; how financed, 113, 123, 132; and governorship of colony, 115; accounts of procurator of, 209–18

—, at Macao: composition of, 44–45, 174–76; changes in, 45–46, 67; how financed, 47, 54, 55, 61, 172–74

Camara Coutinho, António Luís Gonçalves da, 87

Campos Barreto, Julião de, 22

Canarins [pejorative term for full-blooded Christian Indians], 34

Captain of the city: special position at Goa, 13, 23, 161

Capuchin friars, Italian: in Angola, 132–33

Carneiro, D. Melchior (bishop), 59
Carnival, 91
Casa Branca, 50, 51n
Casados [married settlers]: at Goa, 28–29, 34. SEE ALSO *Moradores*
Casa dos Vinte e Quatro: explained, 7–8, 15
Castro, D. João de, 19
Castro, Martim Affonso de: rudeness of, to *mesteres* of Goa, 28, 156–57
Catherine of Braganza (wife of Charles II and queen of England), 79, 92, 188, 192
Checks and balances, government system of, 145
Chinese attitude toward Macao, 51–53, 170–72
Christãos-novos ["New Christians," persons of more or less remote Jewish origin]: prejudices against, 8, 30, 112–13, 153
Church, relations with Camaras: of Goa, 40–41; of Macao, 47–48; of Bahia, 88–90; in general, 143–44. SEE ALSO Poor Clares; Religious order; Religious processions
Class consciousness: at Goa, 16, 26–27, 28; at Macao, 56, 59–60, 62–63, 67–68; at Bahia, 73, 76–77, 78, 93; at Luanda, 116
Coelho Guerreiro, António: criticizes Macaonese, 70
Coinage: and the Camara of Goa, 20; shortage of coins in Bahia, 82–83, 108; demands by Camara of Luanda for copper coinage in Angola, 125–27
Colour prejudice: at Goa, 27, 29, 34–35; at Macao, 68–69, 71; at Bahia, 77, 94–95; at Luanda, 135, 136; in general, 147–48
Congo, kingdom of, 114–15, 123
Conquistas ["conquests"; Portuguese term for their overseas possessions], 18, 73
Conselho Ultramarino. SEE Overseas Council
Contador [accountant], 5
Convicts as colonists, 62, 73, 119, 120, 197–209 *passim*
Convoy system: criticized at Bahia, 83–85. SEE ALSO *Armada da collecta*
Corpus Christi, Feast of: at Lisbon, 11, 39, 143, 144; at Goa, 39, 40, 158–59; at Macao, 48; at Bahia, 73, 89–91, 181–82; at Luanda, 137
Correia de Sá e Benavides, Salvador: recaptures Luanda, 111, 114; relations with Camara, 117; advocates copper coinage for Angola, 126; admits Italian Capuchins, 132
Cortes (Portuguese Estates or Parliament): colonial representation in, 24, 108–9
Cotton: failure to cultivate in Angola, 121
Cova [holes for planting manioc], 106
Cron, Ferdinand (Fernão de), 162n
Crown: attitude toward Camara of Goa, 13–14, 17–18, 20, 23, 24, 27–28; attitude toward Camara of Macao, 44, 48, 49–50, 53, 67, 70–71; attitude toward Camara of Bahia, 80–81, 85, 87–88, 93, 106, 108–9; attitude toward Camara of Luanda, 116–18, 126–28, 139–40; general reliance on Camaras, 141; conservatism of, 142; procrastination of, 142–43; indebtedness to Lisbon Camara, 143
Cruzado [Portuguese coin, originally of gold, later of silver, but with a theoretical fixed value of 400 reis, roughly equivalent to 4 shillings (English) in the 17th century], 19, 22, 114

Cunha, Tristão da, 115
Curandeiros [quack doctors], 136

Degredados [exiled convicts, banished criminals]: at Macao, 62; at Bahia, 73; at Luanda, 118–19; forcibly recruited as soldiers for Angola, 134; typical deportees to Angola, 197–208
Despacho [official decision or answer to an application or petition], 164
Dias Davilla, Francisco, 177
Diu, Camara of, 18
Dote de Inglaterra e paz de Holanda: explained, 79–80; at Bahia, 79–80, 144, 188; at Luanda, 114, 118, 144, 191–92
Doutel, Francisco Xavier, 68, 168
Dutch, war with, 31, 74, 84; in Angola, 111, 112

Elections, municipal: how conducted in Portugal, 5–7; at Goa, 16, 159–60; at Macao, 167–68; at Bahia, 176–79; at Luanda, 189–90
Epidemics: at Goa, 31; at Bahia, 102; at Luanda, 133
Estorninho, Carlos, 71n
Evora, 44, 45

Falta de justiça ["lack of justice"], 86
Fernandes Vieira, João, 139
Ferreira do Amaral, João, 51
Festas del Rey [statutory processions at Bahia], 90–91
Filipuchi, Francisco Xavier, S.J., 172
Finances: of metropolitan Camaras, 9–10; of Goa Camara, 21; of Macao Camara, 54–55, 172–74; of Bahia Camara, 78–80; of Luanda Camara, 113, 209–18
Fonseca de Sampaio, Luís de, 31
Franco da Silva, Gaspar, 167
Freyre, Gilberto, 146
Friars: criticism of colonial, 94–95

Gama, D. Francisco da, Count of Vidigueira, 18, 160–62
Geribita [rum], 121–25
Goa: in its decline, 31, 165–66; in its heyday, 37
Gonçalves, Gregorio: account of founding of Macao by, 42–43
Governors: rivalry with High Courts, 145
—, and cooperation with colonial Camaras: at Goa, 18; at Macao, 49; at Bahia, 87; at Luanda, 117–18, 120
—, and friction with colonial Camaras: at Goa, 16–18; at Macao, 48–50, 70; at Bahia, 75, 85–86; at Luanda, 115–16; in general, 142
Graft: at Goa, 22; at Macao, 52, 53, 54, 62; at Bahia, 78, 95; at Luanda, 115–16
Guild system, 7–8. SEE ALSO *Mesteres*
"Gunboat policy," 53
Gypsies: deported from Portugal, 119; exiled to Angola, 199–208 *passim*

Hamilton, Alexander: account of Macao by, 50–51
Homens bons: explained, 5–6

Hospitals: at Goa, 21, 25–26; at Macao, 43, 47, 54, 63; at Bahia, 94. SEE ALSO Misericordia, Santa Casa da
Hygiene, public, 7, 101, 138

Ilha Verde, 52
Ilhéus, 103–4
Indemnity. SEE *Dote de Inglaterra e paz de Holanda*
Infanções de Santa Maria: explained, 44

Janeirinhas: explained, 7
Japan: trade with Macao, 46, 47, 49, 54–55 *passim*
Jesuits: at Goa, 17; at Macao, 47, 52–53, 55; at Peking, 49; at Bahia, 89; at Luanda, 137; importance and ubiquity of, 149
Jesus Maria, Fr. Joseph de, O.F.M., 63
João III, king of Portugal (1521–1557), 15, 85
João IV, king of Portugal (1640–1654), 14, 23, 74, 83, 108
Juiz de fora [district magistrate], 75, 113
Juiz do povo [people's tribune or judge]: at Bahia, 76–77, 179, 181; at Luanda, 112
Juiz dos orfãos: explained, 5
Juiz ordinario: explained, 5, 22
Justice, maladministration of: at Goa, 22; at Macao, 62; at Bahia, 82, 86

Kindersley, Mrs. Nathaniel: account of Bahia given in 1764 by, 102
Kinship: theoretically a bar to municipal office-holding, 6, 67–68

Labour, free: at Goa, 26–27; at Macao, 59; at Bahia, 76; at Luanda, 113
Labour, slave: keystone of Portuguese empire, 131–32. SEE ALSO Slaves and slavery
Lavrador, vil [an ordinary peasant in Portugal], 106
Lavradores de canas [tenant sugar-planters in Brazil], 77, 105–6
Lawyers, Crown: and friction with municipal councilors – at Goa, 22–23, at Bahia, 85–88, in general, 144–45; and cooperation with Camara at Luanda, 144n. SEE ALSO *Relação*
Leite Pereira, Manuel, 68
Lencastre, D. João de, 87, 117, 178
Libongos: explained, 125
Linhares, D. Fernando de Noronha, Count of (viceroy of Portuguese India, 1629–1635): and the Camara, 18, 19, 23, 26; and Convent of Santa Monica, 38; criticizes Macaonese, 70
Lisboa de Almeida, José, 61
Lisbon, Camara of, 7–8, 143–45 *passim*
Lopes de Lavre, André, 54, 176
Lopes de Sequeira, Luís, 135–36
Louvados [umpires or arbitrators], 107
Luanda: founding of São Paulo de Luanda, 112; Dutch occupation of, 112; as a penal settlement, 119, 120, 133; and the slave trade, 120, 129, 130–33

Macao: origin of, 42–43; in its heyday, 46–47, 70; in its decline, 61–64; loyalty to Portugal, 71

Macuta: explained, 125
Magalhães, Henrique Jacques de, 133
Malacca, 19, 55
Manioc, 103–7 *passim*, 121
Manuel I, king of Portugal (1495–1521), 39
Maragogipe, 106
Mascarenhas, D. Francisco, governor of Macao, 46
Mascarenhas, D. Francisco, viceroy of India (1581–1584), 44
Massangano: rivalry with Luanda, 139–40
Mastrilli, Marcello, S.J., 56
Mattos, Gabriel de, S.J., 52–53
Mecanicos [artisans, manual workers]: 59, 192n–193n. SEE ALSO *Mesteres*
Menezes, D. Fr. Aleixo de, 36
Merop, Martha, 61
Mesteres [workers' guild members], 5; at Goa, 27–28, 155–58; at Bahia, 73–76, 77, 105, 179–82 *passim*; in general, 147
Mestiços [half-castes or mixed bloods], 34, 148
Metello de Sousa, Dr. Alexandre, 56
Military orders, 80, 105, 106
Militia: at Macao, 54; at Bahia, 108; at Luanda, 135
Mina (Elmina), 129, 194
Miscegenation: at Goa, 28–29, 34, 39, 41; at Macao, 63, 65–66, 69; at Bahia, 77; at Luanda, 128–29, 135, 136
Misericordia, Santa Casa da (Holy House of Mercy): at Goa, 24–26; at Macao, 43, 47, 54, 59–62 *passim*, 173; at Bahia, 95; at Luanda, 128, 139; at Massangano, 139, 140
Mombasa, 108
Monopolists and engrossers: at Goa, 20; at Macao, 57; at Bahia, 103; at Luanda, 116
Moradores [heads of households]: at Goa, 28–29, 153; at Macao, 46–47, 64, 67, 69, 173, 174; at Bahia, 108; at Luanda, 121, 127, 128, 139, 196–97
Muitsai [Chinese female bond-servants], 66
Mundy, Peter: at Goa, 36; at Macao, 65
Murmuração [fault-finding]: typical instances of, 86–87, 146

Naik, or Naique (subordinate Indian official in Portuguese service), 165
Native clergy, 35, 94
Naturaes [natives, in the sense of indigenous inhabitants, with little or no European blood]: at Goa, 35; at Macao, 69
New Christians. SEE *Christãos-novos*
Nobre [a vague and elastic term for "noble"], 67, 93
Nuns, 145. SEE ALSO Augustinian nuns at Goa; Poor Clares

Oficiais da Camara: explained, 5
Oman, Arabs of, 31
Oporto, municipal privileges of, 44, 45, 74; Macao fails to obtain, 44; granted to Bahia, 74; granted to Luanda, 112, 118
Oporto-born friars in Brazil, 94
Ormuz: taken by English, 19; besieged by Turks, 27; compared with Macao, 52

Ouvidor [Crown judge], 6, 9, 85; not necessarily a professional lawyer, 167*n*
Ouvidor-geral [chief justice], 113
Overseas Council (*Conselho Ultramarino*), 54, 142–43

Pangim, 31
Pardau [Indo-Portuguese gold coin], 159
Pauta [electoral roll], 6; [shipping list at Macao], 58
Peça de Indias [standard for valuing slaves], 194
Peixoto Viegas, João, 81, 95, 182
Pelouro [voting list], 6; at Goa, 159; at Macao, 167–68; at Bahia, 176–77; at Luanda, 190, 197
Pereira, António José, 44, 45
Pereira, Manuel, 62
Pereira, Dr. Pedro Alvares: on the *armada da collecta*, 160–62
Philip II (of Spain, Philip I of Portugal), 14, 15
Picul [a varying weight, but usually equated at 133⅓ lb. avdp.], 169
Pinheiro da Veiga, Tomé, 142
Pinho Teixeira, Diogo de, 49
Pombal, Sebastião José de Carvalho, Marquis of: and the colour-bar, 69, 94–95, 135, 148
Pombeiros [itinerant slave-traders], 118, 132
Poor Clares: at Macao, 54, 64–65, 173; at Bahia, 92–94
Population decline: at Goa, 31; at Macao, 61, 63, 67; at Luanda, 127, 131, 133, 136, 137
Population growth: at Goa, 37; at Macao, 46–47; at Bahia, 73; at Luanda, 128–29
Porteiro [doorkeeper, porter], 5
Posturas [municipal statutes or regulations], 10
Povo [people, populace], 6
Procurador [municipal procurator or attorney], 5; of special importance at Macao, 45–46, 68; downgraded at Bahia, 78; and reluctance to serve at Luanda, 192
Propinas [perquisites or emoluments], 10–11
Pumbeiros. SEE *Pombeiros*
Pyrard de Laval, François, 26, 36

Quinas [royal arms of Portugal], 11
Quintandas [street markets], 129

Raças infectas ["infected races"]: ineligible for municipal office, 148
Race relations, 34–35, 147–48. SEE ALSO Colour prejudice
Ravasco, Bernardo Vieira de, 95, 105, 106
Ravasco Cavalcanti e Albuquerque, Gonçalo, 95
Real de agua, 162
Reconcavo: explained, 98–99
Regidores [Spanish term for aldermen or councilors]: compared with *vereadores*, 77, 147
Regimento [set of rules, orders, or instructions], 5
Reinol [European-born Portuguese]: at Goa, 34, 35, 41; at Macao, 67, 68; in general, 147

Relação [High Court], 9; rivalry with Camaras — at Goa, 22–23, at Bahia, 86–87, in general, 144–45
Religious orders: accused of tax evasion, 89. SEE ALSO Augustinian nuns at Goa; Jesuits; Poor Clares
Religious processions: at Lisbon, 11, 143; at Goa, 39–40; at Macao, 48; at Bahia, 89–91; at Luanda, 137; in general, 143–44. SEE ALSO Corpus Christi, Feast of; *Festas del Rey*
Renda do verde [tax on fresh provisions]: at Goa, 21; at Bahia, 79
Rocha Pitta, Dr. João de, 87
Roza, Manuel Vicente, 68, 168
Rum: in Bahia-Luanda trade, 113, 121–25; contract at Bahia, 183–85

Sabugosa, Vasco Fernandes Cesar de Menezes, Count of (viceroy of Brazil, 1720–1735): clashes with Camara of Bahia, 75, 100–101, 103, 142
Safra [sugar crop or harvest], 84, 107
Saldanha, Manuel de, 55
Salema de Saldanha, Diogo Fernandes, 49
Salvador, City of: used interchangeably with Bahia, 72. SEE ALSO Bahia
Sánchez, Alonso de, S.J.: praises Chinese women, 65–66
Sandalwood: in Macao-Timor trade, 57–59, 169–70
Sande, Dr. Francisco de: account of Macao given in 1582 by, 43
Sanitation and public hygiene: Camara responsible for, 7; at Bahia, 101; at Luanda, 138
Santa Anna, Fr. Diogo de, O.E.S.A., 38
Santa Clara, Convent of (convent of Poor Clares at Bahia), 92–94, 173
Santa Maria, Fr. Agostinho de, O.E.S.A., 29–31 *passim*
Santa Monica, Convent of (convent of Augustinian nuns at Goa), 31, 35–39 *passim*
Santa Rosa, Fr. Hilário de, O.F.M. (bishop of Macao, 1739–1752), 57n, 62
Saõ Vicente, 62
Senado da Camara. SEE *Camara, Senado da*
Senate. SEE *Camara, Senado da*
Senhores de engenho [owners of sugar mills]. SEE Sugar-planters
Sertão [backlands, hinterland], 98
Sertão, Domingo Affonso, 178
Siam, King of: and loan to Macao, 55, 173, 174
Silva, D. Pedro da (bishop of Bahia), 89–90
Silva Correia, Elias Alexandre, 137n
Simões, Julião, 21
Slaves and slavery: at Goa, 13, 26, 38–39; at Macao, 57, 60, 61, 65; at Bahia, 94, 95, 101, 102; at Luanda, 129–33, 193–95; mistreatment of slaves by colonial powers, 60n
Slave trade: dependence of Angola on, 113, 114, 120–21, 124–25, 129–33, 193–95
Soldiers, drafts of: in Angola, 133–34
Sousa, Francisco de, S.J., 25, 63
Sousa Correia, João de, 115
Sousa Coutinho, Innocencio de, 120
Sousa Pereira, João de, 71

Status-seeking: at Goa, 25, 26, 27, 29; at Macao, 68–69; at Bahia, 89, 90–91, 93, 95; at Luanda, 115–16

Sugar: staple of Brazil trade, 84, 98, 103–7 *passim*, 186–89; price fixed by Camara, 107

Sugar-planters (*senhores de engenho*), 100, 104–6; of Brazilian aristocracy, 73, 77, 83, 98; and the rum trade, 183–85; and the sugar trade, 186–88

Tavora, Bernardo de, 115

Tavora, D. Francisco de, Count of Alvor: popularity of, in Luanda, 117–18, 124

Taxation: at Goa, 21; at Macao, 51, 54, 70; at Bahia, 78–80 *passim*, 82, 105; at Lisbon, 82; at Luanda, 114, 127–28

Tax evasion, 80, 89, 174

Tesoureiro [treasurer], 5

Theatines: admit Indian novices, 35

Timor: trade with Macao, 57–58

Timorese slaves at Macao, 60, 65

Tobacco, 103, 186–87

Trade, seaborne: dependence of Goa on, 29; dependence of Macao on, 47, 54, 56–57; dependence of Bahia on, 84; dependence of Luanda on, 121, 124

Tso-hang [Chinese mandarin], 51–52

Van Dune (or Van Dunen): family, 189n

Van Zil: family, 189n

Vasconcellos, Manuel de, 46, 168–69

Veador de obras [foreman of works], 5

Venereal disease at Bahia, 102

Vereador [alderman or councilman], 5

Vereador fidalgo, 12, 15–16

Vereador nobre, 12, 15–16

Vieira, António, S.J., 23–24, 81–83 *passim*, 105

Vilhena, Luis dos Santos, 75, 86, 95, 107

Wines, colonial duties on, 113, 123. SEE ALSO Brandy; Rum

Women: marriageable and otherwise at Goa, 37; surplus at Macao, 63; origin of Macaonese, 65, 66; at Bahia, 92; white in Angola, 128–29; and entrance to nunneries, 145. SEE ALSO Poor Clares; Santa Clara, Convent of; Santa Monica, Convent of

Xerafine [Indo-Portuguese silver coin theoretically worth 300 reis, but which varied greatly in weight and consequently in intrinsic value], 166

Zayton, 51